SERPENT SONGS

Serpent Songs

AN ANTHOLOGY OF TRADITIONAL CRAFT

Curated by Nicholaj de Mattos Frisvold

SCARLET IMPRINT MMXIII

Published by Scarlet Imprint 2013; curated by Nicholaj de Mattos Frisvold.
Edited by Peter Grey, copy-edited by Troy Chambers; typography and
design by Alkistis Dimech. Set in Satyr with Paris Verand initials.

ISBN 978-0-9574492-2-0

© 2013 the individual authors and artists.
All rights reserved. No part or parts may be reproduced by
any means whatsoever without prior permission being
obtained in writing from the copyright holder.
SCARLETIMPRINT.COM

Contents

The Other Blood: A Prelude
NICHOLAJ DE MATTOS FRISVOLD
vii

The Witch's Cross
GEMMA GARY
1

The Spirit of True Blood
SHANI OATES
11

Lezekoak
ARKAITZ URBELTZ
32

A Gathering of Light and Shadows
STUART INMAN & JANE SPARKES
42

The Fall and Rise of an English Cunning One
TONY MACLEOD
62

Stregoneria: A Roman Furnace
NICHOLAJ DE MATTOS FRISVOLD
69

But the House of my Father will Stand
XABIER BAKAIKOA URBELTZ
79

Bucca and the Cornish Cult of Pellar
STEVE PATTERSON
96

Exorcists, Conjurors & Cunning Men in Post-Reformation England
RICHARD PARKINSON
119

The Liturgy of Taboo
FRANCIS ASHWOOD
138

Trolldom
JOHANNES GÅRDBÄCK
147

The Bogomilian and Byzantine Influences on Traditional Witchcraft
RADOMIR RISTIC
167

But to Assist the Soul's Interior Revolution
ANNE MORRIS
178

Passers-By: Potential, Crossroads and Wayfaring on the Serpent Road
JESSE HATHAWAY DIAZ
193

Mysteries of Beast, Blood and Bone
SARAH ANNE LAWLESS
204

BIOGRAPHIES 219

The Other Blood

A Prelude

*So what it boils down to is the fact that
as times change the Craft changes with them.*

– Robert Cochrane

HE CUNNING MAN who charms away a wart, the astrologer who casts an election and fashions a talisman for a given purpose, or the lonely walker who blesses a barren womb are all people who practice parts of the plethora of the Craft. Yet there is a tendency to limit what is referred to as traditional witchcraft to just a few groups. As a result of this exclusivity the great diversity of the craft, its richness, risks becoming lost. Yet, when you call upon the spirits and they answer, who can deny you this connection?

Traditional witchcraft is a set of practices born from need, land and blood. It is the art of working one's fate and the art of working hedge, hill and mound for one's benefit or that of a group or conclave of people and their needs. The witch in the traditional sense is someone who is aware of their pedigree, the particular blood that sets them apart. Because of its diversity traditional witchcraft remains misunderstood.

Some even see it as a vacant term that can be filled with whatever meaning one chooses. That is not my intention. Even if Traditional Witchcraft varies – sometimes dramatically – in its expression, there are vectors of commonality to be found. It is those vectors that brought together this gathering of serpentine voices under the traditional witchcraft landmarks: blood, night, land and crossroads.

The other blood can be passed on horizontally, blood to blood, flesh to flesh, it can also be awakened by the celestial fire. Within whom and where this fiery blood is quickened is bound to give a unique expression, because traditional witchcraft is a poetic reality of night and nature that, whilst adopting various guises, gives form to the possibility of the incursion of the other. It is here we find the nerve of the Craft. It is the song of those who cross hedge and veil, it is the fire of those who make their fate and it is the memory of blood and need making signs across the scales of the earth. My own perception of traditional craft has developed over nearly two decades. In this time I have been blessed to meet pilgrims and masters of what I term the craft of the wise. Like many I became aware of the term 'traditional witchcraft' through the letters and writings of Robert Cochrane and my search was rewarded by encountering a host of wonderful practitioners of the art, where kinship was mutually recognised. Some of these individuals are bound into the book which you now hold, others have informed it in more subtle ways. This collection of songs surely testifies to the burgeoning diversity of traditional craft in all its expressions. It is with great pleasure I give to your hand and eye the song of fifteen of these serpentine vertebrae.

Nicholaj de Mattos Frisvold

❖

The Witch's Cross

GEMMA GARY

UT, AWAY FROM THE VILLAGE, on its far outskirts, where the everyday world of everyday man gives way unto hill and hedge, valley and wood, it is here that tradition illustrates the character of the witch; living in her cottage, in abnormal or eccentric reclusiveness and solitude, nestled betwixt the civilised and the wild; keeping a watchful eye on the one, and immersing herself in the other. It is in such a situation I am glad, blessed and blissfully accursed to find myself in today.

It is a situation I have always longed for. Upon my early steps in pursuit of the old witch's path, I made many little journeys, out from the small family cottage, and away from the village as dusk began to creep across, transform and moisten the land and the very air. Along little-travelled, narrow footpaths I slowly passed, flanked by tall Cornish hedges; thick with thorn, furze and bracken, with long, vicious tendrils of bramble spanning the way and impeding one's progress. Out upon the high windswept carns, or the dramatic granite bolder-strewn and towering sea cliffs, or through the many mist shrouded fields, bordered each by their black thorny hedges, breached here and there by old granite stiles. It is here, in these lonely places, amidst the dancing bats and ghostly owls that I immersed myself in and imbibed deeply of the spirit of place, via which much of my path and Craft was received and assimilated, building over time into fuller realisation.

Those things thematic of the betwixt and liminal are old and recurrent threads within witchcraft, and they are avenues via which the witch accesses and employs the power, virtues and wisdom of the *other* as the source of all that informs their Craft and Arte.

As the veil of dusk falls, the land is betwixt in anticipation of its parting through which night emerges; bringing another world of subtle voices and mystery that speak to those with the inner quietness to listen. These things and those who have a natural affinity for them are for profane and 'normal' society however, often viewed with suspicion, fear, and even revulsion.

Normal society's aversion to the night and the other, is revealed in its desire to keep its civilised urban areas in constant light, and its desperate rites to banish, fend off and exorcise the mysterious and subtle virtues of natural night via the vulgar and loud exuberance of urban nightlife. The participants in this rite arm themselves with a thumping cacophony of noise, flashing lights of multi-colour and chemical intoxication to a climax of violence amongst themselves, and rolling around in their own and other participants' excreta in the gutters of civilisation. Such are the rites that indeed repel the witch.

Many are the ways in which the Other is sought in the witch's Craft, but our First Way is the witch's exilic and lonely pilgrimage to the places of intersection and power. In the tradition of the Cornish witch, and indeed in that of the witches of other areas, such places include the crossroads, the churchyard, the lonely and wind-distorted thorn, the potent stone, the holy well, the hill, and in the caves of sea and land, and the wooded valleys and streams of spirit force.

The lonely places to which the witch may make her nocturnal pilgrimages are liminal in nature, for it is the purpose of these journeys to encounter the virtues and wisdoms of the other, and the liminal and betwixt has always served as an intersection between the worlds. It is here, in the places wild and between, that the witch seeks to commune with and receive teaching and guidance from the spirits and the faery, and here the telluric serpent is drawn forth that intoxicates and brings vision and power to the witch.

Thus it is that the wild and lonely place calls to the witch and is her true home; the earth is of her bones and the bones of her ancestors, and carried within the witch-blood is the chthonic and animalistic wild wisdom to be realised, fed and nurtured via the witch's arte. Thus it is also that the witch displays a kinship with animal familiars, each being liminal in nature and character.

Astride the hedge

Perhaps most visually suggestive of liminality is the hedge, and in particular the old stone stiles that grant passage from one side to the other. As dusk seeps across the land, the Cornish witch settles upon the old stile, there to draw upon the potencies and visions of the spirit paths, and there to wait for a passing spirit to draw wisdom from. It is also from the hedge that the witch may receive the gifts of working tools to aid the working of her Craft and of course the herbs and plants to stock and empower it.

The plants that give unto the witch the gifts of vision and nocturnal spirit flight are there to be found also in hedge and wood. Reviled by the profane for their poisonous reputations, it is fitting that these green gifts should grow in exile in the haunted wilderness. Thus may their wise use by the witch be seen as a careful partaking and witch's sacrament of the wild and other itself. Again we see that those things shunned as evil by the profane are in fact keys to vision, flight, power and gnosis.

A point potent also of otherworldly intersection is the crossroads, a location with a rich and ancient association with the dealings of witchcraft the world over.

To the crossing of the ways travels the witch, to find the meeting of the worlds of the living and the dead. It is here in the crossroad's sacred midst that one finds liminality, and unity of the opposing, for here rise the spirits of the dead and the other into the world manifest, or it is here that the witch may shed her physicality to ride forth upon the spirit paths of night. Here, betwixt All, at the point of One is true communion made.

It is for good reason that the centre of the crossed ways is spoken of amongst the witches as the fertile plot, for where all conjoin and emerge in unity is the true point of all potential. The circle, the cross, and the point teach that All is One, thus the fertile plot is a place of life and death, creation and putrefaction, the receiving of gifts and the giving of sacrifice, and here may the witch, by arte, conjure forth or cast away in banishment. Always in such work must the crossroad's nature as a point also of sacrifice be remembered, where the cost of our decisions and choices must be contemplated – for there is always a price to pay for dealings at the crossroads. Here kindles the witch the hood-fire that consumes and bears forth; the flame of wisdom, sacrifice and transformation, and here raises and reveres the witch the old signs of the phallus and of the skull, the signs of fertility with its requisite virtues of growth and repose, the signs of the Old One of the light of life and the mysteries of death, crowned with the horns of the duality's union. Here, at the old fertile plot and the crossing of the ways, dwells the Devil indeed, he who stands at the threshold of All, and chases death into life and life into death at the thinning of the veil.

The figure of the Devil, and the old god of the witches, shall be found most often to be represented in liminal form, intermediate between man and the bestial, with horns, cloven hooves, and a tail. The flame-eyed and fur-thighed wild spirit of nature, fertility and death, he is often also blackened as night – the black bull, hound, goat or toad, or riding a black mare – thus is the Devil depicted as a vivification and avatar of the night and the other. Also one may find that his eyes *burn* with a strange fire, or that smoky fumes issue forth in his breath, and of course there is the luminous flame set betwixt the horns. Such imagery conveys to the witch the light of union and gnosis concealed within the Devil's mysterious and darkened form. Thus black tapers are burned by the witch in offering to the Goat of the Sabbat. Here is an occult embodiment of the spiritual illumination concealed within the night's wild, lonely and haunted places of the other.

With the crossroads, the churchyard overtly shares its associations as a place where the worlds of the dead and the living meet, and where the West Country witch may hold patient vigil, or make active conjuration for the spirits to reveal wisdom. Both crossroads and churchyard are set apart and taboo, keeping the spirits of the dead contained and separate from the world of the living. To this place the witch may also travel under night's cloak to hold conference with the Devil, who has appeared to the Cornish witch who calls him forth in the guise of the black bull, or the great dark toad. Akin with the crossroads, the churchyard is also a place of rites and witch-magic, for the receiving of gnosis, for transformation, and to make banishments of illness and things undesired.

In addition to the witch's dealings with the Devil and spirits of the dead, we find in Cornish lore that the witch not only communes with and obtains power and wisdom from the potent and lonely places betwixt, but also from otherworldly and intermediate beings such as mermaids, toads, and the faery folk who grant sight and convey gnosis.

In Cornish folklore, we find what appears to be a pellar foundation myth in an old man of Cury's encounter with a mermaid. In Robert Hunt's version of the tale, the man is walking in a day-dreamy, meditative state of mind upon the sands in one of the Lizard Peninsula's coves, where he happens upon a mermaid stranded by the receding tide. A bargain is struck with the half-human creature, and for returning her to the sea the man is granted the ability to exorcise black witchcraft, provide cures, and to divine the identity of thieves and recover stolen things. These abilities were also to be passed to his descendants, thus have many Cornish magical practitioners traditionally claimed to be of the pellar bloodline of Lutey.

The toad, one of the forms taken by the Devil, the witch's familiar, and the witch herself, is also encountered by the magical practitioner as an initiatory source of witch-power and gnosis, notably in the famous tradition of the nocturnal churchyard encounter. Beneath the lonely and wind-distorted whitethorn is where the Cornish witch will go, under night's cover in genuflection to seek the magical assistance of the faery folk, or there to dream in hopes of receiving their wisdom and knowledge of such things as the curing of illness and other artes.

Witch-emblems of the night and of nocturnal spirit flight are the owl and the bat. As well as their associations with the witch's secret journeys, and passage into the other, night and spirit flight are important aspects of traditional witch-magic. The witch's magical intent is sent forth, often under the secrecy of night's cover, through the air, and upon the winds to its target. It is often carried forth by the witch's familiar spirit, or conveyed by the witch herself, traversing the spirit paths in bestial form.

Curse magic is, in the West Country, called *owl blasting* or *owl blinking* – descending with fixed focus upon its target with the stealth and silence of the owl. Malefic magic, or evil spirits that fly through the night were guarded against by all manner of precautionary charms and countermeasures. In Cornwall, it is interesting that one charm to guard against all evils that travel forth by night, consists of a pair of bat's wings, enclosed within a small bag and hung above the hearth, the chimney being a traditional point of entry into the home by spirits, witches and their magic.

Travelling, and sending their magic forth upon the winds of night, alike unto the movement of spirits, or traversing the ways in bestial form, it is not surprising that the witch should be seen to be not entirely human, but of the family of spirits and beasts. The boundary between the witch and the familiar spirit is very blurred indeed; the great toad making a sudden appearance to frighten those who have done some wrong unto the witch, may be the witch's familiar or it may be the skin-turned witch herself. The witch-lore of Cornwall and beyond is full of stories of the toad being wounded or killed, or the strange white hare being shot by the hunter, only for the witch later to be discovered in a corresponding state.

The very body of the witch was itself a spirit house for her familiar spirits, for she carried them within her. This was the belief of the modern English Cunning Man and Witchcraft Museum founder Cecil Hugh Williamson, who encountered and gained knowledge from many of the West Country's working wise-women and witches. Between the witch and her familiar spirits there is only unity, any separation or distinction would be very difficult, if not impossible to make.

Concealment, secrecy, and the keeping of silence are central tenets of the traditional witch's Craft, one of the old skills of which was the ability to turn invisible, the highly useful ability to pass by and go about one's business unnoticed.

Just as the being of the witch is a concealment of her Craft and Arte and her familiar spirits, it is also very difficult to make distinction or separation from the night, a concealment of the other and the light of otherworldly gnosis and spirits. Between the witch and night there is only union, and it is in invocation of this union that the witch enters into the night, concealed by cloak and mask. By such an invocation does the witch seek herself to become a living avatar of the night, the other, the fertile plot and the dark womb of Chaos from which all magical potential of the witch's craft may be born forth in magical creation. The witch's envelopment in the cloak, the transformation into bestial form via magical rites and the donning of masks, skins and horns, are sacral acts of the dissolving of one's self into the night, to become one with the other and the hidden. Clad so in the skins of the night, the witch becomes a vessel for its wisdom, its powers and its spirits, and these, treading the sinistral dance of return, she calls forth in silence to be made manifest, stirring the dark depths of the cauldron that hangs above the fire at the crossing of the ways.

The invocation of, and communion with the night made, the witch's mystic vision and second sight is opened, aided further by the serpent-tides of the year and the observance of high nights, being themselves times betwixt. Thus may the channels of otherworldly communication be brought to flow.

Emblematic of both the stripping of self, and exchange with the world of spirit, is the presence within the witch's circle of skulls and bones, of either man or beast. Just as the witch becomes a vessel for the night's gifts, so do the flensed bones that serve as tools of the witch's art, set upon the cross-marked earth in the north of the circle, become re-fleshed as mediating vessels for the presences, spirits and virtues of the other.

The northern direction is the dark portal of spirit wisdom, divination and whisperings on the wind. The flame set there to burn by the witch is kindled for the illumination of the flow of the otherworldly, spirit presences, and gnosis; a shedding of light upon the un-manifest, unknown and hidden, and a flame of devotion to the other.

Set into the earth, at the crossing of the ways and beneath the hood-fire, is the iron witch's nail; the serpent-seed and lightening bolt, uniting the worlds and drawing the hidden upon the paths of spirit into the centre, into manifestation.

The flame kindled in the North is also maintained in honour of the North's status as the source of mystic light, and is in acknowledgement also that the dark northern direction of death mysteries and transformation is the direction of the birth of light. Midwinter, whose direction is North in the witch's round, gives birth unto the sun and the increase of the year, the dark bears forth the light, as from the womb, or the seed bursting forth to emerge from the dark moist earth. The dark of the north and night bears the light of spirit gnosis, the dark of midwinter bears the light of the sun anew, and the dark of the witch's cloak conceals the body of witch-fire.

To the witch who sees that *All is One*, the divine seed is present in all things from the highest to the lowest. The wisdom of the interconnectedness of all is expressed within the witch's reverent finding of the divine light within those dark things commonly viewed as evil and unworthy by the profane. A classic symbol of this within the old craft of the witch is of course the toad, that dark creature passing with impunity between the worlds. For the witch, unification, the presence of the divine within all, and light from the dark, forms part of the occult arcana of the toad. Thus does the witch revere toad, earth, and stone. By the witch practice of letting forth one's blood upon the black earth, and unto the old stone altars, does the witch feed, enflesh, and unite with the serpent and the fire concealed within.

The traditional witch's nature is revealed in many of the facets of her Craft. The West Country witch was not entirely a pagan in the modern sense in which the word is popularly used, but more a dual observer, in which the Devil was the Old One of the earth and the hidden world within nature. The witch made use of all that was of use, and simply employed Christian themes and practices in a way that suited her needs.

Indeed the witch's apparent dual observance, and use of both Christian and pagan magical formulæ is betwixt; a unification of things thought by others to be entirely incompatible polar opposites, good and evil.

The witch might also be seen to stand astride the ways of good and evil, via her holistic embrace of magic, both white and black. In the West Country, the true breed of witch was known as a grey or double ways witch.

The witch's path is trod with feet in different worlds, and leads to the wisdom and gifts of the physical and the other. Upon this old path of exile, through the lonely, wild and haunted places of the earth, the witch, a creature of nature, is truly at home and one with all between the worlds and accompanied by the hidden; thus never alone, but always One.

A RITE OF THE STILE AND THE CROSS

OR THIS WORK, shall the witch venture forth betwixt day and night unto an old stone stile set within some lonely hedge, or to some other place vivifying liminality. Bearing the lit lantern and the staff, and carrying the blade of arte and a bottle of some good drink, let the very treading of the journey become a meditative act and an inner conjuration of the other and of Oneness, the state betwixt.

When the old stile has been reached, let the witch be settled upon it, there to further the conjuration of Becoming. There shall the witch breathe deep and imbibe of the darkling air, of the black earth and the cold stone, drawing of the fire therein concealed. Let each breath serve to fan the witch-fire; becoming as a spirit-beacon of haunting luminosity in the waxing of night, as the witch merges with the green and black of the hedge, and with the nocturnal creatures, busied creepy-crawlies and hidden presences.

Let the witch, so transformed, with staff mark the cross of One; the meeting of the ways upon the earth path before her. Let her take up then the blade of arte, and draw a drop of her fiery blood to fall forth upon the midst of the cross. Then upon this let the lantern be set as the witch does conjure:

A rider astride the hedge,
A watcher 'twixt the thorns,
A traveller in stillness upon the paths of One,
With eye cast between the ways to the realms beyond profane sight,
I conjure and bid open the serpent paths of night.
I conjure thee O witch's lamp; arise ye O hidden light of the wise,
Illumine the ways of blessing and curse; the crossing of the ways,
Unto my senses all I conjure thee O spirits, presences and potencies,
Who move abroad by night,
To secret vision show, or hid' word convey,
By fleeting shade or fullest form,
By wind carried whisper or a cry to chill the bone!
I conjure thee forth by lamp by rod and blooded cross!
So Shall it be!

The staff is struck thrice on the ground, and there shall the witch, with her own fire kindled by her sacrifice upon the black earth unto her kin, the ancestors, the spirits of the ways, and the serpent fire, imbibe further of this union with the other and her realization of oneness at centre and point of all potentiality.

Seeking vision and word in the dancing shadows cast by the lantern, or in the winds and movements of the wild, the witch is open unto the flow of otherworldly wisdom, the guiding spirits of place and its potencies and virtues. Learning and empowerment via such exchange are traditional hallmarks of the witch.

The Spirit of True Blood

SHANI OATES

F I ATTEMPTED a vague description of *She* who above all others is deemed Ineffable, it might be: the uncreated, bornless, eternal, un-diminishing, all-generating, un-limiting absolute sentient, ambivalent multi-verse of Being. Yet description fails utterly, for, without exception, words and images are self-limiting and finite. Beyond All, She can be neither. Humankind in tandem with all other material form created within our universal existence is a self perpetuating sequential cycle of life and death. Non-material forces are likewise self-generating and eternal; yet *both* force and form arise from the singularity termed (for our recognition and distinction only as) the uncreated absolute. To express this intellectualised perception of perennial philosophy further, in ever more personal terms, humanity instigated the grand pantheonic narrative. The veneer of culture is but a veil to the Truth, the Singularity above analogous mediation.

So could it be rationally argued that archetypes can model those pantheons without pre-existence as divine forces or be-cause of them? Do those archetypes act then as primordial forces; given form and clothed with cultural character, thereafter elevated to a (post-creation perception of a) 'divine' status? Humanity's struggle to comprehend its self perceives these external influences upon things of this material plane in terms of our inter actions with other humans according to our allotted fates. So my question presses deeper; are these archetypes, as emanations of the Uncreated like ourselves, products of manifest creation as form, or are they created as both manifest and un-manifest principles of force and form?

All life is inseparable, our ancestors knew this instinctively. Everyone in the ancient world recognised a pattern of similarities in their perception, in number and quality. Unilateral virtues became deftly woven into all myth and legend as tenets of necessity, granting some measure of validation regarding their 'reality' at some level. Too often, this resource has been forgotten and neglected over time.

All epithets for Wyrd reflect a personification of the inexorable bound through time as a nebulous expression that ironically becomes intimately personalised through specific family spirits, of ancestral links in time. Eventually all views coalesce into fewer and fewer until they become one influential recognisable force. From this we may confidently deduce how twenty-four original tribal ancestors became associated by obscure, elemental forces of nature as active filters and channels for the Triune Exemplars of Absolute Fate. Fate is therefore embodied yet further as an impalpable ambivalence closer and higher even than the Ultimate Creatrix.

Pondering upon these views, we seek their clarification in beliefs that reflect them. Our engagement within the Work is filtered by what we are, in the sense of how we are to be known: definition is requisite. Subscription to either of the following possible examples that label the complexity of our belief as either Henotheistic Panentheism or Monolatrous Paganism (in a totally non neo-pagan manner) asserts that in fact, we are neither. More properly, we should posit an Ecumenical Gnosticism in absolute contra-distinction to any deviant historical corruptions of what essentially describes a non-elitist, non sectarian confederacy of people who speak the word of truth in the absolute sense and who are fully immersed in the Mysteries. To that end we become defined in simpler terms as a Mystery Tradition.

Under that veil, we offer only one of many ways towards the discovery of that reality, whether such be termed Individuation or a Grail Attainment. All things shift and bloom in grace alone. So we neither profess to be The Way, nor hold a definitive apprehension of those ineffable challenges borne of the Faith. Effectively, our Compass is timeless and universal, yet equally it becomes honed to ancestral vision though a collective history forged within Northern Europe. We are in Craft, mystics, pilgrims, warriors, artisans, occultists and shamans. We are also none of these, for all labels stifle growth.

Numerous cultures and past beliefs have been raised upon gnostic foundations irrespective of later developments. It is a discipline of the self, but not in terms of ego obsession, but ego transmutation; it is a purely scientific process. Rigor and stamina provide the stoic reserve of seekers set upon this stony path; for crooked it is not, but arduous, unappreciated, oft reviled and all too zealously polemicised.

In this rapidly shifting arena of tradition and definition, clearly, the question of what qualifies as witchcraft particularly with regard to the beliefs and practises of Gerald B. Gardner and Roy Bowers needs to be reassessed. Moreover, despite in-depth clarification throughout the works of Roy Bowers, whose own frustrated tirades acknowledge the liminality of credulity in matters of faith, his own opinions have been much distorted and misrepresented among the greater occult communities. Time then to redress such ill conceived constricting perspectives. As individuals can we ever define and categorise the totally subjective experiences within the personal and intimate modes of contact with which we engage the other? Surely this would defeat the purpose of growth? This indefinable something may at best be aligned to a stream, a pattern of similarity and no more.

Looking into historical patterns of emergent Gnosticisms during the pre-Christian apocalyptical eras, we may discover how Platonic philosophies infused were artfully lifted by a subtle interweaving of Hermetics to form a base pattern of enfolding oriental mystery traditions. In modern times, vague and subjective categories by example include terms such as Traditional Witchcraft and these do not serve us well. Traditional Craft becomes however an altogether more promising toponym offering progression towards a more succinct definition to distinguish ourselves from the wholly undesirable maledictions that typify historical witchcraft.

The Craft is the thread that thrives as an underground stream. Its fierce abnegation of dogma offers succour that generates a mystical path, of hermitage and evolution. Its source honours the pagan spirit, yet seeks the transcendent infusion that ignites those animisms. It presents to every seeker an objective goal that allows their subjective need for a devotional path to overwhelm and elevate them as journeymen upon a road shared by others of similar vision ... it denies no-one, yet accepts only those who grasp the thorn. It is in fact the magic of the soul, a spiritual alchemy masterfully borne in the crafting of matter.

In this the tenets of Craft shape and hone such a questor. Each and every individual become recognised by ancestral forces as dynamic catalysts for their growth and well-being. The spiritual forces that guide them, better defined as the Egregore, are the intrinsic cellular well-spring of regeneration. As occult potencies these concepts are often mis-understood by many whose personal preferences for all things macabre demean them into the realm of superstition. Therefore the Craft again becomes a means of ingress. But it is not one engrossed in material thaumaturgy, nor maleficent acts, so again defies any label linked to witchcraft in any relative literal or psychological sense whatsoever.

Fundamental to everything metaphysical, the animistic principle remains supernaturally axiomatic to True Virtue everywhere; it cannot be otherwise. In the archaic world any unsophisticated religion outside the imperial or state judiciary, as a non-state religion, would be deemed as pagan. This correct definition is rather different to that defined in the modern neo-pagan sense. Only animism allows and accepts the spirit of virtue in all things, a caveat both Roy Bowers and Evan John Jones were very cautious to express. Mindful lest they be mistakenly considered pagan in true 18th century idyllic fashion, they strived to separate their perception in contradistinction to that same example revived and revamped by Gardner quite successfully.

This contemporary of Bower's rose in prominence to assert a constant reminder of the gulf in belief that separated their praxis. Neither men shared Valiente's vision of a unilateral term, where differences in principle become less important than those which unify the broader spectrum of 'pagan belief.' This issue remains unresolved as neo-paganisms continue to factionalise into unceasingly smaller sub-groups and cultic orders. As the former Magister of the Clan of Tubal Cain, Evan John Jones became influenced by Doreen Valiente during the few years they were called upon to work closely on writing projects that included their book, *WitchCraft: A Tradition Renewed*.

Some of his writings therefore bear opinions seemingly at odds with his own more forthright appreciation of his Craft. Having caused certain confusions for those analysing his collective works perhaps unaware of those brief influences, it is worth remembering both John and Doreen worked closely with Roy Bowers and with each other for a short time after Bowers' tragic death. Hopefully this explanation will dispel all errors of judgment with regard to his uniquely original influence intrinsic to the Clan mythos brought to bear upon the People of Goda, of the Clan of Tubal Cain.

Returning very briefly to things of superstition known as the baneful plight, we discover there is nothing new under the sun, quite literally. Plato especially struggled to explain the presence of all things negative withholding their nature as not divine; and yet his explorations do suggest he found a harmony of sorts, but was afraid to fully express them. In truth but few are brave enough to be martyrs; talkers, walkers even, but not fighters whose end game surrenders all. Ambiguity hints enough to satisfy the need to be heard, but offers a shield to fend off those who do not understand such subtleties; a dead man tells no lies, but neither is he heard.

Change as a necessity offers the idea of choice buffered as an illusory reassurance to protect the ego from accepting its enforced subjugation to anything less than free will. All is meant to be, I believe. So I am of the opinion that no opinion serves, and therefore no answer is correct, nor is it wrong. Change is inevitable, the illusion of choice suggests the persistence of a comfort zone unchallenged by an inability to inflict resistance to any perceptible effect ... the subtle difference lies only in my avoidance of the subject of ego and the matter of 'free' will – outwardly only of course.

Language is so easily a device of ambiguity; direct address is oft preferred, as that, unaided, leaves little room for doubt. All statements are by definition a commentary borne of the flux of necessity, subject to individuality of purpose, idiosyncratic of and subject to the independent right of every individual. Even minor manipulation changes the manner in which words are received, thus shifting their impact. Vision must be sincere and without guile or artifice. But the Word, the gospel of the breath, needs to be delivered with all the subtle and noble arts of rhetoric much loved by all teachers of philosophy, whose faith infuses every lesson with the pure and holy fire of the priest. When talking to those sleepers not yet awakened, the charge to memory requires a different approach, a challenge to predictive cognition. This effects a tactic of confusion wherein the seeker becomes one among many where: *some have no filters, other have too many, some have no need of them for their blindness gives them inner vision.*

It has always been thus. Therefore, even as a thought carried upon the breath that finds expression as syllabic form, the spoken word is no exception to this most basic tenet. Hence, my most valued lesson gleaned from the invaluable outpourings of Thomas Aquinas concerns his realisation with regard to how those who understand his words, do not really have need of them, yet to others who cannot, his words are useless! He had their measure of course, but still conceded that in each piece of writing be it good or bad, at least one person will read what they *need* rather than what they desire or want. Knowing this, how then should we attempt to understand the allegorical complexity of myth, or the moral principle within the fabled stories of renown? Are they literal conjecture or metaphoric musings.

Certainly I feel the Sufis might agree strongly in principle of myth as metaphor. Other sects having a contrasting dualistic foundation might express those same events as historical. On the other hand, Zen Masters profess that intrinsic harmony of and for all derives from the apprehension of truth imbued by the Word in contemplation – *neti neti*. As no single isolated thing it is cumulatively the summation of all these ideas and yet transcendent of them. For All is One. Humankind alone sets a mutually exclusive precedent. In choosing to exclude all forms of itself and the *other* from its totality of *being*, it asserts a negation of unity and of completion, all to serve instead the ego, building upon self and perception of self *ad finitum*. Yet to fully sense all others, we must propel what is within and without; *to be filled, we must first empty*. Few will take that as a gift. For many, it is their greatest fear.

It has been very successfully argued that everything resides in polarity. Beyond that, a third and equilibrating force exists primarily based upon the interactive friction of the two opposing forces of polarization. This fulcrum requires distribution via the flow and ebb of a tide due to the dark and light of shade and radiation. One is void without the other; neither completing their purpose without the other.

Again, Evan John Jones was most insistent upon this primary tenet, claiming it inherent to the dialectical mechanistic methodologies processed all too often within Traditional Witchcraft as occultisms. Devoid of intellectualizations, we strive together, with partners (if possible) and alone to enable us to experience the variant expressions of our Faith. Each dynamic is essential for holistic epiphany. Group dynamics encapsulate the network of Wyrd, an innate sense of belonging, a profound unity of camaraderie and brotherhood within *that inspires our deepest vision*. In our partners, we discover the Self. Alone we discover Truth.

Traditional Witchcraft is essentially a praxis instigated by one person, commonly, and two or more persons but rarely. Gnostic tradition by contrast, avows a brethren. Traditional Craft however is represented by the tau and the crescent, the stand and the arc as a place of meeting and of working where all ritual is prayer. Albeit for many, no longer. A marriage of such intimacy, once infused with hermetic principle, establishes a perfection within the harmonic conjunction of opposites where Self becomes voided through ecstasy. It is Apollonian and Dionysian; the heart and mind. Neither is separate of nor subject to the other.

Consequently, as none of us (including Roy Bowers and Evan John Jones) has ever considered ourselves as Traditional 'Witches,' I am grateful we may continue under the greater and more ambiguous term of Traditional Craft. Both men asserted such descriptive terms were applied by others external to our Craft. Our preferred idiom expounds a collective tradition, a faith, and a craft as pilgrims in pursuit of the Mysteries. This arcane tradition serves well its gnostic heritage, a gift beyond measure and a blessing treasured beyond mundane kenning.

In essence we are not kin nor are we kith to any Craft of witchery. As a Mystery Tradition we properly assert its place in arcane currents serving Truth in preference to illusion, choosing the magic of mystery rather than the mystery of magic. Though, as ever, our radical heresy shall go un-noticed by those who would both profit the most by it and who would ironically profit the least from it. Thus the work shall whisper only to all who might opt to listen, a needful few then, and none other.

> The beauty of service, the humility of poverty, the joy of despair, the pain of love ...

Serving others is worthy of any, but no-one should ever become servile. From within inspiration flows forth issuing the hermit's light. All sentience is Her becoming active form. So when we enter any trance, or contemplation we shift 'in-between' them, thus we become affected in our musings by both to varying degrees deepening whatever mood we entered that state in. Drug induced experiences may become terrifyingly horrific when subject to simultaneous exacerbation generated by the negative emotional residue of depression.

Needful clearance within the mind of all extraneous stimuli thus avoids the worst excesses of fallout throughout the most ardent execution of cultural imperatives. Shamanic integrity is maintained through a careful priming of the apprentice before all undertakings. Sacred journeys begin with mind-ful instruction of requisite cosmologies before venturing forth upon individual or collective vision quests. It is not for nothing the church described idle hands as the devil's work. Just think of Maya and Buddha who wished simply to explore all distraction. Embracing it he was able to better understand the mechanics of it. If then *you see Buddha, kill him,* for it signifies a loss of true focus.

Everyone should provoke, stimulate, inspire and intuit all gems of wisdom deduced from all responses including random or rogue elements. Teaching constructs of us the best students; teaching is truly a gyfu virtue unrealised in vain pontificating condescension. We learn best through reciprocity. If however, we act as the blinkered leading the blind, whatever we said would fail to generate an echo. Through such acts only do we acquire and hone compassionate discernment absent of judgement. Everything that is said or directed should induce an emotional response, which may then transmute accordingly, relative to one's own apprehensions gleaned in wandering the weary road.

But I was once asked if we do not ourselves wither and diminish in our compassionate exhortations, to which I responded that we would not. For if considered analogous to any plant that has strong roots, draws and is nourished by them, is veiled in light and blossoms under the Muse, what finer act of reciprocity is there than the sharing of its perfume with all who pause in passing to study or regard its form? In sharing its beneficence, however brief, the drifter will remember always that small instant of grace; the plant will continue to grow, as it would, un-diminished by its gift.

Our Muse then suffuses Her gifts to us above and below the boundaries of form and force. Hermetics places these realms according to the heavenly division. The sub-lunar realm is of its nature, all illusion, albeit grounded in the manifest. Only the super lunary realms speak truly to the mind-soul as it traverses its way home. What is witnessed there is an elevation of awareness through and of the self within the All, a state of distinction exempt in the sub-lunary realms of Cain. Known as the Man in the Moon, he acknowledges our errors, improperly deemed sins. These we seek always to correct our aim, to realign our self in tandem with our Wyrd.

We judge only ourselves, as it must be, and if we do not attain mastery of our self, then we must affirm acceptance of the self and move on from that point next time we remember it. It is to commit to memory the journey and so lessen the term of each subsequent return. All is lost to the Lethe if we do not at least keep this in mind-ful awareness. So that is the first goal. The moon-sphere is where we use that mirror to see the self truly, inside, to drop all feigned shadow and light, but to know thyself. There is no passage beyond the moon if we seek Her reflection only.

To that end, we have just one guardian, through whom all possible aspects radiate to their relative and appropriate station meeting each departing soul individually according to its own level of attainment. The Hound spoken of by Roy Bowers and Evan John Jones is the Egregore that oversees all, permeating each thread of the tapestry woven by each individual who lighted upon this strand of Wyrd together. As a conglomeration of memory within a protective form via sublunary experience, the hound manifests through the (group) mind, the objectivity of consent. The discerning self is the lack of surrender – in other words, the resistant self opted to remain as that aspect of the group mind required to prevent external and incompatible forces encroaching within. Similarly the guard at the gate is trust, again generated from mind conjoined within the other. That bond masks fear, which is doubt, doubt and fear shatter truth. Only lack of trust negates entrance.

All true pilgrims must prevail. A very wise person once assured me that we are all here because we failed. The object therefore, is to learn and move on. The web draws us together where we gaze through Her veil to envision the same truth. Our scars will fade in the tears shed by memory. Tears of salt are the symbol of man's labour – the work of this realm; sweet tears the symbol of bliss – the work of the other realm. Bitter aloes and honey are the matter of the work. The difference exists only in this realm where the memory of life and its value are borne aloft, a perfect gift of surrender to Her by whom these fruits are rendered sacred.

All is of the one, and all things return to the one... we have returned full circle.

Evan John Jones refers to his own method in preparing a new working site where he states quite baldly that as he throws a handful of salt around himself, he declares it as *a space now duly sanctified as a fit and proper place of labour, for the work.* This affirms the Germanic principle of labour and work as Id/ida. She is simultaneously profane and sacred in this act of marking the working space together with its cleansing and dedicatory act of the libation. All these concepts are the gift and remit of the archaic goddess of sacrifice who taught this function and format to the first of our kind. It is in that space, that moment of time where infused by ancestral wisdom, we draw from its pool to accomplish needful things through learned instruction and inspired direction.

Compound formulae illustrate such wisdoms though symbolic elements and illustrative tableaux. Salt, sulphur and mercury offer three of the five alchemical states that process matter along with the soul and spirit to configure the realms of life, sleep and death. My own instinctive choices place them as follows: salt is the earthly corporeality, all matter; sulphur is the fiery, etheric soul in ascent. Mercury completes the human compound as the mind, quicksilver of spirit and plasticity of the astral. Yet all make up the complex layering of the world tree: the waters of the mercurial well are present as the font of all wisdom, the sulphuric tree as the anima mundi, and salt of the earth as all the crystalline forms of life itself.

She leads and we follow; we are at any one time, exactly where we need to be in order to glimpse that small speck in the formation of our Wyrd. Beyond that, do we need to witness all force? No? Truth is alone profound. Yet we attempt to understand it, but process is inadequate, wholly so and exactly why Roy chose to abandon reason, surrendering to Faith, falling into Her Truth, the absu void. How wonderful is this gift of grace? Some are born knowing and others die seeking; some are born certain and others die perplexed; some are simply aware and others have yet to become. We each perceive best that view which accommodates our present; the future is spun from the weave of that discovery. Personal struggle presents the biggest hurdle to our achievements. We are all seeking, not the fact of or actuality of the divine, but its absorption into our full awareness.

So, having briefly been introduced to the function and purpose of both Egregore and Hound, we may now look to She whose name within our kinship is not widely known without. Her triune form is (perceived) aspected in conjunction with the personal dæmon (divine self) and the

Egregore together. Beyond that She is infinite. The internal dæmon as a distinct part of an individual filters through Her to that innermost part of one's soul, immersed within the World Soul, mind to All Mind. Between both extremes, intermediaries exist as named filters, others as hierarchies of force.

Certain ancestral family names are used to personalise Orlog (duty to Law) as Wyrd (overcoming of Fate). Many epithets are accepted as given names that are best understood as personal aspects of the Fates and of Primal Law. Each one echoes ancestral attachment through consistent invocation, a mnemonic retention in flesh of arcane unity continually manifests co-existent. Without knowledge of these distinctions, the spirit-blood will not bind in troth those who invoke these Virtues in ignorance.

Ancestors are in a sense deified kin and part of Her, through the soul, through spirit, through mind and now in flesh within ourselves as the ongoing product of kinship extant. An ancestor is part of Wyrd; yet Wyrd is also a conjunction of primal law through Orlog. Such vibrant mysteries are impossible to define/express. We can only begin to apprehend them by individual and personal experience of them, directly. In that instant alone, a level of truth pervades the psyche. Thus I may fail to communicate what I *know* and *feel* but cannot hope to convey. Yet that hope pervades as latent desire, a dreamy wish percolating as personal impetus, fuelling remote though not random expression. Because we are a Clan covenanted through its egregore, the agencies within it are required to fulfil the historical and mythical requisites. In a postmodernist world, that is an arduous quest.

As awareness deepens, our visionary connections enable ever greater clarity. She reveals further diversity of form, forging the rainbow bridge between the realms of the manifest and un-manifest realities. Refracted through this bridge of glass, She falls into the spark within, attracted by Her reflection there, completing Her image, but never as we imagine Her. To each of us, She reveals the inner self. The hidden soul we have yet to discover, void of ego, the pool of memory.

One other profound question I was once asked to consider concerned the immortality of the goddess of Love, She alone who is all beauty. Was Her exception to annihilation because as Love, She is the first and last desire? My thoughts on this regard Her effectively as alpha-omega. All forms of love and all virtue survive therein; all forms of their opposites, equally and regrettably so. For though virtue induces aspiration, without balance, without harmony, there is only pre-determination, which is not the same as pre-destination. One is doom, the other its causality.

All things must then survive.

The void is the pleroma of all things.

She/He form the ambivalent fulcrum of desire, the nux and nub of a needful entirety.

We choose instinctively our impetus for love or hate, desire or need. Deny that choice, and we deny the reciprocal promise of evolove. The all is all, and all is one and all alone and ever more shall be so. This bliss is our release. Our conjunction in Truth is a convocation of Love and Beauty. In seeming paradox, *Love conquers all* and that love survives in humanity for we *are* the World Soul. In fact, all the 'gods' exist, thriving in fact, for they are the clothing of spirit in likeness of their primal templates. But of these, love is the strongest and is eternal. Those saturated in Her, sacrifice all and become Her ... *For I am the womb and the tomb together.*

So in a phantasmagoria of projected creation, it is less bizarre perhaps than at first could be imagined to have a wind deity as the apical ancestor of the Clan; for She is, in that final primal and historical sense, deemed as such. From within those noteworthy and sacred twenty four lamps, arcs of heavens, three reign supreme. These ideas, unquestionable among our ancestors challenge irrefutably our modern sensibilities. Yet the very premise of all existence and its creation rests upon just such magic.

Coupled to this we must consider the relevance of the divine self, often discussed in terms of the higher self being that part of ourselves recognised during its conjunction with the Other. To amass 'form' a deific character reflects its essence complimentary and completes itself within, unlike the primal self, the true self; this other is a force that 'fits' the divine self, a harmonic of like, of kindred vibration.

Though we are not divine in the sense that is eternal and uncreated, we form a host for it, if you will, not so much a construct as a matrix that lends form to the divine self is that part always connected in awareness to the Divine. It has no form or identity; the individual divine self perceives an identity drawn from the many emanations of the divine that we are able to harmonise with. Filtered through the Clan Egregore, She flows, undiminished as the personal link bridging communication between the higher/divine self and the divine itself. Many choose to ignore this reality and sublime personal interaction – a true gift beyond measure.

This explanation is the only one that ever made sense to rational intellect also; the divine self is simply not 'The Divine,' as assumed by so many. How could it be? Nor is the Divine the clothes we weave for it, it is all and none of these things. The divine self is only the housing, the layer of the self able to hold the divine in awareness and thus receive a more personal sense of something that is essentially ambivalent.

Ironically, other forms of the divine feminine present in their all too human qualities a deity of uninspiring generality. For example, though Bertcha/Bertha/Pertcha was probably the most conventional form of a goddess across Iron Age Europe, with Freya and Frigga as yet barely known, within a few decades both had surpassed Pertcha's popularity. Due to distinctly 'female' qualities in addition to their archetypal adherence to all former 'motherly' (sic) qualities much as Isis and Venus, they triumphed over others of their own time. Confirmation is rarely so blatant here exemplifies to what extent we clothe our gods according to evolving needs. I think Roy Bowers and Evan John Jones also understood this very well.

Clearly we do not then invent our gods, nor do we re-invent them, we merely remember them, in joyful anamnesis. We need them to access the vast cultural treasures suspended in myth and legend, for in that ancestral world, steeped in a faith we cannot even begin to comprehend, insidious superstition and fear raged rampant. Although we have failed to completely eradicate these fugue ridden filters from the credulous, we may still witness how awe and faith retain their place as knowledge applied through those experiences surrendered in complete trust.

In descent along the golden chain of being, all force is squeezed down the line; once subject to design it imposes itself as form, that we might better know it, accept it and communicate to and through it. It is vast, and we are such small creatures. Yet I know that beneath this momentary overwhelming, it is ultimately beyond our kenning. All we can do is attempt some sensible measure and allow the All to work its magics; its presence and its reality convey its Truth. For though in our own era, we are a vast populace, in simpler times, long past, everyone stoically believed their genesis occurred from just seven or twenty-four tribes. Such hoary memory ascribes divinity of a kind to apical man, whose obligation is to forever act as dutiful intermediary to all who thereafter bear that name.

From within the pages of old diaries recently discovered is described there among my scribblings, a pledge made almost three decades ago to what was then perceived as a triune 'British Creatrix' who was composed of Minerva, Brigantia and Sulis, now cognate in my understanding in essence as Skulde, Weorthunde and Urdhr. All are mathematically tenable through their associated numbers of 24, 12, 7, 3, all rising instinctively from and of the natural forces of this Fair Isle. Furthermore, these numbers relate to man's own observation of patterns and repetitions in nature, bringing our appreciation of them as manifest expressions of the divine to the fore. Her breath is ancient indeed. As Vac in Sanskrit She is truth expurgated as creation. Her name encapsulates these virtues as subjective and inspired media of application.

She has no absolute name; sensing Her is enough. She needs no name to exist, nor to create; remember her maxim: *For I am She who is older than time, I am She, I am womb and tomb together, for I am All, yet I am No-thing.* Many older workers of the Craft would never utter Her name, in devout reverence. She is beyond all, so cannot be limited to a name. So first we go though Him, the challenger, the cajoler, the trickster and tempter.

Our Egregore draws back its own People bringing them home to be *properly prepared to die, recognised and welcomed by ancestors of spirit and of blood.* All are nourished exponentially. This mystical path has little in common with either neo-paganisms or historical witchcraft. Neither pagan, nor witch then, we revel in our Craft as that of a vestigial survival of the (British) Mystery Tradition. It was thus fifty years ago in Roy Bowers' term as Magister, and remains so now under Robin-the-Dart's.

Angelic potencies perceived as ancestral spirits attached to Clan families are cited in ancient source documents that describe Goda in terms of mind, of a protecting rationale, a central intelligence if you will. Semantics all, for Her faculties, in 5000 years as the Egregore remains a tangible ancestral presence, a psychic link between all its people. All that changes is a time-locked descriptive. As mind/intellect it is linked to the source which is Herself, we are all the mother's children, the source is home, point of origin, not Edin, as this is Edin; paradise is within Himself as guide and teacher.

Ida is the root memory from whence it is believed the Egregore originated. Ida is not the creatrix but the source origin of the Egregore held within our mythos. Ida is our personal name for the place of origin, the root of our being as a manifest living entity. The Source of All Being is not that. Ida is the name of our *manifest* origin. So it is easily traced back to Meru, Turkey, all the mythical places people feel they hail from. Ida, better known as the Garden (its fruits and sustenance) of Edin (its boundaries, Mound and Maze) becoming the first place known to the first of our humane fore-fathers.

According to our mythos and ancestral culture, Ida is in one sense the parent of the Clan, its origin, as homeland and birthplace. Ida is (the origin) filtered through the goda (brain and people of) Egregore, via the tutelary deity – named as Tubal Cain, the triune promethean avatar, guiding light and *abba*. As a father (and son) figure, his role is anchored within the law of human endeavour. Through Alcis, the horse and Eiwaz, the twins, both divine and mortal, by whose virtue we stand harkened, are we ascribed to one particular aspect of Him for all time, transcendent, singular and unchanging. As a kenotheistic monolatry, He becomes very much a personal god, of presence and immanence.

She is however the great 'grandmother' the nuclear cell of our existence, the processor of our mind as it were – who we are. But from whence its spirit? We carry Edin within through the Egregore. Beyond that, the Ultimate Source is that venerable obscure liminality of intangible ideals, the meter of silence as void of the lie. Art conceals the mind's eye to reveal; the fragment of no-thing is everything, all beyond and all no-thing. As Mother of all Mothers, She is Fate or Providence. That single thing alone resides above all gods and all being as She to whom all gods bow; subject to the ineffable rule of the universal cosmos, they are all force. Beyond time, they are eternity. This magnificent prayer perfectly expresses these concepts intrinsic to our mythos:

> *thou who created the heavens and the earth,*
> *order from chaos, and time from eternity, i pray to thee*
> *thou who listens to our deepest voice,*
> *thou who inspires our inherited wisdom,*
> *thou who shines forth the pleasing light and*
> *who protects us from the baneful might of the destroyer*
> *i pray thee always to grant me the inner voice*
> *that will speak of spiritual things*
> *and let love always be our guiding light,*
> *in the name of lucifer and the dark mother,*
> *the one spirit that moves all*

Cultural names exampled here as Holda, Gaude or Freya, even Hekate are but mirrored facets of that Greater Light. The patron aspect is a cultural thing, where the Clan becomes in a sense a macrocosm of the microcosm. Of course we know it to be a Faith beyond that cultural lens. She is All there is and can never be more or less than this. She is the perfect crystal, reflected through infinitesimal kalas radiating from each prismic shard of beauty. Fragments suffuse the Universe, each speck reflects the whole. So it is less that Roy Bowers' description refers to each individual facet perceived of Her, but more that we open ourselves to Her Totality, through that very fragment gifted to us, utterly, without reservation. Every fragment is Her spark, Her personal fragment aglow within each of us. All humanity is illuminated by Her soul light. This is why we live in Her and She in us.

Hidden along the lemniscate symbol of infinity are Her eight shades, fallen through Her veils to form the Compass – the Merkabah of Herself as vehicle and destination in One. She imbues the folkloric Valkyrie and the Disir with ancestral rights to call home their own. Then in reflux, through the Mound, each Compass point reflects a deific feminine facet of Her. All is bound to that totality as manifest/unmanifest potencies. It is why death is not where expected and why Her Face of Beauty becomes the *grimmr*, the Mask of Death. It is the portal through which life and death merge, a vesica piscis of sorts.

The round of life reflects perfectly within the Compass Rose of the people of Goda, termed by Roy Bowers as the *necklace* upon which the nine knots forms the brightest jewels. She beguiles us with Her fabulous necklace enchanted by its beauty. Yet I am reminded that as a symbol of Her virtue, it was more probably a girdle, or breastplate very similar to that fiery ornament of authority, the mighty mind jewel worn by Brunhilde. Brisingamen, formed from Freyjas's tears of love shed as fire, hardened into amber beads and then fashioned into Her girdle/breastplate. This means, like Inanna, she 'holds' the law, the authority of the Me and the spiritual intelligence of humankind. She is thus the patroness and protectoress of humanity also.

Inanna's divinely gifted girdle, the supreme emblem of Her status was surrendered in order that She might know death, that is mortality, the affliction of humanity, whose spirit alone is eternal. Official deposition of Sumerian law, the *Ilu* authority to implement the sacred *Me* is envisioned in the status of Her true crown of qayinship. Granted dominion over three realms, Inanna became elevated as the Holy Queen of Heaven, Earth and the Waters of the Underworld. Her gift acquired from Enki shadowing the similar Odinic endowment was relinquished to enter the realm of death, the plane of non-being where the Laws of Manifest Nature no longer exert any authority.

Brunhilde rejected the noose that bound her to those who might dishonour their oaths of fealty. Yet she humbly accepted a Troth ring. Although both halter and noose perform the same function in form, their distinctive forces offer contrary intent. One only apprehends Her girdle of stars where all souls are bound in a love knot of eternity. All bridges are constructs between one point and another. They form the journey without end or beginning, aligning disparate premises that allow the unreachable to attain corporeality in actuality. Simply, this gift of Prometheus, is hope.

Her breath colours and transforms those qualities our senses record as experiences of Him. His role as guide through all form is variable, adapted to the individual, just as perfume forms a unique synergy with each person using it. These adjustments fluctuate organically to facilitate the requisite shift of each individual. Cosmology dictates a foundational framework, a typology corresponding to the topographical criteria for the people looking to these forms for guidance. Absence of diversity fails evolution. If the presiding deity is of water consigned, its message would not be received in the desert.

Something we had been probing, half blind, for some time, recognising but not with full grasp until recently, was this very principle of adaptation. Despite Roy Bowers' lucid explanation of how myth and symbol engender paradigm shifts, we held only an intellectual appreciation of how extreme boundaries are required to retain core integrity. Discernible by general examples, that central tenet can easily become compromised when another seemingly random element is introduced. Taboo becomes a sorely overwrought or underestimated facet of belief; it is one factor that stands proud in modern praxis as random.

The historicity of philosophy reveals its devolution through time and location, absorbed culturally where grafts are not always as seamless as would be desirable. But those nuances have become the subject of study rather than the structure. Just as the divisive praxis of religion/faith has obfuscated perennial truth that myth records, those myths also speak of its complexities and trial in the hearts and minds of humankind. One fine example describes the directive of certain missionaries involved in taking the Edinic myth to Africa, but the people there simply rejected the issue of Adam and Eve's nakedness. They rejected that as not breaking any god-given taboo relevant to them and so replaced it with incest, making Adam and Eve siblings to one another. This fascinating shift in taboo parallels myths concerning everything, having connotations of immense significance within perennial philosophy. As the purpose of any myth is to retain its own integrity, it becomes fascinating to discover how that tenet, despite all apparent changes in structure, truly does remain intact.

That incest as an arcane taboo became intrinsic within countless myths serves to further illustrate with considerable clarity this impetus of a paradigm shift within the transport of myth. Taboo itself acts as supreme example in studies of the rigidity of specific frameworks built around a core principle for its supposed preservation. Quite quickly we are able to subtract the real nux concealed once within taboo through its repetition and patterning within relevant myth. This fundamental reflection asserts an overarching principle of lateral perennial philosophy.

Groping around another myth cycle concerning the dynamic of the Hero, Gawain and the Green Knight offers a superb example of that same core principle, enabling us to distinguish its patterned matrix, its structural pattern of the cycles of death, of fate, of initiation and failure. This classic perspective focuses upon the year cycle at Arthur's court, of the quest of winter and summer. So, what was the central tenet? Taboo again, but this time of fealty, the honour of troth to one's liege lord and lady. The framework for all myth is the formulae of retribution and loss the breaking of taboo unleashes.

All things human interact at a soul level, without exclusive assignment to other humans, but to all those that include animals; in fact, all flora and fauna. We are unanimously compelled towards certain people, sometimes for a moment, sometimes a while longer. Sometimes we are held forever, others never; for all share a collective sentience albeit filtered within each of us along the way. Hence we must choose carefully whom we work with and open to. There is much wisdom in the naiveté of the fool and also in the sage who plays one.

It is written into our cosmology that we must work under the stars within a ring of stones, hedged by trees and by a river if possible for all the above reasons. To feel the burning sting of wind, the play of moonbeam upon one's skin, to be awed by the grand vista of stars and to draw orgone from all around us, including each other is unmatchable by the craft of man. What finer temple than this our world, the seat of Himself ensouled by Her, a fountain of earthly delights.

The temple of the Shekinah is the Self in communion through all those media. For many years ago we have asserted the favourable belief in animism as the greater and more sophisticated of all comprehensions. It speaks to the soul on all levels, where monotheism fails utterly. Panentheism yields the realisation that everything is simply not inhabited by god but *is* within god – *is* god in fact. The only way and the best way to learn anything, how best to understand is to stand under it. There to be taken apart, turned over and come back to, yet beyond with knowing.

This is also why the gnostic like the brahmin once insisted all devotional acts were held in natural environs. In knowing lies true liberation. Many things will always appeal and seduce the mind, yet these things should be engaged and embraced; but never must we forget the needs of the soul to embrace spirit directly in true holy communion. All is *grist to the mill* as Evan John Jones would say; all necessary for our winnowing oddly (or not) a process that engages the kernel being thrown up to the winds.

> It is all such a beautiful dance, this life, but only where we know the tune, the players and the dancing floor ... beyond those bounds, the discordant cacophany jars the soul in flight.

That the Ida priestess as Gaude/Fate instructs mankind on all arts of the Craft, is perhaps the singularly most important realisation achieved recently. As a core principle of resounding relevance, She asserts Her causality as the Chieftain of all Wind spirits, the ancestral Valkyrie. Better, it refers to Her role as Grimmr, a face many fear, and others love.

> *Freyja kept up the sacrificing, for she alone lived on after the gods.*
> (Ynglinga Saga 10)

Within numerous Gnostic traditions and Mystery schools, certain strong figures frequently occur with specific emphases: these are Prometheus and Epimetheus, the divine twins and holders of the flame through their complementary gifts of Charity and Hope. Several stone reliefs depict Iconicised saints as bridges up towards divine liberty through their mutual virtues of faith, hope and charity. Faith manifests in the figure of one saint in particular, that of John the Baptist.

Another layer forges further connections again by the same three virtues albeit via three canonised archangels; solar Mikael, the mercurial Raphael and the lunar Gabriel. Raphael, mentor to the young Tobias in the apocryphal *Book of Tobit,* instructs him in the apothecial arts of alchemy, science and healing. Raphael is habitually depicted carrying a pilgrim's staff and shares both Sun and Mercury interchangeably with Mikael.

The Planet Mercury rules over the Tree of Life Sephirah 8 (Hod – Splendor), the Greek Deity Hermes, the Alchemical Metal Quicksilver, and Reflective Intelligence.

In Gnostic terminology, a fourth, the Holy Sophia as representative of Grace becomes essential in understanding the initiatory baptism administered through John, of Her holy fire. Mercury's vital angelic potency invites the void of intellect, by use of intuition. Starry Venus too beckons instinct for completion. These Three Queens of the Compass offer water, air, and earth. Mikael brings Fire. Through sacrifice of intellect, piety and devotion, a new shift into the origin of all things is facilitated. Remember, the end of desire (as per *Thunder, Perfect Mind*) is our willing surrender to be Hope for others. Our stoic conviction through Faith brings that Hope to others as we openly act as vessels of light.

Through intellect we may fall first into Sophia, the primal other, though not the earthly Mother. We are wise indeed to consider how Sophia bore the soul, and spirit into the flesh of Venus. We voyage around instinct and intuition back towards intellect to complete the rose. Sophia has for that reason alone in Her purity been the one who breathed the desire, the potential, the need. But She is not Hope, She is forever fallen. We alone are hope; this was the divine gift to humanity. It is *the* journey explored through all others that offers the redeeming Hope for Her and all humankind.

Self thus becomes the bearer of light – the microcosmic Lucifer/Lucifera/ Christos – Self as its own vehicle for growth. Self as banisher of all darkness and the void in-between; self as diminisher and conqueror across the gulf of fear. Crossed by the light of hope that sears all baneful shadows into oblivion, only the light of truth remains bright, stark within the emptiness of reality; It alone of all things carries the dark light of liberation.

Hermits akin to St Francis tend to the needs of one's own soul. This radiance of spirit reflects then into the souls of others in the gnostic way of influence. Gruelling abstinence is a path unwelcome and unsuited to most. Beyond those, so many are drawn into various stimuli as solace is sought, though sadly, not where true respite lay.

This presents the onus of a duty of care to maintain an outward presence rather than abandon people everywhere needing the merest support or full mentoring, safely. The luxury of indulgence is therefore denied us; to others then we look within the pastoral nurturing noted in line with the maxim: *Physician, heal thyself.* This uncomplicated duty of service is a reality.

And so in final summary of a living Mystery tradition, of all tenets and praxis intrinsic to a rich, diverse heritage offering certain nostalgia, it should be noted that we may, if we ever have the presence of mind to employ it, present ourselves as gnostic heathmen. Yet however appealing, in reality the People we remain, battling upriver, the underground stream so beloved of all heretics, it's in the blood!

Lezekoak

ARKAITZ URBELTZ

AM A MAN FROM THE CAVES; it is in the caves my soul breaths fire and restores its vitality. There are many caves in the Pyrenees and some are more home than others, but what they all share is that they serve as mouths for mysteries, because in all caves Mari dwells and shields the world from the hunger of the earth's secret centre who breaths fog and flames beneath our feet. It was to the cave that Mari sent her first human twins, Mikelats and Atarrabi, to be taught by the memory of light resting within the cave itself. Humanity was the child of light, a light both obscured and guarded by the many mothers of land and being, and from the cave wisdom and illumination was extracted. In a way we are all children of the cave, the difference is that some of us still have a memory of this, whilst most have forgotten.

In the mythologies of the world the cave represents a place where prophets are born and visions are received. The seven dreamers spoken of in De Voragine's *The Golden Legend* and Qur'an sura 18 were laid to rest waiting for Judgment Day in a cave. Saints such as John the Baptist and Elias gravitated towards the cave, the living tomb of mankind, the uterus of the mothers. The cave is memory. It is here at the gates to the fire at the centre of the earth, which strikes to the inner sanctuary of God, where wisdom dwells. In a world that worships ambition and selfishness, wisdom will often become a scapegoat for all that is wrong, and thus the cave becomes a gate of terror and dread. And so it is from the cave I write about the ways of the *sorgin*, as one who makes his own fate and walks goose-footed across the worlds. Since it is from the caves I speak, riddle and silence will pass between words, because the sorgin exists under the Sun and lives under the Moon, a paradox and a truth which Francisco Goya expressed in his paintings of the world of the other.

Julio Caro Baroja and José Miguel de Barandiarán have written extensively about the mythologies of the Euskaldunak, or the Basques if you prefer. They have demonstrated sensitivity to myth and legend and how it reflects the reality of the sorgin and in this hinted at the multiple possible readings. For us myth and legend riddles original truth and because the blood has given us a twin set of eyes, we can see the form and its essence, just like a bull by day is merely a bull, but under the rays of the Moon can become or be something other. This balance between night and day is fundamental to how we see the world and has little similarity with people out there that have taken this term sorgin, as their own.

The idea of the *sorgin* holds so much more than the current witch beliefs often encountered today. A *sorgin* is born from need and necessity. We are born to carry a burden that belongs to us all, but in order to carry it well we have also been given the knowledge of the necessary tools. This knowledge is not strictly about the pagan cycle of the year, nor is it about rites of worship of anything. We pay respect and reverence, sometimes out of love, but more often because of need and duty.

All things have a name and when something *is* it is possessed by *adur*. The philosopher Andrés Ortiz-Osés makes a parallel between *adur* and *eros* and *mana*. This parallel can suffice to give an idea of what *adur* is. But it still cannot convey how a sorgin perceives, understands and possesses *adur*. This difference can never be spoken, only experienced as it makes part of an arcane perspective of the world and our purpose as *sorgin* and *belagile*, people of the pact and the blood. *Adur* must always be followed by *indar* which is the ability to make use of *adur*, and this power is born from need, a secret fire that belongs to the *sorgin*.

The Basque land held a particular interest for the Inquisition. When Pierre de Lancre came to the Basque country to investigate the many cases of *malefica* for the inquisitorial tribunal he not only did this as a servant of God, but also to make peace with his own ancestry. He found the Basque people to be ghoulish and strange, inconsistent and wicked in their ways of life and sexual lewdness. As his ancestors were calling him back to his house so his awe and repulsion grew. In his notes we find a blend of the grotesque and beautiful slithering on a thin twig of faith and the blindness only faith can give. It so happened, for good and ill, that De Lancre gave the world some of the most detailed and shocking accounts of what he saw as witchcraft practices. He fused truth with horror and diabolism of a Christian cast, and this has coloured the modern view of witchcraft which is seen as some form of paganism or polytheist heathenism and a peasant rebellion against the Church. This is, as I see it, a revision of history as we were doing what we were used to doing until Christianity came and said we worshipped a figure called Satan, a figure they brought, as he was unknown to us until the people of Kixmi (Jesus Christ) came. I have nothing against Kixmi, and so we are not a rebellion against his people, but as I see it, they stole many of our secrets and they tried to make us change the ways of our mothers. Is it so strange that we want to take back what is ours?

There are hundreds of examples in De Lancre's presentation that have a kernel of truth, but they are constantly infested with his fascination with the Devil. Take for instance the following paragraph:

> The Pythagoreans thought that when men were born, that is, men who were to become witches, a certain animal was born with them that they variously called a beast with several heads, discord, inconstancy, and mutability. Iamblichus calls it a beast with many heads, inconstant, and light. They no doubt meant the Devil.

There is truth in this, because we are born with our 'beast' and our *jauna* (lord), and indeed this beast has many heads and forms, like the soul itself. But we can perhaps disagree in his postulate that Iamblichus and Pythagoras saw in this the Devil of Kixmi's people.

De Lancre called his treatise *Portrait of the Inconstancy of the Witches*, but I question whether the inconsistency he read in the Basque ways were really his own and those of a changing society, as Julio Caro Baroja suggested in his treatise about the witches' world. The *sorgin* is rather a stable element; he or she does not give in to the fancy of the world or change his or her clothes to make society comfortable. The *sorgin* walks the road of fate with tongs and hammer in their hands. And as the Moon goes through her gardens and the sun through the signs of the horoscope, so also does man and the world go through a cosmic rhythm and growth in order to remain true to its core. The inconsistency is more with those that resist the natural flow of the world and want the Sun to be the Moon and the Moon to be the Sun.

The *sorgin* is a child of night and the secret fire that is veiled within the spirits of night and caves, he or she is the child of need, he or she is therefore someone that constantly keeps the chaotic powers in a state of peace. Hence, he or she is a mover on the outskirts of the world. In saying this I do not intend to claim that the *sorgin* is engaging in some form of altruistic act; the stability of the world is merely a consequence of the stabilising work with chaotic forces that in turn makes the *sorgin* flow into the balance of Sun and Moon in harmonious ways. The Sun (Eguzki) and the Moon (Ilargi) are the two poles of the dynamic of all things. For us they are children of Mari, two daughters placed in the heavens to serve as Janicot's eyes, ensuring that God sees all and watches over all as God of Day and God of Night.

Ilargi is *adur* and Eguzki is *indar* and so it follows that all things breathe life and death in a constant dance of death and birth, and this is mirrored in Mari's first human children, Atarabbi and Mikelats. The night is refuge and contemplation and the day is action and accumulation. Their mother, Ama Mari, is the animator of cosmos and creation and brings all into being.

Anthropologists constantly deem Mari to be a demoness who shows herself in red, white or black, depending on the degree of mercy or destructive power. Yet she is not a demoness, but is instead the merging of opposites, or rather their origin. Naturally, the symbiosis of all there is will hold these oppositions as a unified globe of movement alternating destruction and becoming, because that is the very essence of being named and being.

From this arises the famous Akerbeltz, the Black Goat of the Sabbath, Mari's lover and son. The goat, as well as the bull, is a masculine symbol of fertility, strength and protection. Mari loves the Bull and the Goat because of this power they hold to protect and bring forth progeny. The goat as the mediator of what moves between Ilargi and Eguzki is deemed to possess all knowledge. He is equally demonised because of this and seen to represent one who fails to understand that the spirits of night are not the spirits of the day.

Hence, the *akelarre*, the celebration in the field of the goat, is a celebration of the powers of *adur*, repose and contemplation. It is the Sabbath given by the spirit of dream and also the Sabbath as danced out across the body of Mari. It is veneration, a living sacrifice and a soothing of the worlds, a celebration of the eros that binds Ilargi to Eguzki and brings ecstasy, joy and hope.

The world under the light of the Moon as well as the Sun has many masters or lords and of most importance are perhaps the Basajaun and Basandere, the Lord and Lady of the forest which are creative spirits and great protectors of the wildlife and greenwood. In a way it is these lords and ladies which ensure that we can still commune with the *jaunak* (lords) of the night and be on good terms with Ama Mari.

The veneration of Mari is also replicated in the household. The house, and in particular the kitchen where the fire of the house burns, is the domain of Mari and the lady of the house, the Etxekoandere, is a living manifestation of Mari in a particular point of nature set aflame by Mari's protective powers.

Mari is said to live in caves, and several in the Pyrenees are said to be her dwelling: Zabalundi, Urkiola, Amezketa and Orzoko amongst others. Some have found this to be inconsistent and confusing, but Mari is by her nature everywhere, so naturally a great number of caves hold her presence. It is the same with her forms of manifestation: she can be seen as a tree shooting forth flames, as a vulture, a bird-footed woman, as a horse or a goat, as a fire serpent, as a woman dripping fire or riding a pig or a ram, but most often she is a reddish woman holding a flaming sickle with snakes crawling beneath her feet. Mari often take zoomorphic forms, because she is all there is, and these animal forms testify to her richness.

Mari is said to have one husband (but multiple lovers), Sugaar or Maju, both being snakes, but of a different kind, though people usually make no distinction and see either of them as diabolic *sugeak*. Even those prone to the Christian superstition of good and evil often name Sugaar as Lord of the House and treat him with deserved respect, whether or not they see him as a devil. In token of this, it will serve the house well if an axe is placed over the door with the blade facing upwards.

Barandiarán tells in his *Mitología Vasca* that Mari condemns lying, theft, pride, boasting and the failure to keep one's word, disrespect of others and neglect of the need of others. We summarise these demands of Mari in the proverb: *ezagaz eta baiabaz*, which means *with denial and with affirmation*. There are several legends and stories telling of how Mari manifests to sow

destruction upon people who fail to keep her commandments by allowing the person to fall foul of his own lies, pride or robbery. To keep one's word is considered extremely important; it is better not to promise than to promise and not be true to one's word.

The *etxe* (house) is a sanctuary and must be treated as such, because this too is where Mari dwells, in the cooking fire, where she infuses the Lady of the house with her creative fires of renewal and destruction. The Etxekoandere is the guardian of the woman and the tomb and this is what the hearth fire seals. All negotiations should be done in the kitchen with Mari's fire burning, the Etxekoandere being heavily involved in everything, this will bring Mari's attention to whatever business is being done. Any house should be treated as the sanctuary of Mari, and how do we treat Mari's sanctuaries?

The rules for consulting Mari are as follows: When you find a cave where she resides you must address her respectfully before entering and offer water, wine and milk at the entrance, stating why you have sought her out. You must state that you are coming to her with no deceit in your heart, lest she strike you down and make you one with Ama Lur (the earth). You will then walk into the cave and bring to her milk, wine and water. When you leave the cave, you leave in the same way as you entered, meaning that if you entered walking forward you will leave walking backwards without turning around. You are forbidden to sit down in her presence and should either stand or kneel in such way that your buttocks are not touching the ground. You can than state the nature of your visit and wait for her response there or later in dreams.

Mari is also the Queen of *laminak*, or *lamias*, usually seen as riverside sirens and nymphs that often fall in love with humans. This relationship can be good or bad depending on many vectors concerning the rules of the old ways of the land. We are here confronted with a term which is not alien to us, as the *lamia* were popularised by romantic poets in the 18th and 19th centuries and depicted as vampiric seductresses. This does hold some truth, but as with so much, has been polluted and distorted by a flying fancy and a supercilious adoration of something that is other than what it seems. The *laminak* can kill you by draining you, by making you disappear or go mad, but they can also open roads and gates to unfathomable riches and rewards; as long as love is present.

Mari loves the thunder and the storm; hail is her punishment and fog is her grace. Especially dear to her are the storm spirits Odei and Itsai, which are the thunder and the lightning as found in the profundity of the cave's darkness. In this lies a great mystery as profound as the deepest cave and Akerbeltz, the Black Goat is its vehicle and mouth. There is no worship in this, but reverence and communion, and this is what the infamous akelarre is about. In Zugarramurdi we go to the Akelarren Lezea, the cave that is at the meadow of the male goat but today it has been overtaken by people of a pagan disposition that drive the spirit of the cave deeper down, closer to the heart of the earth.

The world under the Sun might be seen as pagan, but the world of Night belongs to the *sorgin*. Here we find the chaotic forces that threaten the pagan order and these forces must also be kept in their rhythm so chaos doesn't flood the world of the Sun. But let me return to the caves of Lezea. Martinez de Lezea in his collection of Basque legends concludes that the rituals of the witches had one common denominator: that they were banned by the church. He also gives some ideas about the nature of the rituals that can bestow the witch powers upon a person. Amongst these he mentions circumambulating the church, rejecting baptism, and receiving a *kuttuna* which is usually translated as amulet, though it possesses a mystery far deeper than this. He also mentions that one can kiss Etsai and make the sign of the cross with one's left foot and make the following declaration: *Por la se, zalpate, funte fa, funte fi, txiri, biri, ekatzu, ekatzu, amen, Sasi guztien gainetik, hodei guztien azpitik*. In this or similar declarations one swears to be one with Etsai in some form or call upon Etsai to open a state between states. In the latter charm which calls Etsai above the bramble and below the clouds it is used as a key for congress. Many of these riddles encoded in charm hold power both because of the intonation, and the reference they make through myth and legend which calls back to the memory of the world.

Etsai has many names like, Gaizkine (Malefic One), Yusuri (Scourge), Galtzagorri (Red pants), Kapagorri (Red Corporal/Captain), Txerren (Bad, Traitor) and many others, these being either epitaphs given to Etsai under the influence of the Christian Devil who was syncretised with him, or names of other nocturnal spirits. The name itself, Etsai, means *enemy* or *opposer,* and with the advent of Kixmi in the Basque country, this role was demonised, with Etsai and Satan seen as the same spiritual force, no doubt helped by the linguistic similarity.

For us Etsai as the enemy is not understood in the same way as the biblical Satan. For us he is not a beautiful rebel angel, but the image of God reflected in the mandrake as it lights up the cave in memory and dreams. Etsai is old, almost as old as God – he is (t)his forgotten state, and naturally with the advancements and evolution of the world of humans he turned into an enemy; because he represents something forgotten, namely wisdom. He is also said to walk with spirits like Odei (spirit of night storms), Amets (spirit of dream) and Gaueko (the spirit of Night). By the same line of association Etsai was also seen as the dragon St Michael held under his foot. This is an image we find cause to celebrate, but not in the ways Kixmi told his congregation! In many ways, Etsai can be seen as an adversary because he is one of the prime powers Mari uses to execute punishment upon those sworn to her that break their vow and code of honour. The *modazaharrak*, or old ways of the land, are strict in their demands of truthfulness, of keeping one's word and avoiding lies and deception of any kind.

Etsai can come out from his cave in Lezia or other caves where he dwells in the form of a snake, bull, horse or a pig. He is usually red, like his lover, Mari. When he comes out it is to watch over the world, to visit his children or to make love with Mari; and thus infuse all being with forgotten light. It was to Etsai that Mari gave her first human children, Atarabbi and Mikelats, to teach them the wisdom of the world so humankind would be wise and crafty.

The way of the *sorgin* is about upholding the order of the world, the world under the Moon. Because of this we rarely speak words, as the rays of the Sun multiply in joy what we say. Eguzki is wonderful and perfect, but we are not of her world, though she is of ours. Because of this we find our home, our etxe, in the embrace of Gaueko and Ilargi where the water of the moon serves as a constant reminder. We are not of this world, but the world is from the cave, the place of origin, the daybreak of the ages.

Once in a while Mari comes to my cave with her laminak and the land grows moist with fog and night dew. She takes my milk and wine and I go out from my cave to hear the mighty heavenly snake Herensuge strike the earth voluptuously and I lose myself in love and ecstasy. In this moment I turn into leaf, wood and dew as the night blazes red, red as the eyes of the bull watching the nightly renewal of the world and its mysteries.

BIBLIOGRAPHY

BARANDIARÁN, JOSE MIGUEL DE, *Mitología Vasca*. Txertoa, 1979.
BAROJA, JULIO CARO, *The World of the Witches*. University of Chicago Press, 1965.
LANCRE, PIERRE DE, *On the Inconstancy of Witches*. ACMRS, 2006.
LEZEA, TOTI MARTÍNEZ DE, *Leyendas de Euskal Herria*. Erein Argitaletxea, S.A., 2002.
MARLIAVE, OLIVIER DE, *Pequeño Diccionario de Mitologia Vasca y Pirenaica*. Alejandría, 1995.
ORTIZ-OSÉS, ANDRÉS, *Los Mitos Vascos*. Universidade de Deusto, 2007.

A Gathering of Light and Shadows

STUART INMAN and JANE SPARKES

RADITIONAL WITCHCRAFT, despite that 'traditional' prefix, would seem to be a volatile and protean thing and difficult to pin down. I'd go as far as to say that from one perspective the name 'traditional witchcraft' is something of a misnomer as it can change, develop and evolve with great rapidity, reinventing its traditional roots which very frequently, although they certainly exist, are from traditions and groups that did not call themselves witches. Some strands of the tangled web of traditional witchcraft are undoubtedly lacking in any kind of tradition, and it is frequently these very people who affect to despise Wiccans, despite the fact that Wicca has a proven lineage that goes back at least as far as the 1940s, something most traditional groups lack. More reputable and sensible groups and individuals are likely to respect Wicca and are content to differ. They will no doubt show both a great respect for tradition as well as a refusal to be enslaved by it, after all there's little point in cleaving to a tradition that lacks meaning or that needs to change in order to uncover that meaning. For instance, among the main transmitters of the ritual known as *The Waters of the Moon* are the East Anglian Horsemen. It is certainly true that one can learn a great deal by studying everything available about them, but in order to become an effective toad-witch it is necessary to go beyond the bounds of their traditions, to delve into older, possibly more primitive influences, and to bring them into the present time without compromising the essential nature of the rite. The Horsemen were also entirely masculine, swearing never to divulge their secrets to a woman, but a study of their traditions is very useful to a woman who seeks to be a toad-witch.

It is that essential nature that we need to seek, not some dead traditional form which might do more to hide and stifle the essence than preserve it. Neither cleaving to mere form, nor abandoning the spirit within the tradition, it is necessary to negotiate between these extremes and arrive at one's own synthesis, a lifetime's work for anybody, regardless of whether or not they inherit a stream of traditional craft.

In my own case I do have something of an inheritance, but mostly one of responsibility. I have frequently reiterated that Joe Wilson was far more concerned with transmitting, to anybody capable of understanding, the essential method of 1734 rather than a ritual form. He asked that I should be one of three guardians of the 1734 stream, not strictly speaking in lineage from him, he was clear in his last days that there was no such lineage, but of the methods and basic principles that could be applied by anybody willing to undergo that discipline and capable of grasping the method. This doesn't mean that within 1734 there are no lineages, but their relevance and authority are self-contained by that lineage and have no relevance for others. So, if I establish such a lineage it will no doubt be of benefit to those who inherit it, but there will be others outside of that lineage who will be just as much 1734 as my lineal spiritual descendants.

The current essay is an attempt to chart the development, firstly of my own study and then its development into the Clan of the Entangled Thicket alongside its founding and current Maid, Jane Sparkes. I originally intended to write all of it, but found that I needed to incorporate lengthy quotations from Jane as well as rewrite many passages at her suggestion, so I have tried to allow her voice to come through in a slightly unorthodox manner, neither quite as a full co-author nor merely as a quoted source. I feel that this allows a different perspective to communicate itself within this text that might be of value to somebody who is serious considering the study of the 1734 method.

During the time I have studied 1734 it is inevitable that my understanding of it should change; although I can't take too much credit for that transformation as although I have striven to understand its many dimensions, and often worked very hard at this, much has been beyond my control or intent, an influx of information and inspiration from many sources, each transforming the possible understanding of 1734 and reflecting off each other. Some of these sources have been outside of 1734 itself, I must mention here the inspiring and poetic work of Shani Oates, the Maid of the Clan of Tubal Cain as among the most important examples, and also John of Monmouth's publication of many of the texts of Roy Bowers' group under its various names and offshoots, Thames Valley Coven, Royal Windsor Cuveen, The Regency and Clan of Tubal Cain. Both the Regency and the Clan fed into the 1734 stream, some ways are very apparent, others less so. It is well known that Joe Wilson was the recipient of a series of letters from Robert Cochrane that inspired many aspects of 1734, including its name, but many seem to have ignored the contribution of The Regency and Ruth Wynn Owen. In some ways this is understandable, Wynn Owen's group, Y Plant Bran, although it remains in existence, remains publically very quiet and comparatively little can be seen of it in that most public of realms, the internet. One may gather certain things about it by looking at the website of an allied group Y Plant Dôn, but one should not assume or presume too much by the common link between the two groups without a degree of inside knowledge, which, frankly, I lack. What we do know is that Ruth Wynn Owen was a major influence on Joe, a fact that he acknowledged in his final version of the 1734 website.

In the same website Joe discussed his first teacher, 'Sean,' who remained such a shadowy figure that it was possible to assume he might not have existed or that he might be an amalgam of several people who had influenced Joe's early development. Any such ideas were thoroughly scotched when a cache of letters from Joe to 'Sean' were sent to one of the Guardians of 1734, Aisling, by Sean's widow. It was immediately apparent that, far from being an imaginary figure or even one greatly embellished on by time and memory, Joe had presented Sean in a very factual way, had studied with him for several years and remained a close friend for several more, nearly ten years in total. Sean emerges as a fascinating and still enigmatic figure who attempted to bring together the different aspects of his heritage, Scottish-Irish and Native American alongside local folk magics. It is also worth mentioning the appearance of a mass of notes, substantially written by Joe for an early 1734 group The Pantheon. This was preserved by Dave Finnin of The Roebuck and later broadcast by him as a scanned document which he referred to, somewhat erroneously, as *Joe's Book of Shadows*. None of the texts in this document mention Sean, neither do they directly mention Ruth, although they refer to, and briefly quote, her teachings.

In his last years, Joe Wilson had attempted to impart the essence of 1734 rather than its form. He had always intended the form to be fluid, but had often found that many people were always happy to throw away the baby, but would hang on to the bathwater with grim determination. For example, where Joe had used Wiccan elements as a sort of scaffolding for the more traditional material from his early teachers, some people seem to have done their best to 'wiccanise' 1734. Although it is important to recognise that some individuals and groups did indeed work in a valid manner, continuing to employ the Wiccan influence in the form of their workings, others bastardised it unforgivably, making the riddles and questions into a petrified dogma set in a neo-wiccan landscape, the very opposite of his intention. So, the question for Joe's last students was what was 1734 when all that formal structure was stripped away? What was the essential method and how could it be built into something that was closer to his central concerns at the end of his life? Joe spent a long time seeking the essence of shamanism and folk magic, not trying to take from other people's traditions, something which is often done without proper respect for the traditions, spirits and people from whom they are taken, but starting with where one is. This begins with a simple relationship with sun and earth, nothing sentimental, just the recognition that without them we would not be here. From that point one seeks a direct relationship with spirits and Spirit and in order to find this one needs to set out in the open and wilder spaces, the paths, fields, woods.

My own induction into 1734 seemed very different to this in that I was caught up in attempting to solve a series of mythopoetic riddles and puzzles. Of course, as I was trying to absorb the lessons of Metista and Toteg Tribe my rather intellectual and poetic strivings had a very different context to mere mental acrobatics. There is certainly intellectual effort involved, but that is something like a launch-pad for a more informed intuitive approach, a holistic approach one might say, in which intellect and intuition are brought into balance. Some people have understandably made the mistake of supposing that 1734 is based on Graves' *The White Goddess*. This is not the case, but the initial tests often are, drawn more immediately from the so-called *Robert Cochrane Letters*. Cochrane's own tradition the Clan of Tubal Cain is, in turn, not based on Graves, but, although it sometimes leans on his work for support, its origins and meanings are quite distinct. So, the Cochrane method uses his work as a series of examples and explorations of possibilities, it is a poetic method rather than the content that is at stake. Without the poetic method all is dully literal; rather we need to learn a twilight language.

It is fair to say that the method is also used as a way of helping people to develop discrimination between enchanting ideas and the often gritty truth. It is in this friction that we can best develop real poetic insight. So it was only gradually that I was able to really develop a praxis that started to respond to my own understanding of 1734's essence, and then only when I started to work regularly and cohesively with Jane who was to become the Maid of our tiny clan. We increasingly abandoned anything that belonged to Wicca or to Druidism (an important part of Jane's background) and attempted to identify the principles of each working so that we could work spontaneously around those principles. We sometimes made mistakes and sometimes found that the mistakes worked better than the way we had considered correct. We worked mostly in the garden, a lovely and secluded spot, but were increasingly drawn to the nearby woods. Traditional elements sometimes emerged within our freeform praxis, for instance, I had, some years previously, found a single antler tine that I had used as a wand or pointing tool. I then found out that there were several in the Boscastle Witchcraft Museum. They had originally been used in sail-making and because of this connection with harnessing the wind were subsequently used in weather magic. The tine therefore seemed very appropriate to use in summoning the Wind Gods. This idea came to me only gradually, as my notion of who and what the Wind Gods are was transformed by practice and meditation. Although they do relate to the elements, they are not primarily elemental guardians, but the Winds, and it is their force that drives us around the Mill towards the realm of the Queens or the Rose Castle. Therefore they become essential to our practical, as well as philosophical understanding of the Mythos.

At this point I would like to quote extensively from Jane's notes to give a different perspective:

DOORWAY TO THE MYSTERIES

Jane Sparkes

LTHOUGH Stuart's entry point was through the magic of the riddle, such things did not grab my attention in quite the same way. My way through was via a different gate. At first, I had spent a lot of time and energy trying to prove that Robert Graves' obsession with the tree alphabet was really only practical from his personal standpoint, as someone who spent a lot of his time away from these shores. As I have a long-standing personal relationship with the trees he examines, it made me dig even deeper to prove he was mistaken in some cases. However, in my dogged determination to prove a point, I discovered something rather important. It is not the validity of the actual information that is so important, but the path you are on whilst seeking. In other words, it is not the questing beast that opens the doors, but the quester herself.

So as a child of Cain, born to wander, searching for a resting place, always seeking truth and wisdom, I am up for the chase, but in so doing, my awareness needs to be in the here and now, never taking my eyes off the prize. And as Joe Wilson said, *experience is the only real teacher*; and I seek that experience, not in my case through the solving of riddles, although that is still a valid gateway, but it is not one that all may find. Personally I have found that: *the answers to all things are in the Air-Inspiration, and the Winds will bring you news and knowledge if you ask them properly. The Trees of the Wood will give you power, and the waters of the Sea will give you patience and omniscience, since the sea is the womb that contains a memory of all things.* (Robert Cochrane) (*Amen and amen again*, I say to those words. JS)

Once we began to work the woods there were various places that seemed either natural 'hot spots' or symbolically relevant to us. For instance, there was a beautiful old tree with a hollow trunk that looked like a table, so we started to make offerings there. We had already used the little river that flowed nearby for various workings; we now looked at various sites in a more complex way, identifying mythic factors, crossing the little bridges on the river, walking the paths that ran by the cemetery. Eventually we identified a crossroads that seemed just perfect. It aligned with the cardinal points and just slightly North-East there is an oak.

When we attended the Scarlet Imprint 'Summer of Love' event in the Summer of 2011 we were struck by Jake Stratton-Kent's talk, not only for its intrinsic interest, but how he described a magical landscape that in many ways, including some small details, related to the mythic landscape that we had built up and worked with in the Clan of the Entangled Thicket. What Stratton-Kent was talking about was something very different either from regular temple-based ritual magic or from neo-paganism. He seemed to be describing a magic that was earthy, but not earth-bound, sensual, understanding that the otherworld and our world might overlap or even be the same, from a very different perspective. What we are discussing here links to Stratton-Kent's talk only tangentially, but in a way that it might open doors for a few people. I shall discuss both the ritual or mythic landscape and the connections between Joe Wilson's late expression of 1734 and the Afro-American tradition Hoodoo. The two meet, wouldn't you know it, at the crossroads.

ROOT AND BONE: FOLK MAGICS

OW I WANT to back-track a little. In the last two years of his life Joe Wilson had become increasingly interested in Hoodoo. There were several reasons for this. Firstly, his last wife (there were several) Cher, was an African-American woman who practiced Hoodoo. Secondly, he said that although it was not the same, it was similar in many respects to the sort of folk-magic he had learned as a young man. Thirdly, he had enrolled as a student on his friend Cat Yronwode's Hoodoo course and he was recommending it to his own students.

I was a bit surprised when Joe seemed rather insistent that I should learn Hoodoo; after all, I was not only white, but British, what sort of connection would I have with an African-American tradition? Although Joe had founded 1734 in the 1970s he had gone through a long phase of disenchantment with the way 1734 developed and a fascination with American Indian practices. To some extent this was a filtering through of influences from his first teacher, Sean. Sean had been of mixed ancestry, part Celtic, Irish and Scottish and part Amerindian. He spent much of his time with the local Indian tribes and the influence was strongly felt in his teachings. Perhaps Joe was trying to reach back into this aspect of his mentor's work, but seems to have gone overboard for a while and studied with controversial Indian teachers such as Sun Bear. I think it is reasonable to say that Joe was to feel a sense of remorse later and when he set up Metista the focus was on not taking from the practices of other cultures without permission and without cultural context, but finding within one's own inner and cultural resources the essential nature of one's own spirituality. Joe spoke scathingly of those forms of cultural appropriation all too often found in new-age groups and books that were too often merely theft and frequently led to eclectic mish-mashes that lacked any kind of integrity. Although Joe came to espouse a kind of shamanistic practice, he very deliberately distanced his version from new-age neo-shamanism as well as the so-called core shamanism of Michael Harner. For him the problem with Harner's work was that it took tribal practices from very different, usually Amerindian, peoples, and put them together regardless of cultural context. Therefore the degree to which they might mesh together mythically was limited and thus so was their potency. And what spirits might come, summoned by people not their own, not having the connection to the land or the people and spirits of that practice?

Metista, and later on Toteg Tribe, were in large part an attempt to develop not only a community of people who based their spirituality on their own internal and cultural resources, but one in which they could consequently access the inner realms on these terms and without taking from exotic traditions. Now, given this, why on earth was Joe suggesting I should study Hoodoo? On the face of it, Joe's enthusiasm for Hoodoo might have seemed contradictory, but I think there were good reasons for it. Firstly, as I have said, Hoodoo has many similarities to the kind of folk magic Joe learned in his youth. Secondly, as it is not usually an initiatic tradition, it is, as it were, an open source in many ways. Beyond this, it is important to realise that as a syncretic system, Hoodoo has never been purely African American, having many traces of European and Native American influence and indeed, historically, there have been White practitioners of Hoodoo for a considerable time. So, for the American members of Metista and Toteg Tribe Hoodoo constituted a living tradition of herbal and folk magic that could be learned and practised with at least some sense of harmony with their dominant culture, although the very history of Hoodoo reveals a degree of antagonism as well and I will discuss this a bit later.

My early experience of Hoodoo felt both very limited and rather abstract. I could read a certain amount, but had few supplies and had little idea where I could find more. I heard rumours of two botanicas in Brixton, but nobody seemed able to tell me quite where they were. Some Hoodoo ingredients were easy to find as they were common or garden herbs and oils, others seemed extremely exotic. Somebody finally showed me where the Brixton shops were (actually only a few doors away from each other) and then something changed my view and my experience completely: I actually met a rootworker living in London.

Dr Beetle was a young African-American woman who had grown up in New York, then lived some time in the South before marrying an Englishman and moving to London. She had been taught Hoodoo by her Godmother who lived in Brooklyn, but had originally come from South Carolina and was of the Gullah people. What was initially a rather cautious friendship became, over a period of time, something like an informal apprenticeship. I don't want to over-emphasise this, but there was a gradual building of trust and then sharing of information and then, rather unexpectedly demands were made of me, that I should help with some piece of work or should read certain books. These books were usually not the rash of new and popular works on Hoodoo practice, usually rather shallow and frequently 'Llewellynised,' but mostly historical works, for example Yvonne Chireau's *Black Magic*, an account of the origins of Hoodoo through slavery and oppression. It became obvious that Hoodoo is not the rather pleasant new-age herbal magic portrayed in Stephanie Rose Bird's *Sticks, Stones, Roots and Bones*, but a weapon, the only weapon of the unarmed and helpless, in a war fought over centuries. To be more precise, it is many things, but if you ignore this aspect of Hoodoo, its use to dominate, jinx, hex or curse, you deliver an emasculated version of it that is reduced to the same new-age eclectic mess that every other magical system seems to end up as.

This is not to say that every Hoodoo spends all their time cursing their enemies and attempting to dominate everybody around them, but because these are real and living issues in communities that practice folk magic, you really need to know about them if you are going to be effective in counteracting dark workings. For instance, if somebody has been working on a person, undermining their confidence, drawing them closer to their own inner darkness, will they really feel much confidence in someone who just draws a few pentagrams in the air? Even at a purely psychological level the work would seem to need to be more physical, more embodied, where the practitioner might do something for their client but also give them something to do that will enforce the psychological message. Baths, washes, powders, all have an element of physicality that gives the magic a sense of reality. When Dr Beetle asked me to help her in a house clearing we visited her clients to find them living in wretched circumstances. They believed that they had been hexed by the grandmother, apparently well known in her community for working negative Obeah. Even if they had not been worked at they were very definitely stuck in their situation and were reinforcing it themselves. We made a spirit bottle for them to trap and eliminate negative forces. It contained layers of goofer dust, glitter, pins, roots and other materials making something designed to counteract whatever worked against them. In a short while their situation changed for the better. While they had been utterly stuck in their grim flat in an even grimmer estate, their lives gradually shrinking around them, they found ways out, new accommodation, relief from their negative personal situations and renewed strength to deal with their difficulties. The difference manifested throughout their lives, physical, emotional and psychological. I think that what was important here was that the work was tailored to suit the needs of the clients; it was not a one size fits all approach, and I am sure this is a major reason why it worked.

More recently we came to know another rootworker living in London, Miss D. She was rather different, specialising in love and lust work, her background was not African American, but neither was it very English. Born in the Philippines, she had been adopted by a British couple, but had led a sometimes itinerant childhood and her mother had picked up elements of Hoodoo tradition on her own travels and transmitted them to her daughter. D. had then started to study on her own and while not having the same basis in tradition that Dr Beetle had, she was able to use what she knew very effectively. At Lammastide that year Jane and I invited her to join us in our seasonal working and it was happy and successful enough occasion that we then decided to do a collective working in a crossroads in the woods. In fact, our working was oddly eclectic; we were all going there to do something of our own, but together. Miss D. needed to go to the crossroads to work with St Expedite and carried a statue of him to the crossroads. Jane needed to call on Hekate and I wanted to work with one of the spirits of the Toad Bone Rite. Normally I do not like this sort of eclectic approach, as it tends to confuse things. Each working was valid in itself, but didn't necessarily mix or fuse with the others, so it could have all fallen flat. Nevertheless, it was a night we still frequently talk about, it felt like a real night of power.

I want to change tack at this point. So far it has been mostly a narrative; now I would like to examine more closely some of the issues that seem relevant to this curious relationship between 1734 and Hoodoo. It is not, as you must have realised by now, straightforward, but while I never wish to avoid complexity or brush problems under the carpet, I don't think we need to be overwhelmed by these problems, far from it. This sort of complexity, addressed with a certain straightforwardness, does not resolve into mere simplicity, but it is something that becomes very direct and real and fantastically rich. So the remainder of this essay will break into brief sections, each addressing some of these issues on their own ground. Some are comparisons, finding of common ground, some are tensions or problems; all are a part of the fabric of my own branch of 1734, for better or worse. (*For me, the important part is to be able to examine things in a different way, and which gives me a clearer view of what I have and hold.* JS)

THE FAMILY, THE ANCESTORS AND THE HIDDEN COMPANY

IT IS WORTH MENTIONING that the ancestors play an important part, both in Hoodoo and in all of Joe Wilson's work, not just 1734, but Metista and Toteg Tribe as well. One should not really speak, as many do, of ancestor worship but certainly of respect, of veneration and of contacting and working with them in different ways. Certainly the ancestors are central to traditional Hoodoo as indeed to most folk magical systems and it is they who give the magic their power, so this would seem to be an area we need to examine in more detail.

According to Joe, we can break the ancestors down into three fundamental categories: firstly biological ancestors. Most cultures have a great deal of regard for the people of their own bloodline, they are literally our family and are often those most likely to help and support us, protect us from negative works and harm. But at the same time they are still who they once were, even if they are wiser and more powerful. Also, it has to be acknowledged that not all ancestors are benign and many might baulk at workings of magic and witchcraft.

The second, almost equally important category, is that of spiritual ancestors. We need to consider our late teachers and their teachers, even if they do not constitute a formal lineage. It was an important experience for me to learn something about Joe's first teacher 'Sean.' When Joe had spoken of him I didn't actually have any evidence that he really existed. Joe spoke of him as if he did, but he remained shadowy and unreal to me. Imagine my delight to find that Joe's account of Sean had in fact been very factual and direct, apparently not romanticised or fictionalised at all. I certainly could not claim Sean as official lineage, but he was my teacher's teacher and the revelation of him to me seemed to make a sense of contact with him a reality. At the very least he gets that moment of veneration when I pay homage to my ancestors. In the realm of spirit, and most especially where there is no bloodline involved, the notion of spiritual adoption is of paramount importance. Within many forms of Traditional Craft one is not simply inducted into a group, rather one is adopted into a family. This is an important reason why we speak of clans rather than covens. By this act the initiate can, with right effort, find access to the ancestral and tutelary spirits of the stream. Within this scheme the ancestors especially, but also the tutelary spirits, relate to the egregore of the clan. Within the wider scope of the stream we might find a great degree of variation here. Obviously some of the ancestral spirits will be particular to the individual, their own ancestors and the spirits with whom they forge bonds or make pacts. Others form, in different ways, some kind of lineage. In 1734 there is no lineage as such, although the different clans and covens within the broader 1734 family do have lineages. But 1734, as a method, allows direct access and development of one's own relationships with ancestral and tutelary spirits and it is difficult to make any definitive claim as to how this might be expressed in any group or individual.

So, all 1734 groups derive, directly or indirectly, from Joe and his teachings. Joe is always therefore in ancestral relationship to 1734 as its founder. Some might have inherited particular ancestors and guardians from working with Joe, others might have forged relationship with quite other spirits. Everybody will have ancestral spirits of their own, even if they were adopted. The ancestors are always with us. In my own case I have my own mix of biological and spiritual ancestors, human spirits who seem to be in some kind of relation to me, and various other, possibly non-human spirits, such as the genius loci and the patron spirits of the Toad-bone rite.

A GATHERING OF LIGHT AND SHADOW
Tutelary Spirits and the Genius Loci

YPICALLY, MANY SPIRITS that one might encounter in various ways might be considered non-human. While the ancestral spirits, in the context I have discussed them in, are specifically our human ancestors, by blood or adoption, many others are of a different order of being. Among the more important ones are the genius loci, the spirits of place. As our work developed, we became increasingly aware that we needed to form relationships with, and not just placate, the spirits that inhabit both the physical and the mythical landscapes in which we practice. While some might be more or less generic, they are mostly particular to the locality, which is, after all, why they are spirits of place. This stream, this tree, this clearing, field, pond. Some would appear to be more transitory, moving as animals do, maybe are indeed animals, actual or not, others seem rooted to the spot. We started to make regular offerings, mostly of cake or bread and wine, sometimes other edibles, also smoke, perfume, brandy, whiskey or rum, even water. We also quickly took up the practice of leaving coins as offerings at certain places. (*These spirits can become helpers even when not performing a working. On an individual basis, my primary connection is with the spirits that reside in a particular place. These spirits can also lead you on a dance and get you lost, the lapwing dance is always present!* JS)

If I think of the various guardian spirits of which I am aware, the first is Mortimer, an ancestor doll made for me by Joe Wilson. Mortimer seems to have something of Joe's character and curiously winning ways, in his origins he might have been thought of as a servitor, but he seems to be far more than that, very much his own person, but never a human being. He travels freely between the realms. He is a go-between, almost a psychopomp, and can help forge relations with the spirits of place. They, in turn, can be either well defined or vague, according to our experience of that place. Some can be more or less synonymous with the spot they are spirits of, effectively are that tree or whatever, while others can have a wider sphere of activity. An American colleague recently discussed the question of a tradition rooted in British myth approaching the indigenous spirits of the Americas. It seemed evident to me that an indigenous spirit of place would not be 'Indian' or First Nation but would precede the Indian tribes, possibly by millions of years – to some degree depending on the nature of the place. While we would all experience these genius loci through our own cultural filters, in themselves they would no more be Indian than Celtic or Saxon or African.

On the other hand, the spirits that belong to a stream of Craft will, in different ways, be profoundly shaped by our culture, but then it is necessary to consider both what that culture is and how they might depart from our expectations. Too many depictions in the pagan and occult communities have gods and spirits wafting around in 'timeless' gowns or looking like refugees from a heavy metal album cover. But would, say, Tettens, really look like Gandalf, or would he look quite other? To some extent their appearance is dictated by how we visualise them, but as they develop a sense of reality for us, these beings, gods and spirits alike, move into a more reciprocal relationship and shape our perception of them. For the group it is important to agree upon the appearance of these beings. This was hammered home for us when we read John of Monmouth's *Genuine Witchcraft Explained*, where Roy Bowers expresses his frustration at the group's inability to arrive at this agreement and imposes a form for their 'Hermes.' This agreement allows the proper development of the egregore, the group mind.

THE MYTHOS

UR PERCEPTION OF the gods and spirits rests to a great degree on our understanding of the clan mythos. A bare outline of the mythos is included in the document *The Basic Structure of the Craft*, but it would be a mistake to suppose that this is the entirety of the mythos or that we do not deviate from it. As is so often the case, I cannot speak for other branches of 1734, but our starting point was that document and from it we elaborated a great deal more at various levels. At this point it is useful to mention the publication of a work by Shani Oates, *The People of Goda*, which gives an unprecedented insight into the mythos of the Clan of Tubal Cain. This has been extremely useful

for us, not only in seeing how we resemble a related tradition, but how we depart from it. The simplest explanation might be that we understand our mythos as a whole to consist of many levels of related mythic cycles. This is necessarily open-ended, the mythos is not static, but rather a growing thing, dependent on our current understanding. It is not the same as it was a few years back and in a few more years it will have transformed again. Within this one might discern a 'pagan' level, almost in the currently understood usage of the term, but also a more Christian level, albeit one that most Christians would probably not recognise. One might speak of Hermetic or alchemical levels and also of both Luciferian and Cainite understandings, especially in relation to the rite known as The Waters of the Moon – the Toad-bone Rite.

So, if we consider the yearly cycle and the relation between the Horn Child and the Lord of the Mound, the battle of the Twins, we also consider how they might relate to the way we experience the Goddess, as Rose Queen, or Pale Faced Goddess, as Hekate or Lilith. We find a path that takes us across the River and through the Wasteland and finally to the Rose Castle. This much is established, but for each person the path is different and has many byways unique to each of us. On the one hand this means I would not wish to over-define the mythos in a dogmatic way, because the outline may remain constant, but it will be different for you than for me. It is also essential to our way of working that while the realisation of the mythos awaits the discovery of the landscape that can accommodate it, the mythos is also in some ways shaped by the landscape, at the very least in as much as it plays a fugue on the mythic components as we discover them played out within the actual land. The myth takes on flesh, real encounters and imaginary merge and change places. Clearly this is an evolving work and much would change if there was a permanent change of location, but the clan work is also a moveable feast, elements of the mythos would change and others remain, but as ours is very much an evolving work, much will change as we grow in understanding.

THE MYTHIC LANDSCAPE

E HAVE ALREADY referred to the notion of a mythic or ritual landscape in which the ritual forms of the working are played out. The actual land becomes the focus for different kinds of working and different forms of the compass. But more than that, the land becomes hallowed through working with it and new relationships, between the practitioner and the land, and its spirits, develops. While we have a compass area within a secluded garden, in which we can work and feast and elaborate the mythic landscape in miniature – an important aspect of the geography of the compass – by entering the woods, even though they are very managed and heavily populated by joggers and dog-walkers in the day time, at night the woods are transformed. We can wander from place to place, use particular trees that are relevant to our mythos, oak and holly among others, features of the wood, the clearings, a bridge, a crossroads and a place that signifies the Castle. By pacing this landscape we are not only walking in this world, a suburban wood, but also the Otherworld, the ground becomes sanctified, or perhaps its sanctity becomes recognised. It reveals a different aspect of reality, the process involves the body and the mind, emotion and sensation together. At one of the key points we find a crossroads and slightly to the north-east an oak. This has become one of the key places of how our mythology plays out for us, not as a single sacred tale, but as an interplay of real and imaginary and a natural intersection between the worlds. We need to emphasise, however, that we are not working in just three dimensions, but several more in that there are many levels and worlds and different modes of access according to the kind of working.

COMPASS AND STANG

HE STANG IS probably the most familiar symbol of traditional witchcraft and has been known to be adopted within Wiccan and neopagan circles. It has usually been described as representing 'the god' and this is true as far as it goes, but like a lot of things in Traditional Witchcraft, only as far as it goes, and in fact it goes a lot further than that. Recent publications have shown how the stang

has various other names, including the Horse which suggests that it might be regarded as a vehicle, and indeed there are engravings of the 15th and 16th centuries that show witches on forked poles, much as they are shown on broomsticks in popular illustrations. I would suggest that it must, like many things in traditional craft, reveal itself as polysemic which is to say that it contains many meanings which cannot be exhausted by any single description, and if this is true of the stang it is even more true of the Compass.

While I have heard of people describing the compass as *what traditional witches call the circle,* it is in fact something quite different; or rather its meanings are far from exhausted by such a description, it is many other things besides. In particular the compass can be understood as the map of the other worlds, as the territory of those worlds and as the vehicle by which on can travel the worlds. It can be a circle, a square or a crossroads, Cain's blood-acre or the Castle of the Rose Queen and much besides. At the most generic level we are speaking here of sacred space, but it is not just that it is declared special and *sacer* (Latin: apart) but it embodies a flexible symbolism that charges it with meaning. Actual symbols might be used in various combinations as a kind of memory theatre, mnemonic devices for triggering associations, this, of course, is common to many kinds of temple work, although here the symbols can be both man-made and natural and to a great extent include the nature of the location. For instance, Evan John Jones refers to several different kinds of location used in the rites of the Clan of Tubal Cain, a hill, a cave, an abandoned chapel and so on. In The Waters of the Moon one keeps vigil in a graveyard, some rites are held in woods by certain kinds of trees.

Apart from the actual location the nature of the rite is announced by the tools used in each case. The stang is most commonly positioned in the North, but in her book *Tubelo's Green Fire,* Shani Oates reproduces diagrams showing it in the centre and in the South of the compass. In our own workings we move the stang for some of the seasonal festivals, so for the cross-quarter festivals it remains in the North, while for the equinoxes and solstices it travels round the compass through the year. So it can be seen that the stang can provide different foci within the compass according to purpose, but it would seem to do far more than that, and it is only one of several tools that we commonly employ.

If somebody was so inclined they could create an experiment quite easily, either by bringing together a collection of tools or by making a set of cards of those tools and moving them around the compass in different combinations. If cards are used this can be done in miniature and this is indeed a very valuable exercise, although no substitute for getting out and working with this idea in the flesh as it were. Start by considering the directions in the traditional compass. Although we use the names of the Wind Gods as given in the *Basic Structure of the Craft* document we see them as fundamentally forces, potencies, rather than statically as personifications, or rather they are both. Although they do also embody the elements, they are not primarily elemental guardians, but Lords of the Winds and much can be learned if you consider just how many winds there might be. Nevertheless, they do also embody the elements as a part of their function, Lucet for Fire, Carenos for Earth, Node for Water and Tettens for Air. So one possibility is what happens if you put a symbol for water in the fire quarter? This question is true in any symbolic system that employs elemental correspondences. If you put water with water, clearly there is a harmony, if fire with water there is a tension or friction, or maybe just steam! Consider though how, in the Golden Dawn they employed complex combinations of the Tattwas in order to explore and work with different aspects of the elements. It is possible to do this with the tools of the Traditional Craft, albeit in a possibly more homespun manner.

So, if by positioning tools along the compass one can portray shifts in the seasons or develop combinations of elemental power, this still only seems to give the compass two dimensions; it has far more than that. It is said that the Compass is the map of the Otherworld, the Otherworld itself and the vehicle by which it is traversed. Put simply it is not just the flat circle on the ground (actual or imagined) or indeed a sphere, although this too could be a part of what one works with, but it also has height and depth so that one can enter the Underworld or attain the Upper Worlds through different ways of working. The symbols are laid out in a way appropriate for the world one wishes to explore; the necessary inner work is done so that one can enter. This is where the Stang helps to mark out the territory in a quite different way. We know that other names for the Stang are the Horse and the Tree. Again we find that a symbol is open enough to be both the territory and the vehicle that takes one to that world. One of the important aspects of Cochranian Craft that has become publicly known is the correlation between the Stang and the mysterious diagram known as the Mask. That there should be some point of identity should not be a great surprise, but the degree of detail and sophistication in this system is considerable. Again I point to Shani Oates' book *Tubelo's Green Fire,* where she makes it very clear that Cochrane was thinking in terms of analogies with Qabala and the Tree of Life. It should certainly not be thought of as identical or simply rebranded, but as an analogous system in which one can ascend the worlds through the Stang's symbolism.

Imagine then a mobile and flexible symbolism in which the static magic circle is replaced by something like a kaleidoscope whose meaning is determined by the position of the relatively fixed items used in the working. For example, in a more or less impromptu working some months ago, we used among other things a fox skull, deer antler and toad bones marking out the compass. We could have easily used other objects, depending on what we had found or what we carried with us. Also, it is more variable than this as you might arrive at a different symbolism to us, through different circumstances and different promptings of Spirit or the spirits.

VALE: TWILIGHT TONGUE

HE SYMBOLS OF our craft reveal many different meanings, according to need, season and our own predilections. While we might be firm in the observance of a principle: *We have no hard and fast dogma that we adhere to, what we do hold fast to is change itself, carried along by the winds, and if we fall we arise stronger. We embrace our heritage, found in the hills, woods, forests and streams of this land. It cries out from the very roots of the plant that live here, and blossoms forth in their flowers, and laps over our feet as we stand on the shores of the sea. They are my teachers, and I listen to their voice.* (JS)

I spoke earlier of the Twilight Language of the Tantras, also known as Intentional Language. It would seem to be of two forms. The one is the inner meaning of the symbolism of the tantras, something that might be common to all to whom it is imparted. The other is whispered by the dakinis, especially in liminal states of meditation, dream and trance. While there are obvious differences between our Craft and the tantric traditions, I insist that at this point there is a similarity. The poetically understood symbolism of the Letters and the Basic Structure of the Craft, once brought together with the art of listening to the winds, the trees and the waters, and to the voice of Spirit, constitutes our Twilight Tongue, heard imperfectly now, but ever more clearly.

This also has some bearing on our final point; Jane asked a question in her notes: *So where does that leave us as a group?* And she began to answer: *This is the never-ending quest for answers that fires our clan engine, and drives us ever onward. It means that nothing is fixed, all can change. However it has also become clear that for clan workings we need to develop the egregore, the group mind. So although we might have different interests, influences and leanings, when we work together we pull together, so our focus becomes complete agreement on the working we will undertake, and the shape of the images called to mind.*

The egregore is fundamental to much of occult work, but sometimes seems to get overlooked. In our case we were strongly aware of it, but it remained a bit nebulous until we read *Genuine Witchcraft Explained* and saw just how we had avoided something fundamental and obvious. But however obvious the egregore might be on one level, it can't be taken for granted. It is not a passive form, but something that, once activated, speaks the Twilight Tongue and thus in dealing with it one must become increasingly proficient at speaking and reading a language that may or may not have words, hieroglyphs or visible symbols, endlessly variable and eternally constant. There remains so much to do, each stage of the way opens up at the proper time and we tread a path that is happily and proudly our own. We have found few companions so far, but we have not sought any, until now. We have felt for some time the need to open out to those who can understand this path and who find sympathetic resonances in what we have to say and who might then walk a way along with us wherever it should lead.

The Fall and Rise of an English Cunning One

TONY MACLEOD

T IS SAID that those whom the gods would destroy they first make mad. But what do we define as madness in an upside-down world that is governed by arbitary seeming social conventions? An outsider would consider these conventions to be madness, yet society does not. The ego strives to find its place amongst the crowd and denies the spirit its journey, stumbling blindly, distracted by the noise and confusion.

By civilisation's own rules it is often a madness that frees the man, a fall from grace that silences the ego. Delusion melts away and in the distance we start to see the answers, they were there all the time and like so much Craft knowledge, hidden within plain sight. My own story follows this path.

From a young age I had a sense of the other and the need to reach out and touch that which I could not see. Laws may be broken but to break with human convention is a sin, to pursue this quarry is to willingly cast yourself away from acceptable society and places you in the company of others who would also attempt to touch the gods. Confused beings stumble upon these crooked paths, would-be guides and mentors seek to add to this confusion, as there is power in keeping the dispossessed in this bemused state. Many follow these leaders, content in the knowledge that they finally belong to something; occasionally glimpsing the other and assuming the words of fools are the truth. It is a heresy of sorts to question your guide and yet I have questioned all and have found myself an exile even in this strange land.

For many years the questions persisted, close to answers sometimes, yet further from the truth in others, the ego still in control and the true self a subdued being fighting for air beneath a sea of discontent. A searching, fuelled by anger and the need to fit in somewhere. A feeling that I could not be a man alone on this path or I would likely fail in this quest for the grail. To fall here would render my existence pointless, my acquired knowledge worthless and my life's work a waste of a life.

Then I fell.

This fall was no slow descent into the realm of madness, I was in freefall down a well of utter despair. My ego clasped at the sides of the well as I fell, desperate to find a hold yet the walls were smooth and steep, the light disappearing from view. Added to by the pain of failure, this inability to hold all that I was together, this was a self-destruction created by a noisy ego, my own fault and divine justice, and stinging tears burnt the skin upon my face. That was that day I died for the first time. None saw the corpse, yet many could observe the gaping cracks that appeared in my personality. The corpse was hidden, like the knowledge I sought to embrace, this man was broken and there were none who could repair him.

All things must die; this is a divine truth that is universally recognised and this creature that we call the ego is no exception to this rule. For a new beginning there must be an end. I see this now, though at that time the helpless cries of this dying monster of my own making blocked out the sound. My dearest and most beloved heard the cry and yet there was no tear shed for this passing, as she knew in herself the seed of creation was starting to stir.

There I stood at the crossroads once more, many possible paths spread out before me. Behind I perceived a wasteland, a past that no longer belonged to this lone figure at the meeting and parting of ways, a choice to be made that in all truth was no choice at all, for amongst the destruction there were gems which I had carried for many a year, beneath the dust they still shone, that sense of the other, those connections to the greater whole, those very jewels that the greater population considered to be the signs of madness, or at best the products of a deluded mind.

> I know that I hung on a windy tree
> Nine long nights,
> wounded with a spear, dedicated to Odin,
> myself to myself,

> on that tree of which no man knows
> from where its roots run.
> No bread did they give me nor a drink from a horn
> downwards I peered;
> I took up the runes, screaming I took them,
> then I fell back from there.
>
> (From the Hávamál)

With what I now held in my hands, the journey of the fool began as I set forth upon the path that few choose to walk with absolute honesty. To separate the lies from the truth I had to re-examine all that I had, the tools of the Craft, the learned words of others, the trappings of life and love. The books I had acquired over many years had little meaning now, the wisdom of so many reduced to pulp, much of which was fit for the fires of need and little else. Yet there was inspiration within the piles of dead trees, two men, whose words still rang true even here in this dark place, lost voices that still did beckon in the wilderness that was my soul. I owe my debt to Roy Bowers and Evan John Jones, calm voices within a storm of noise, men whom one could see were truly inspired by She who would show us the light, searching souls who gave all of themselves and took only what they were given. They were the foundation for this would-be cunning man to build upon anew, and that is exactly what I did.

It is need and not desire that drives the human condition. Desire leads us back to Ego and to return to that path is to deny one's own evolution. To stand within the compass and to assume to know all that these realms have to offer is heresy at best. A far simpler answer is to be a child, a blank slate, one who is prepared to listen to that knowledge that flies upon the wind, then and only then will She open her arms and gather you home again.

> Upon the rough twisted edge of the abyss I stand.
> Dawn breaks the change of man.
> Beyond the reach of the beloved and upon the wings of destiny, we fly.
> Head long, straight into the arms of fate.
> To stand upon that distant land,
> To knock upon the castle doors.
> Many rivers to cross, many mountains to climb.
> A road less travelled to a destination rarely seen.

That blessed isle, that perilous realm.
Pray be with me now,
for this holy fool does stand or fall at your will.
An infant soul, to the arms of his mother goes.
I would beg you now to be kind, to hold me in your love,
not brush me aside as autumn leaves to the wind,
Ash to this storm.
I am the clay to be shaped,
the sword in the stone.
Mould me, temper me.
I am yours.

No compass was marked upon the soil just my simple stang and a pile of tools that had no meaning, the quarters were realms to be explored, to listen and look and see what I found there. Spirits of place gazed down through the swirling mists at this hapless fool who stumbled from north to south, east to west, picked up the knife and kicked the cauldron, yet for all this I could feel that connection had begun to grow. Those shining stones which I held were as sparks from the forge. The Rose unfolded once more within my life, a solid foundation. To dream was to build an understanding based on instinct and not doctrine. From the fire of need the rose did grow and bloom.

Yet I was alone, if Fate herself had decreed this was to be, who was I to argue with her plan? Perhaps as the solitary man I would have to serve, yet I yearned for companionship within those dark nights of ritual, to celebrate in the company of others, but desire will always lead you back to delusion, so I left that one in her hands and concentrated on the work at hand. The call went out, green fire to light the sky of any who had the eyes to see.

This wind of change blew away that which I had thought I had in common with the general pagan community of our isle, many of whom had stopped looking forward, content in their own little worlds, becoming as indoctrinated as the followers of the modern church and as inspired by the same vices as popes, cardinals and bishops had been before. Witchcraft was for sale on huge commercial levels; a taste of the lie for the sake of a coin, and I was not prepared to buy. Wisdom was free for those with an open heart and an open mind. My own place was not among the sheep and I had no wish to become the shepherd either, the path of the hermit would suit just fine until the time when, and if, the gods would bless this one with a true Family.

Traditional Craft in the sense of working groups/clans/families is not open to all, its practitioners come from many walks of life and anonymity serves to protect those individuals from the attacks and petty concerns of the masses. These orders are closed and they are not for sale to even the highest bidders. Yet blood still calls to blood. We all have this gene and it is not something we inherit as a gift. Not all of us choose to engage with it and turn it on, it is a decision we make from which there can be no return, once one has switched on there is no way to be switched off.

The call came, slowly at first, when offensive remarks about people I had never met, made by those I did not know, struck home as personal insults, acid vitriol that cut to the bone. The bitterness of those who have been denied the blessings of gnosis, family and heritage led to circumstances where beneficial contacts were made. Friendships formed, discussion groups shared information and finally mentorship from people whom I could really respect.

This was my call, I was coming home to roost, to know at last as I stood beneath the stars in wind and rain that I was not alone, that there were those I knew who would be doing the same beneath and among the same. A family of sorts, separated by place and what seemed impossible distance, although joined through blood and cause. Who I was and what I was doing was verified by those who were becoming dear to me, the questions were beginning to be answered. I was whole and this was a blessing indeed, a flame that was to become part of a far larger fire.

Although a path I no longer desired, would need drive me further? I have gone further than I ever thought possible, steadily the boat sailed, driven by her blessed wind. Not the hurried journeys of today's want to haves, but an immersion into a current, a stream to which I belonged. Yes I had fallen, but Faith had brought me safely into her arms, she held me, she showed me her way. She gave me passion and purpose within the light of her love, and we travelled forward together.

Connections to others of my kin grew and grew, until that time, beneath the map of our existence, in the space between the worlds I stood, arm in arm with my brothers and sisters of the craft, there by my own free will, oath sworn and bound to the law, open to this new world of promise, companionship, company and the love of family. The patterns of the year began to take on new shapes, different perspectives and shared experience, true blessings force the lies to become as dust to the wind, chaff from the wheat.

Another part of me died that day as well, need moves us on through a series of deaths until we are ready to face our own true end. Together we go, straight and true down this unwavering path, for it is worth remembering that there is no crooked path after all, only crooked people upon it. But family is not achievable by all, the path of the holy fool is an honorable one and a gift in itself. It is no more or less valid than any other voyage. However, do not consider this or any true path to be an easy ride, for it is work that pays the dividend. For every door that is opened there are a multitude awaiting discovery, and no one can open them for you. When my own life was turned to ash I was left with one thing: Faith.

I have walked in the realm of the dead and returned, stood in the hall of my ancestors, I have been illuminated by her divine light, cradled in her love, I have seen his passion and glory, stood humbly at the door of his house as I stand before you now. I bear the mark of Cain upon my soul and carry her own within my heart. But perhaps I always did.

An unspoken when.

So, when exactly did she come to you my boy?

At what point among the confusion of your life did she pluck you up and mark you as one of her own?

Was it the Sun's rise upon a crisp autumn day, or perhaps that night you sat and watched the lunar spectacle as she travelled from east to west, radiant reflection upon black water and golden sand, sea spray illuminated bright white as it bubbled and foamed along the shore.

Was it that lone piper who gently serenaded you and yours as the sun rose above the mists of Avalon, those notes that carried you far beyond the realms of men, further still than Arthur's quest.

Maybe it was the broken man, whose own quest for shelter left him cold and desolate, asleep at night beneath the eves of the local cinema, gone soon after dawn's break, his whole life consigned to a pair of scruffy polythene bags intended for groceries and not much else. Empathy, compassion and anger were her gifts to you that day, and like the bags, you carry them still.

Could it be the day when you found an injured bird, shaking in its terror, broken wing and eyes as wide as the hub caps of the car that struck it down, the injustice of it all, the lack of reason in this senseless world, you thought a night in an old shoe box with some food freshly dug from the garden would resurrect this fallen angel, yet in the morning, the dull and lifeless body lay upon the old towel, surrounded by dried up worms intended to fix it's broken wing. Nature was cruel that day as is her way at times.

Was it that time within the bustling metropolis, when across a sea of concrete, of lost and lonely souls, you first set eyes upon your beloved. That single moment in time when that sense of wyrd was so strong, you knew then that this was a forever moment, a joining. Fate's busy plan in action and fruition, that which was alone would never be so again, a kiss beneath the sodium light to seal that bond for eternity with never a regret, every precious moment a gift from her.

Was it this vagabond tribe that gathered around you both, the sense of absolute love that came with it, blessed with the company of like you found your own, or perhaps they found you. Still the result was always the same, an oath unspoken yet you are tied to it. Was that when she marked you as hers my boy?

Was it when you took another's life to feed your children, did the blood on your hands make you sad, was the sacrifice worth it my boy? It may not have seemed so, yet it tied you to her in ways you did not know, reaper of souls, pale faced wanderer.

Was it within the cloak of darkness, where you deigned to meet her, never a demand, and yet he took you to her, the crackle of the need fire, music of the night, that acceptance at the crossroads, that divine gift from you both, she told you there would be others, that you would find your family and you did. You never doubted her for a moment.

Was it then my boy?

Well, the truth is my boy!

Are you listening?

You were hers all along.

That breaking light upon a spring day, when you were unceremoniously expelled from your mother's womb, kicking and screaming, into this world of mixed blessings and hurt, before then you bore her mark and will carry it ever more.

You were hers from day one my boy.

As was I.

Stregoneria: A Roman Furnace

NICHOLAJ DE MATTOS FRISVOLD

Stregoneria is the art of living strategically, with passion, dedication, desire and intention, taking into their own hands the responsibility for their lives by transforming the death of the physical body in the birth of the luminous body.

TREGONERIA is the warriors' way of god-making and self-deification. It is an absolute rebellion against enslavement, where the world above and the world below are treated with equality. There are no bended knees or prostration for the Stregone, just the word honored by blood and determination in the name of freedom. It makes demands upon those of a certain character and disposition; the disposition of a god who sets out to forge his or her Fate and build a world of subjective truth, someone who accepts challenge as fuel for his or her fire. This essay is based on the works of the Maestro Fulvio Rendhell and I will at times make his words my own, and as such this article can be also considered a tribute to him.

There is a widespread tendency to present stregoneria as a sinister deviation of stregheria, similar to what Carlo Ginzburg speaks of in his *Ecstasies*. Ginzburg tells how the witches in Friuli in the 16th century went out to protect the fertility of the land with fennel stalks. These witches were called benandanti (blessed or benevolent ones). We find accounts of skin-leaping and going forth in the numinous body. These same witches can in their punitive form appear as malandanti (wicked ones), the enemies of fertility and the grain. This distinction seems similar to what we find with St Claus and Krampus. It is also important to take note of the many comments Ginzburg makes of the malandanti being associated with the *loup garou* or werewolf. Here we have a connection to Stregoneria as the people of the wolf.

Stregheria is peasant craft; it is a view of the world and nature that spins across the two pillars of certainty: birth and death. It follows that Stregheria is about fellowship and family, whether of blood or with allies in the flora and fauna. A *stregone* might be part of a clan or family, but stregoneria itself creates family, one based on the recognition of kinship, not family in the literal sense we find within many houses, clans and families of traditional witchcraft. For stregheria, the sanctity of home and hearth is important; it is a beautiful and stabilizing current of power and truth.

The connection between stregheria and stregoneria is found in the term Roman, because the *stregone* holds a distinctively Roman outlook on the world and being. By this I mean the attitude born from the Roman furnace as a people who were fed on the milk and blood of wolves. Rome that captured the Sabine women, Roman as in a warrior who twists whatever is found between the pillars of birth and death to the full extent of his or her numinous consciousness. Roman in finding a way where there appears to be none.

Stregoneria is not about worshipping gods, but about becoming a god. Such an apotheosis is readily available in the very dynamic of the stregone's art. This is also why the vulgar interpretation of stregoneria is that it is a satanic current. It might be so, but we need to then agree upon a context and meaning for terms like 'God' and 'Satan.' An understanding of this dualistic dichotomy is found in the context of ecclesiastical theology. If we want to understand stregoneria as it grew in the shadow of the Church, we need to return to the time from Charlemagne to the papal bull of 1231 spelling excommunication for heretical clergy as well as baptized commoners now considered witches and troublemakers.

Until Charlemagne the Roman Catholic church was truly catholic, with room for nearly all heresies and interpretations. The great purge of Church doctrine, followed by schism and later the reformation holds significance as it tells of the turbulence of the time. Here then is a glimpse of those conditions. In the biography of Wala, Charlemagne's advisor, we can read about the many accusations and scandals related to poisoning and malefica surrounding the reign of King Louis the Pious (814–40): There was witchcraft everywhere. Policy was based not on sound judgment, but on auspices, and forward planning on auguries ... Lot casters, seers, interpreters of omens, mimers, dream mediums, consulters of entrails and a whole crowd of other initiates in the malefic arts were driven out of the palace.

Due to the scandals at the castle involving King Louis and the evil acts of Louis' eldest son from his first marriage, Lothar did what he could to take the throne and it ended with Lothar inaugurating a campaign of slander and gossip directed towards Louis' most influential advisor, Bernhard of Septimania, together with the Queen Judith and Bernhard's sister, Gerberga, a nun who was practicing magic. She was drowned in a river together with two other nuns. The important point here is that during the Carolingian reign an awareness of magic became widespread. In 899, two people were executed because it was believed they had killed the emperor Arnulf with venefica. In 1028 several women were tried and executed for having killed King William, Count of Angouleme with magic. Exodus 22:18: thou shalt not suffer a witch to live moved into the forefront of ecclesiastical paranoia and judgment.

In the same period we also find stories of clergy venerating and communing with spirits considered hostile and sinister by the Church, even Lucifer himself. There are also monks, popes and bishops like Gerbert of Aurillac (Pope Sylvester II, † 999), the monk and Bishop elect Theophilus († 538) and Pope Caelestinus († 432) who were accused of making pacts with the Devil and being more well versed in magic than was considered proper. We even find a story from 1323 telling how some Cistercian monks in St. Denis had offered up a black cat to Lucifer/Satan/the Devil in the hope of finding a thief. These monks were – along with the cat – burned at the stake in consequence of the 1231 papal bull of excommunication that gave the death penalty for the practice of unlawful magic. Stregoneria and the grimoire tradition is intimately entwined in this and we find Stregones like Cornelius Agrippa instrumental in the preservation of mysteries though veiled in an acceptable neo-Platonic format.

Some have suggested that the Ordine della Luna, passed to Alex Sanders in 1979 by Prince Paleogus is tied to this succession of stregoneria by virtue of being 'the oldest coven in the world' dating to AD 328. The story of such old covens like Ordine della Luna forming in the time of Constantine do hold some truth, but if so, this must have been a conclave of philosophers and warriors, people of a Roman bent that saw in the Church just another illusion of truth that they had no problems entering into. The value of Ordine della Luna for this essay is not to verify its claims, nor to dismiss them, but simply to state that it is not unreasonable to believe that a group of likeminded Romans gathered together under the Cross. However, if such a meeting was a reality they were not a witch coven, more a monastic warrior conclave, a Roman fraction. After all, Christianity is just another mythology to be accepted or rejected.

Still, we cannot say that stregoneria is Christian or that they were for a time a Christian denomination, rather we might say that certain clerics were stregones that took advantage of the public religion on their own terms, with their own truths. We need to understand that stregoneria is a path of sorcery focusing on the ensorcelment of the wizard or witch in the making – so he or she can be truly divinely free, like a god.

It follows that paganism is also a problematic term to apply to stregoneria. It is not paganism. In fact, paganism did not exist for those that were called pagans; again we find it to be an insult, like witch or sorcerer being attached to people and practitioners refusing to submit to the demands of taming the people and their practices. What is clear is that these people whom we today call pagans, be they Greek, Roman or Egyptian had no concept of evil, nor accepted that an institution like the Church had a 'god-given' right to limit their expansion of consciousness, or to bar their becoming a god.

Naturally such inclinations do not harmonize well with religions like Christianity that aim to sanitise and civilise people who insist on being free, and thus biased terms such as Satanism get easily attached to stregoneria. It is the condemnation of the untamed, those that insist on personal freedom who are vilified and it is perhaps in this prejudice we can detect a pure and legitimate flame of the original mysteries. It follows that stregoneria has nothing in common with modern renderings of witchcraft passing themselves off as stregoneria or stregheria as cults of nature worship. Stregoneria was never about this; it was the path of the enlightened individual, the enflamed warrior that sought godhood for himself. Stregoneria took a more formal format when Roman legions saw in the Lugh of the Celts their own god of magic and necromancy, Lucifer Invictus – a solar consciousness – father of stregones. From this time an unbroken tradition can be traced. Hints of the existence of this clandestine cult are found scattered in Roman crypts and ecclesiastical documents for those who know what they are looking for.

In the Roman myths, Lucifer is seen as an epitaph for any deity that gifts an increase of consciousness or light. It is also the name given to a minor god, associated with the torch, as light bringer. He is the torch of the underworld in the hands of Phanes, Diana and Hecate, but in truth he is the Sun fallen black, the Sol Niger, and thus it is in the mysteries of Mithras his cult found a succession as it was patronised by stregones. Lucifer is an impulse, a constant explosion of light, a big bang if you will. His legacy has little to do with modern materialist ideas that see Lucifer as the antithesis of God. Lucifer is his own truth, a particular form of consciousness in a succession of forms that dance across matter in constant bursts of light.

Deities such as Lucifer have been coloured, re-coloured, understood and re-understood in a succession of cultures, all of them bringing their subjective perspectives. By mentioning Lucifer you might assume that there are gods who belong to the 'pantheon' of stregoneria, but they only belong insofar as the stregone can demonstrate the importance of these gods in their lives. Gods and spirits make up the world and the type of relationship we build with the world is always personal. The personal relationship we forge with the spirits and gods that make up the world will in turn be forces useful to our freedom and our chosen path. Hence, we cannot speak of any pantheon of gods in the modern neopagan vernacular.

The stregone will never kneel to any god, unless he or she kneels to their own reflection, this is done in reverence and respect, never in worship. By bending your knees in worship you resign your fate, your light and your fire to someone else, and this is anathema to the ethos of the stregone. Because of such considerations there is a tendency to view stregoneria as antinomian. It might be so, but it would be misleading to see a path of spiritual freedom and deification as antinomian per se. It will only be potentially antinomian if the tamed and civilised hinders the freedom of the stregone. This does not mean that stregoneria is a form of anarchism or nihilism. Rather it is a hermetic discipline of sorcery that demands intuition, knowledge and awareness of need and fire. It is not about violent acts upon the world and its political systems and religious institutions; it is a path of knowledge that insists on unveiling the secrets nature holds so they can be utilised to the stregone's benefit both as a social actor and as a god in the making.

It should also be mentioned that there is little relevant in the work of G. Leland to stregoneria. If anything is relevant in Leland's *Aradia* it is the connection between Aradia, Herodias and Lucifer. This is also found in Paul Huson's *Mastering Witchcraft*. Huson speaks of how the Great Darkness, Diana, divided herself into two equal and opposite forces, night and day. Diana assumed rulership over the night as the moon and gave the day to her brother-son-lover, Lucifer. With feline seduction Diana begot a child with her son and Huson says this was Aradia or Herodias. This holds relevance for stregoneria as we shall see, but this child, Herodias/Aradia was solely a continuation of the theme of Lilith and holds a very different value for the stregone than for those who worship her.

The inspirited human is composed of myriads of particles of consciousness, we are literally legion, and this opens up an endless plethora of possibilities in our self-deification. Therefore the only worthy rituals for a stregone are those that call upon the gods of belonging that fit with our consciousness, the consciousness ruled by need and instinct. It is from this we can form true intent. We take what is objective and abstract and through the bond we make, we make it a part of our own expansion as we build the best conditions possible for this to manifest. Change, transformation and ordeal are our scythe-bearing allies in this brutal yet delicate work of self-deification. After all, if we fail or if we are found victorious, if we veil ourselves in the illusions of Maya or explode into consciousness, it is our choices that make it happen. Nature is as she is, it is up to our ability to understand how to use her secret storehouse that makes the difference. Nature is like a furnace, what we gain from it depends on our perspective and the constitution of our consciousness and intuition.

In truth, there are no secrets. Everything is there for he or she who dares to uncover what is veiled. It is about the urge to be free – a freedom consistent with one's 'atmosphere,' or state of consciousness as being. The secret is simply how to follow the path that you choose. We know the path is right when it leads to freedom. It is about freedom from ignorance as we grow wiser with each step. It is about freedom from the prison of reason; freedom from social obstruction and institutions of shame and captivity. We are speaking of the freedom to fulfill your divine promise. Freedom changes people around you, by sharing the light of freedom you will never disempower people, but rather inspire them.

By living for the challenge you will be in a constant state of illumination, your torch will flicker and blaze in the air of freedom and possibility so you can both take and attract what is rightly yours. Be wise, but never forget to be overwhelmed by the passions of existence, to be intoxicated with life and pleasure until you feel you cannot take it anymore, then, take it further.

It is by taking matters to the extreme and then crossing over that you can realise the world is not singular. Rather, what is perceived as singular is composed of an endless gathering of forms that are in motion and adapt to the world dictated by their own strategies for existence. These forms, specters of conscious light and stars are what we call gods.

But let us return to nature. After all, it is nature that gives us the possibility of making our path. Nature is She who appears as a mirror. We can, for instance, see her showing herself as Diana when social systems are in jeopardy and as Juno when renewal is taking form. We should however remember that Diana is a fierce goddess, she is virgin.

All of nature is of a female orientation. She is a panorama of expressions, a garden of stars and possibilities. The male quality however is a violent force, almost an intrusion (by fire, force and direction) that holds the capacity of adapting and transforming this panorama. Because of this violence Lilith in one form or the other tends to be intrinsic to stregoneria. It is also here we find attempts at defining stregoneria as left hand path – which in the proper context of vama marga and its veneration of woman and yoni is correct – but also Satanists tend to rise up and mirror themselves in the stregone. This is quite understandable, but there is no Satan as such in stregoneria. If 'Satan' is used, if 'antichrist' is used, they are used as references to magnetic forms of consciousness, a way of explaining and understanding a point, not a reality. By logical dissemination: if Satan is God's adversary we need to admit some sort of relevance for this God he is opposing. This in turn depends on the acceptance of the Christian mythology, and with this rejected, Satanism in its modern form tends to be meaningless. It is still possible to use such terminology to bring more light to the matter so to speak, so Lilith can be the courtesan and wife of Satan if we ensure that the premises underlying our understanding are correct.

If we return to the Bible we see that the figure of Satan represents a very different perspective upon matters, and his role as a challenger is exactly the kind of power the stregone deems necessary on the path of self-deification. Satan becomes the power of contrast, it is not the power of our opponents; no, it is the power that refuses to kneel to an unhappy fate or institutions void of light and consciousness. But in the Bible he is given a distinct personality, and a direction that goes counter to everything that is good. Well, this is one perspective, but surely not the only one.

Similarly we find Ishtar and Astarte, deities far older than the Bible, who in ecclesiastical writings have been introduced as prostitutes and deities of ill repute. These were deities that outside the Abrahamic perspective were seen as dignified manifestations of stellar potencies. Accepting Satan as the enemy of man and Ishtar as a whore depends upon whether you accept Christian mythology as true or not. What is clear is that these deities predate the composition of the revised and re-revised Bible we have today. Perhaps their massive influence and their call for freedom was the reason for editing them out from the holy books pulled together by civil religion?

There are clearly significant gaps in the Bible, where traditions like Stregoneria have secured a transmission of the knowledge that it attempted to eradicate. For instance in Genesis 1:27 we read:

> So God created man in his own image, in the image of God created he him; male and female created he them.

Then in Genesis 2:7 we read that God breathed life into Adam and that God created woman from his flesh and bone so he would not be so lonely. So, in the first chapter man and woman are created as divine manifestations, mirrors of God. Then one chapter later only man is made, from earth, and given divine breath. Later comes a servile woman that god made to be Adam's submissive partner – a creation myth proper for any civic religion that seeks to tame passions and intuition. Clearly we have a variety of creation myths already in the first two chapters of Genesis that for the stregone speaks of the obvious: the predominance of Lilith. Lilith is important in this context, because she is a cosmic manifestation of the spirit of earth – a transcendence of matter if you will – that replicates the self-deification of the stregone. Lilith did not cause a transformation in the world, she transformed herself. She did this so she could move better in the worlds of her choosing. As such she became a mirror that reflects how a particular truth can be achieved, attracted and integrated. We hold the potential of transposing our light caught in matter onto our numinous body upon death. As Lilith achieved this, then it can be done again. This is the path of the *stregone*.

For the stregone, Lilith is the cosmic terrorist, she is what explodes in renewed essence constantly; she is the stellar succubus and the black moon. She is the frustration of the worlds because she recreates herself anew. She is chaste as a whore and holds as many lovers as any mother. She is found to be exceptionally active in what is known as the via lilithia which concerns the 15°, 16° and 17° of the sign of Libra. She is Algol when the Moon is new in the signs of Venus and she loves the four towers to be filled with Mercury. These are auspicious stellar junctures for the work of the stregone, as it is here the Stregone recreates themselves.

The constant transformation that takes place on the path gradually fills us with intuitive knowledge, and wisdom grows from this. This process begins when we gestate in the womb and enter this world; our first magical act. The question is, whether we have sufficient awareness and knowledge to make this happen at the birth of our death.

This leads to the power of need, as it takes the form of determination. Need is the very forge that defines the *stregone*. In the execution of need we must be aware that there seems to be a barrier between reason and intuition, or perhaps there is a polarity there that if one enlarges reason, intuition will also grow. The goal must however be to break the bonds of reason, because it is only outside reason we can meet other gods. There is a particularity with reason, which is about obscuring the individual with ideas of power and domination. Reason is not an ally of the *stregone*, but the prison guard. Breaking the boundaries of reason will set free the original flame of intuition that breeds knowledge. It is only in this field we can start to grasp the 'divine beings' as they appear in their many forms. Intuition is the fuel for growth. The child does not grow up because of reason, but because of intuition. Reason is considered the product of a sanitized and civilized human being. Naturally, this is not how reason is – just one of its many modalities – the way the modern era understands reason and this overarching understanding of this faculty contaminates us with restraints.

The *stregone* is very well aware that our strategies and the magic we use to alter and control life and fate are tools we are using to move in the world more elegantly, with more cunning. But this does not mean that this offers a possibility for escaping the responsibilities we have in this world. Even if the *stregone* lives in a world of dreams, the planes are never confused and the realities are approached on their own premises from the given perspective of the stregone. No matter what world the stregone moves in, he or she will move in an absolute and intense fashion. Every world, every challenge, every paradox is an opportunity to learn how to attract the best things possible. The world of dreams, the other world, is what builds us in this world, and it is from the world of intuition ruled by the moon in which actions are formed and can reveal knowledge.

A *stregone* must be intensely aware to be the best of his or her ability, so he or she is constantly the summit of the possibilities of expansion. Stregoneria is about finding the path that expands your consciousness; it is the art of deifying yourself. It is about freedom and the meeting with gods as an equal. It is about transforming yourself, like Lilith transformed herself – to become, to be and forever be – true to yourself in constant self-creation as your consciousness expands and explodes like the light we know as Lucifer.

BIBLIOGRAPHY

GINZBURG, CARLO, *Ecstasies: Deciphering the Witches' Sabbath*. Penguin, 1991.
HUSON, PAUL, *Mastering Witchcraft*. Perigee, 1970.
RENDHELL, FULVIO, *Alta magia pratica evocative. Rituali di magia moderna.* Hermes, 1987.
——— *Magia spiritica: Lo spiritismo allá luce della Scienza Magica.* Hermes, 1997.
——— *Trattato di alta magia: Nera, bianca, rossa.* Hermes, 2006.

Aditxkidentzat lehenik,   *To friends, first of all,*
heltzen denean pobreric   *to the poor when they come,*
Etsaier, nor gabe denik,   *To enemies for who is without them,*
dener nago zabaludrik.   *to all I am open wide.*

Lintel inscription at Ibarrolle

Nere etxeko kea, auzoko sua baino hobea.
The smoke of my house is better than the fire of my neighbour's.

Basque proverb

The Basque language is a country, almost a religion.

Victor Hugo, on a visit, 1843

But the House of my Father shall Stand

An Exploration of the *Etxe* as Temple of the Land in Traditional Basque Craft

XABIER BAKAIKOA URBELTZ

HEN ONE IS ROOTED in the land, the mere act of walking becomes a pilgrimage and seemingly mundane comings and goings become opportunities for flashes of revelation. These are the lightning strikes of serpent-born inspiration that light our way through the mists of the mind. For us the mist is divine, it is the unformed potential from which all things emerge. In the mountains, fog can hide the sure road and the precipice; angel and demon await us in the fog, always present, waiting to be found and named. We are constantly wading through the fog of our mind, seeking to name our experiences, seeking identity. For my people, there are ultimately two expressions which are essential to our identity: *euskera*, the Basque language, and *etxe*, house.

Our mother tongue, Euskera, gives us voice, shaping how we see the world, and perhaps even how the worlds see us. Our identity as a people is so wrapped up within it that our name for ourselves, Euskaldunak (Basques), means those who speak Euskera. To be Basque, you must speak Basque, and to speak Basque makes one Basque. But the metaphor of language can be extended to all aspects of life, examining all aspects of culture as types of language, including religion.

The *etxe* is the true temple of the Land, built upon the ways of life which find their truest expression in *modazaharrak* (the old ways). Each of us carves out of the world a place of our choosing, and the *etxe* in turn is not only the physical structure, but an intersection of land and shelter, sustenance and solace, temple and tomb, the living and the dead, forming within it a community of reciprocity that outlives the individual and yet informs their journey in life.

There are those that might debate whether a house is truly a sign of traditional craft, and I would propose that all too often in our search for ourselves we ignore that which is right in front of us, favouring the fat over the meat, the coarse over the subtle. For basques, it is Euskera that gives us mind, and when given form, *modazaharrak* become manifest as etxe – a true expression of traditional mindset in Euskalerria (the Basque country).

As a named, living entity, the *etxe* is more than the material building. Echoing the three principles of alchemy it is composed simultaneously of the physical house – *etxe* (salt); the property – *etxeondo* (sulphur); and the inhabitants – *etxekoak* (mercury).

ETXE · THE WALLS THAT GIVE FORM

Ikusten duzu goizean,	*Do you see, in the morning,*
argia hasten denean,	*At the first light of dawn,*
Menditto baten gainean,	*Atop a little hill,*
etxe ttipitto aintzin xuri bat,	*A small house, white-faced,*
lau haitzondoren erdian,	*In the midst of four oaks,*
xakur xuri bat atean,	*A white dog in the doorway,*
iturrino bat aldean?	*A little fountain at the side?*
Han bizi naiz ni bakean.	*It is there that I dwell in peace.*

Jean Baptiste Elizanburu

THE FIRST DWELLINGS of our most ancient ancestors were the cliffs and caves of the mountains themselves, and there is much in traditional Basque thought that seems to have inherited the worldview of these ancient mountain dwellers. Shared resources under an established matriarchy centered around a cult of fire, and deep reverence for the ways of the bear (embodied in the stories of the Hartzkume) as a model of behavior and good judgement for mountain forest survival. We find the old ways still strong today. The caves at Santimamiñe in Bizkaia show continued occupation from the Middle Paleolithic until the Iron Age, just before Roman occupation. Whilst a definitive record for such continued Basque presence in these caves is lacking (but not implausible), in our cultural memory, the identification with the caves, peaks and valleys of our beloved Pyrenees will always persist. For these mountains, that in the ancient mind grow and age as living beings, with characters all of their own, have given birth to our people. Even the Sun and Moon, the daughters of the Earth itself, must return to the folds of the Earth, retreating to their own houses beneath the surface, echoing the cave-homes of our forebears. While Eguzki (the Sun) lights the daytime and the world of the living, her sister Ilargi (the Moon) lights the night and the world of the dead. This separation of responsibility is reflected in the division of labour in the house as well, for both the living and the dead play their part in the maintenance of the *etxe*.

Our ancestors found a stone tower to be easily defendable – a place where the inhabitants of a given area could retreat to in times of conflict. Many included courtyards which provided insular storage and more defensive capabilities. These types of structure are not uncommon in medieval architecture; stone towers, either round or roughly square, with an elevated entrance whose wooded stairs could be burned for defensive purposes in times of danger. These *dorreak*, from the Castillian *torre* (tower), are necessarily related to the *casa-torre* of greater Spain. However, these larger structures received heavy attention from the Spanish and French governments, seeking to end centuries of territorial partisan conflict. Dorreak were either razed or converted to more peaceable dwellings. The average peasant did not live in these fortifications, but rather in wooden huts tightly clustered together that housed people, animals and hay, with additional shacks for other livestock, cider pressing, and granaries. The defensive *dorreak* combined with the needs of the mountain farmers and led to the *jauregiak* (manor houses), and eventually to the *baserriak* (Basque farmhouses).

The *baserriak* allowed the people whose needs were dependent upon mountain agriculture and animal husbandry to truly become established. By the 15th and 16th centuries, new enterprises in Andalusia and the Americas brought wealth and an influx of New World crops, most notably, maize. Shifts in law codes allowed private division of land and the *baserri* became the standard form of Basque mountain life. While there are those that moved to the larger cities, themselves urban expressions of the dream of Rome, manifested lavishly in either Spanish or French form, even the *kaletarrak* (city dwellers, derived from Latin *kale*, street) looked to the *baserritarrak* (country dwellers) as representatives of the older ways, the quintessential Basques. It is ultimately the baserri that manifests the tradition of the etxe with singular expression. It is the *baserri* that helped preserve our language and culture despite the assaults of the wolves of politics and modernity.

The wild land and forest becomes ordered by the *baserri*, whose very name expresses this, from *baso* (wild) and *herri* (settlement, town). *Baserriak* generally follow a set layout and construction. Traditionally facing east or south-east, both to protect from the winds of the north and west, as well as to face the rising Sun, symbol of life and victory, the stone and wood constructed building is almost always rectangular. The earlier constructions, a stone-built ground floor houses livestock, all family members, and a large sloping gable-roof provides a spacious attic area which serves as a drying and storage area, often open on one or both sides to allow for ventilation. In time, the baserri became three stories: the ground floor housing the stables for cattle, storage for carts and tools, the kitchen; the first floor housing the human inhabitants; the attic reserving its previous use as a storage and drying room. It is this typical *baserri* that most basques will have in mind when we speak of the Basque *etxe*. The sacredness of this structure is evident in beliefs that are told of both Church and house, which caution against circling either three times – which will grant one the ability to see the dead, or knowledge and union with the Devil, or the company of witches, or even death.

Sugabeko etxea, gorputza odolgabea
A house without fire is a body without blood

NOT ALL HOUSES are created equal. While the physical structure is what qualifies a house, for the traditional Basque this place must have *su*, fire. In the strictest, most literal sense, this refers to the *subazter* (the hearth-fire) the seat of power in a house, located in the *sukaldea* (kitchen, literally fireside). But beyond these necessities of cooking and warmth, the hearth fire is considered the dwelling of the spirit of

Mari, the very numen of the land. A spirit of order and mountain survival, Mari demands honesty and responsibility, a sharing of resources and upright character, herself reflecting the conduct demanded by fire. The hearth-fire protects by its very presence, and guarantees the sacredness and authority of the *etxe*. In the physical building, this protection extends to the *ate* (door) itself, traditionally stained with ochre, oil and ox-blood, making a protective and vitalizing colour that also hints at a deeper understanding of the old *jaunak* (spirits) – for is this not an echo of the mighty red bull Aatxegorri – defender of the ways of Mari, guarding the entrance and preserving the sanctity of the house? While Basque houses are often bare in decoration, the front door and the hearth both retain a similar sacredness. There is *indar* (strength) in this fire that gives warmth and light to the *etxe*, easing the cold of night, and *adur* (magical force) flowing from the living flame embodied in the *subazter*, that extends not only to the *ate*, but to the entire *etxe*, shedding light upon the unknown. Tended by an older woman, the *subazter* must be cared for with respect, and great care must be taken to see that it is lit according to ritual tradition, and by the preparation of food at the hearthfire, a communion of flame is extended to the inhabitants of the house itself through the food eaten. Indeed, the scraps of food that fall by the fireside become food for the dead of the House, whose presence is reified by the same elders, lighting candles to aid their way on the spirit roads, and making additional small food offerings on the windowsills so that they may find rest within the walls of the house they once lived and died to support, keeping their presence strong, extending the fire of the house to all its inhabitants, living and dead.

The fire is not only maintained by these actions, but can be extended as a protective force through the use of certain plants and tools. We can harness the force of *arantza* (thorn branches) to protect the house and guard its fertility, *lizarra* (ash branches) to keep it strong and the hearth fire burning, and *eguzkilorea* (wild thistle flower, literally sun flower) to ward off those spirits in the night that seek to harm us. We can plant *intxaurondo* (walnut) and *erramu* (laurel) for protection from lightning and curses and place an axe by the door for protection during storms. This harnessing of the *adur* and *indar* of the world around us is where traditional craft finds its expression – for each of us seeks to be master of ourselves. This starts with the *etxe*, but one might ask – where does the *etxe* truly begin and end? Is not the fire kindled in the heart of each person? It is these walls that truly give us identity. I am brought to wonder, which boundaries are mutable, and which are firm?

> *Izena duen guztiak izatea ere badauke.*
> *Everything with a name exists.*
>
> Basque proverb

Each *etxe* has a name, one bestowed upon it, not ordinarily chosen by its residents. It may describe the physical characteristics of the house, or its location, or age. A newly built *baserri* may be called Etxeberria (New House), one nearest a bridge may be Zubiondo (By the Bridge), one in a muddy stretch of land may be Loiola (Muddy Place). What is evident though, is that the name of the *etxe* is ultimately more important than the names of the inhabitants. In rural areas, a person is first known by the name of their house, and secondly their first name. If you move into a house, you will assume the name of the *etxe*, whether temporarily or permanently. The dead of the house also become the responsibility of the current owners. This is in contrast to most naming systems in Europe, where some version of inheriting the father's surname in combination or apart from the mother's is the norm. In modern times, although patronymic surnames are used with greater frequency, in the more rural areas, it is still the name of your *etxe* that is important. In a craft environment, this name will equally extend to all those adopted as a part of the family's ways. All labour and effort supports the house, for one's identity finds expression within the *etxe*, not apart from it.

The mere act of receiving a name from the neighbouring houses imbeds the *etxe* and its inhabitants in a larger community. Thus it is identification with an *etxe* that gives one a sense of collective, an act which by its very nature grants one a certain benefit, and hints at a larger concept of *legea egin*, keeping the law, which can be interpreted as positive engagement in societal contract. Just as membership in an *etxe* benefits the individual, the *etxe*'s participation in the larger community grants that *etxe* a certain power. These roles can be examined and weighed both for their benefit and detriment, and ultimately participation in societal norms is expected to reap the benefits of the same society. While what happens in my etxe is for me and mine, outside my *etxe*, I will be expected to act in a way that does not bring dishonour to my house, and when visiting another, to honour the ways of their etxe. The autonomy of each *etxe* is important and the good name of each *etxe* reflects that – for anything named exists by the power of that name.

ETXEONDO · THE LAND THAT DIES TO LIVE

THE PYRENEES, those mountains which shelter and give strength to the *euskaldunak*, have shaped our identity and how we relate to property. In addition to the physical house, each *etxe* sits upon land for which it acts as temple and caretaker, the *etxeondo*. This land is an extension of the *etxe* itself, or, more correctly, the *etxe* is naturally an extension of the land. The word *etxeondo* itself is telling of this subtlety, for *-ondo* translates to trunk or tree. If a fig is *piko*, then the fig tree is *pikondo*. The *etxeondo* is the tree that supports the *etxe*, which is its fruit. Similarly, as a fruit contains all the potential for an entirely new tree (the wishes and lives of each inhabitant), such potential exists in each and every fruit it bears. In this way we remember that an etxe is an outgrowth of the tree that is *etxeondo*, having the characteristics of the tree from which it grew, but it is the tree that must be maintained and made to thrive, not the fruit at the expense of the tree.

The land, of which the *etxe* is the temple, will ideally be self-sufficient and produce food and wood and necessities for those who work it. This emphasis on self-sufficiency is the ideal, but it is part of a greater belief that growing food is an act of communion with the land. Even in the cities, where small apartment living has become the norm, it is not uncommon to see memories of the *etxeondo*'s fecundity in window boxes and small garden plots that will always grow at least a few edible items. This driving concept of *lurlandu*, working the earth, reflects a deeper need to generate and to give life to the land that in turn gives us life. The barns which house the larger livestock were, and often still are, part of the ground floor of many baserri, and even when a separate building is employed, it is still considered part of the *etxe*, and its inhabitants, part of the *etxeondo*.

There is more to the *etxeondo* than just the fields and portions of woods surrounding the *etxe*. It is the story of the soil itself, of the *etxe* and its former inhabitants that animates the land. For the mystery of the *etxe* is not that one inherits the ancestral blood dead, but rather, the *etxe* is responsible for the dead of the house, and they are eternally part of that etxe, for it is upon their shoulders that the house stands. In ancient times, we know the *etxe* was a tomb itself, and this practice is echoed in the modern era where unbaptized infants are buried just under the eaves of the roof, still protected from the elements by the physical house. The previously mentioned offering of bread, money and candles upon windowsills for the dead also hints at the relationship of the dead to the walls of the house. As the ministers of the *etxe* are the revered etxekoandreak (women of the house), in death the collective force has come to be known in traditional craft as Amak, the Mothers. These dead mothers and witches of the land are contained in the soil itself – they receive due praise and are the means by which the land can express its wisdom in a means understandable to those with ears to hear. It is here the ancient mystery of Erditse is encountered, that veiled First Mother, who ensures the land will be tended, and the dead will have their voice.

The *jarleku* (place of seating) may have originally been incorporated into the *subazter*, and while the physical evidence of it is limited, our oral history tells us that the bones of the most recently departed dead of the house were kept there. It was here that the *etxekoandre* would commune with the dead of the house and land. After the arrival of Christianity, the practice of burying the house dead adjacent to the physical building was replaced by burial in the churchyard and the *jarleku* became a part of each Church. Here is where the institution of *etxe* prevails – for in death, as the members of a house belong to the house eternally, so too does each *etxe* extend its *etxeondo* in the *jarleku*. The *jarleku* is a sacred space, a slab of stone with the name of the *etxe* on the floor of the church, which in some parishes still entomb the most recent dead of the house – this slab is part of the *etxe* whose name it bears, and while physically in the church, is part of the *etxeondo*. For while the priests of Mother Rome may believe they control the churches, high in the protective folds of the mountains, Basques will be Basques, and the *etxe* will prevail.

Not only are the *jarlekuak* part of the *etxeondo*, but so too are the *hilbideak*, the paths of the dead. The route that the coffin is carried from each respective *etxe* to the church is unique, and it too, is contained in the *etxeondo*. These spirit roads are essential as they connect the *jarleku* to the *etxe*, ensuring that the dead know their way to and from the house. In some areas it is still traditional that when a new bride moves into her husband's house, she will circle the *subazter*, walk along the *hilbide* of that house, circle the *jarleku* and return by the same route to the *subazter*. While these are the traditions of the *etxekoandreak* as ministers to the dead of each *etxe*, the *etxeondo* also extends to the mountain high pastures where the shepherds graze their flocks.

The *sarobe*, or alternatively *sel* or *olha*, is a means of marking land used for grazing or demarcating a part of the forest that, although possibly separated from the physical *etxe*, could still be part of the *etxeondo*. Using a circle of border stones, the *sarobe* marked an area of land that was claimed, whether privately or in common between certain *etxeak* in an area. In its center we find the *autsarri*, or ashtone. This pillar of rock is a monument of stability and claim to the land, directly linked to the steadfast North Star, and the border stones to the very cycles of the year. The *autsarri* is the *buru* (head) that draws the *sugeak*, the serpent powers of the land, and burns with the fire of sacrifice that is, for the outside, what the *subazter* is for the inside. This division of land by circles of stones echoes an ancient means of claim, and expresses the ideals of cyclical rotation, or *aldikatzia*.

Aldikatzia is the means by which community takes care of itself. Just as the name of a house places it in the larger context of community, a property of the *etxeondo* is the concept of *lehen auzo*, or first neighbour. In addition to caring for the *etxe* and the deceased members of the *etxe*, each house is responsible for a neighbouring house with regards to the distribution of ritually blessed items, usually to the right, proceeding clockwise and mirroring the mysteries of Eguzki (the Sun), whose beauty gives life to the world. Similarly, in the instance of death in a house, one's closest neighbours will assist the house in the tasks needing doing, and, as the office of *lehen auzo* is overlapping, the help proceeds to the left, reflecting the mysteries of Ilargi (the Moon), the light of the dead, and for some, death herself. Thus the rings of mutual aid and distribution, division of labour and ritual office are interwoven, and the larger concept of *etxeondo* is firmly rooted under the watchful eyes of Janicot (Jainko, the On-High Lord).

ETXEKOAK · THE BLOOD THAT WALKS

Jan behar baduzu, lan egin beharko duzu.
If you must eat, then you must work.

           Basque proverb

HE LAND CALLS TO ITSELF. It will either be of the *baso* (the wild), or through the process of *lurlandu* (working the earth), that it gives rise to *etxe*. While the *baso* is highly respected and seen as a place of great natural power and resources, when the land is worked it is here where the blood of the land becomes manifest and the ministers to this temple assume their place. The true caretakers of the land, the intermediaries of the flow between etxe and *etxeondo*, are the *etxekoak*, meaning those that belong to the house. In *euskera*, the inhabitants of a house belong to that house, not the reverse, which itself represents a departure from common conventional ideas of ownership.

  The oldest traditions have three generations living together, the oldest generation being supported by the efforts of the two younger. The elder pair are the *etxekoandre* and *nagusi* (master). Often the epithet *zahar* (old) is added to signify them as the elders of the house, the middle generation uses the same titles, but often with the epithet *gazte* (young) or *berri* (new). The *etxekoandre* and *nagusi* are most often husband and wife, but this is not always the case, especially with the *zaharrak*. The youngest of the three generations are the children of the middle generation. One of them, often the first-born or one deemed most competent, regardless of sex, will be chosen to inherit the etxe in time. These particular laws of inheritance go back centuries, and directly contradicted the feudal laws of the time. The ability of a house to perpetuate its legacy was and is of extreme importance, and was a prime example of the *foruak*, or old laws, that the Basques demanded be protected by the Crown of Spain, embodied in the Mighty Oak, tree of Truth and Oath, which at Gernika (Guernica), is a testament to Basque autonomy as well as its subjugation.

  Clad in black from head to foot, face obscured by lace and holding the coiled wax serpent whose tongue gives Light to the Dead, there is no person that represents the *etxe* more strongly than the *etxekoandre* (woman of the house), chief spiritual leader of each *etxe*. She is first among the ministers of the cult of *etxe*, for it is she that extends the blessing of the Dead, she that maintains order within the House, she that holds the financial control, she that maintains the traditions of reciprocity to the larger community, and she that educates future generations in tradition. It is she that observes the subtle relationships of land and blood between the living and the dead, and tends to the black earth that is the Dragon beneath our feet. Her authority extends not only in the *etxe* proper, but in the *jarleku* and *hilbideak*, presiding over the religious life of her fellow *etxekoak*.

When the *etxekoandre* of a given etxe cannot be present at the Church to serve at the *jarleku*, it is the *serora* that takes over. Just as each *etxekoandre* serves the *etxe*, the *serora* is herself perhaps a compromise between the church and *modazaharrak*. It is she who holds the keys to the church (as protector and guardian), and serves the needs of the *etxekoandreak* of the community, filling in where necessary for obligations at each *jarleku*, and tending to the physical needs and organization within the church in tandem with the priest. While this office has greatly declined in the last half century, especially when coupled with the *etxekoandre*, it speaks of the high place of women in the affairs of the Basques.

> Both should be physically and emotionally strong, hard-working, and willing to co-operate with each other, as well as with the other members of the household. Considerable emphasis is placed on strength of character. Extreme submissiveness in either sex is deplored, for it allows one sex to dominate the other.
>
> – Sanda Ott, *Circle of Mountains*

Men and women are said to be *bardin-bardina* (equal) in responsibilities. Other than the set offices of *etxekoandre* and her assistant, called *neska* (girl), and the rank of *nagusi* and the duties of the men as shepherds in the *sarobe*, work is assigned and duty assumed based on ability with regards to the farm work regardless of sex. *Etxekoak* are expected to provide *alkar laguntza* (mutual aid) inside and outside the house with regards to chores.

When death strikes, the house bands together. Elaborate funerary traditions seek to unite the recently departed with the honoured dead of their etxe. The older expressions involve interment in the *jarleku* until another of the etxe dies, their *gogo* (spirit) now acting as a messenger between the world of the dead and the world of the living through the *etxekoandre*.

The deceased *etxekoak* make their presence known by rising out of earth as lights, flames, clouds, winds, shadows, draped figures, or patterns in the ashes of the hearth, and their wishes are interpreted by the *etxekoandre* of each house. They may be enlisted for blessing, advice, defence just as the living may, and are also said to help with *eginbeharrak* (tasks that must be done).

One could wonder if in ancient times the title of *etxekoak* was applied also to animals, or to certain types of animals. Consider the keeping of *erleak* (bees), who are held in such high esteem, that upon the death of a house member, the *etxekoandre* will process to the *erletxe* (beehive), drape it in black cloth, and inform them: *Jauna il dek, ta eizuelan ari argi eiteko* (The Master is dead, and we need you to go to work to make light for him). They must be asked to assist, not coerced, and their presence or absence in the hive can speak to the strength of the etxe itself, and should they be offended, they will leave.

The spheres of influence between men and women vary from town to town, and certainly in the higher mountain enclaves there is less French and Spanish influence and it is here where we see a mutability in role. However, during the height of the Basque whaling trade, men often left the *etxe* in the hands of the women to pursue wealth and prestige, and eventually, as navigators and crewmen on expeditions to the Americas to the same end. It is here we find a grave self-dug, and whether from religious zealotry, desire of property, or even ethnic cleansing, the Church began a crusade against the Basques and 'witchcraft.' Much of the evidence used against the Basques reveals those unique expressions of culture that mark the Basques as other. It is cultivation of this other blood that drives the current expression of traditional Basque craft, always based in the concepts embedded within *euskera* and *modazaharrak*.

In traditional Basque craft, men may find a calling as *gizonbeltzak* (men-in-black), often times called by the Castillian *culebros* (serpents), who along with select *etxekoandreak*, are the Dragon-Ladies and Serpent-Men who work the black and red currents of the land for loss or gain, balancing the horizontal pull of the land itself with the vertical stellar pull of desire. Here in this fertile intersection we find the Black Goat, the preserver and advisor of animal and man. Here too are the twin lights, Eguzki and Ilargi, the Sun and the Moon. Our oldest creation myths speak of us being born of the sparks of a great breath of fire, not the origins in clay professed in Christianity, for burning brightly in the center of it all is the living flame,

Mari – who for some retains her traditional name and powers, and for others is now St Barbara, St Marina, or the Virgin Mother herself. And it is that flame that guides us, existing in the depths of the secret caverns of the earth, in the burning hearth-fire of each etxe, and in the beating heart of the *euskaldun*.

A RACE APART

Kanpoan erdera, etxean Euskera.
Outside, Castillian; inside, Basque.

The truth is that the Basque distrusts a stranger much too much to invite someone into his house who doesn't speak his language.
– *Les guides bleus pays basque français et espangol*, 1954.

WITHIN THE CONCLAVE of families that seek to preserve specific expressions of *modazaharrak* (the old ways), there are to be found both *jentil* (pagan) and christian houses, but the labels of religion are of little import here. A Basque is a Basque first and foremost, and while one house's ways may not be identical to another's, one is not better than the other – the house's ways must serve the house first. Expanding from this centre point are duties to the community as participants in communal identity, all based in common interests. There is much power in *legea egin* (social contract), and while the individual may find the restraints of community confining at times, the benefits of partaking in it are ultimately a choice that is reified through experienced blessing or curse.

Our own belief in our history as a race apart is engrained within every Basque, regardless of affiliation with traditional craft on a formal or informal level – for every Basque is, first and foremost – Basque. We are both *euskaldunzaharrak* (Basques whose mother tongue is Euskera) and *euskaldunberriak* (Basques who learned Euskera later, often by choice). But we are bound to each other through that commitment to the tongue of our ancestors. The institution of the house, the *etxe*, allowed traditional Basque ways to be secured across a landscape whose borders are defined only by a language and the memory of that language. The political divide between Hegoalde (Spanish Basque Country) and Iparralde (French

Basque Country) is merely that – a political divide, not a cultural one. In
a world where others have moved borders around without respect to the
ancient stones, claimed mountains when no mountain can be claimed, and
tried to eradicate the living heart of a people – Euskera – through government mandate, it is the etxe that must stand firm. Outside the house, the
ways of the outside prevail. Inside the house, inside the temple, we are
ourselves. To our ancestors, the soul was as a flock of birds, gathering or
diminishing in size and strength throughout our life, and we are all able to
gain *indar* and *adur* to allow our lives to be our own. This is the power of
the *sorgin* (witch), coming from the words *zori* (fate) and *egin* (to make). A
sorgin is one who makes their own fate. They chose how they wish to live,
and it is this independence which the *etxe* protects. Pride in and preservation of one's *etxe* is an act of rebellion. It is an act of service to the
community. It is an act of communion with the dead. It is an act of hope
for the future.

THE HOUSE WILL STAND

Nahiz ez den gaztelua, maite dut nik sorlekua, aiten aitek hautatua.
Etxetik kanpo zait iduritzen nonbeit naizela galdua, nola han bainaiz sortua
han utziko dut mundua, galtzen ez badut zentzua.

Although it is not a palace, I love the place of my birth, chosen by my
ancestors. Away from home, I find myself lost. There I was born,
and there, if I don't lose sight of myself, I will die.

– Jean Baptiste Elizanburu

HEN THE TRIALS of daily living become opportunities for insight
into our character, when how we interact with every moment,
every person, becomes an observable fulcrum of growth, we are
starting to understand our own house. Threats to the *etxe* come from all
sides – the character of each member either gives strength to the walls,
or acts as a decaying force that threatens familial security. It is through
upright character, *zinztasun*, that the house maintains its very structure.

Storms come. Thieves come. Poverty comes. And how will you face
these threats? Are your walls secure? What do you let in, and what do

you deny? For many, the 'temple' is always elsewhere – in the established places of worship, in the woods, away from our day-to-day life. But what is the world created when purpose and spirit are always elsewhere? It is here where the measure of each person's craft truly is; for wherever we walk, we bear the name of our *etxe*, and divine fire burns within our heart. By this measure we live. My etxe is both the house I support through my works and actions, and my relationship and reputation with the land itself. May the strength of your character and deeds be the measure, and may you be supported by the name of your house! May every footstep we take in the world become as holy pilgrimage, strengthening and defending our etxe. For deep within the fires of the hearth lies each person's truth, and I shall defend it, by what adur and indar I have – not only in thought, not only in word, not only in action, but with my whole being.

Hitza hitz. Hala bedi. Hura ia!	I shall defend
Nire aitaren etxea	the house of my father,
defendituko dut.	against wolves,
Otsoen kontra,	against draught,
sikatearen kontra,	against usury,
lukurreriaren kontra,	against the law,
justiziaren kontra,	I shall defend
defenditu eginen dut	the house of my father.
nire aitaren etxea.	I shall lose
Galduko ditut	cattle,
aziendak,	orchards,
soloak,	pine groves;
pinudiak;	I shall lose
galduko ditut	interest,
korrituak,	income,
errentak,	dividends,
interesak,	but I shall defend
baina nire aitaren etxea	the house of my father.
defendituko dut.	They will take my weapons,
Harmak kenduko dizkidate,	and with my hands
eta eskuarekin defendituko dut	I shall defend
nire aitaren etxea;	the house of my father;
eskuak ebakiko dizkidate,	they will cut off my hands,

 eta besoarekin defendituko dut   *and with my arms I shall defend*
 nire aitaren etxea;   *the house of my father;*
 besorik gabe,   *They will leave me armless,*
 sorbaldik gabe,   *without shoulders,*
 bularrik gabe   *without chest,*
 utziko naute,   *and with my soul*
 eta arimarekin defendituko dut   *I shall defend*
 nire aitaren etxea.   *the house of my father.*
 Ni hilen naiz,   *I shall die,*
 nire arima galduko da,   *my soul will be lost,*
 nire askazia galduko da,   *my descendants will be lost;*
 baina nire aitaren etxeak   *but the house of my father*
 iraunen du zutik.   *shall stand.*

– Gabriel Arresti

BIBLIOGRAPHY

JOSE MIGUEL DE BARANDIARÁN, *Mari, o el genio de las montañas*. Impr. de la Diputación, 1928.
——— *Obras Completas, Tomo I*. Bibiloteca de la Gran Enciclopedia Vasca, 1973.
——— *Mitología vasca*. Txertoa, 1979.
JULIO CARO BAROJA, *Los Vascos*. Ediciones istmo, 1971.
——— *De la vida rural vasca*. Txertoa, 1974.
——— *Brujeria Vasca*. Txertoa, 1992.
ROSLYN FRANK, *La serora vasca: documentos y archivos*. University of Iowa, 1997.
RODNEY GALLOP, *A Book of the Basques*. University of Nevada Press, 1930.
SANDRA OTT, *The Circle of Mountains*. University of Nevada Press, 1981.

Bucca and the Cornish Cult of Pellar

STEVE PATTERSON

N THE MID 19TH CENTURY a shadow passed over the land, a shadow that seemingly transformed all that it touched. In Europe the forces of rationalism, Capitalism and industrialism were reaching fever pitch; heralding phenomenal feats of destruction, creation and human endeavour and laying down the infrastructure for a brave new world. The rail road swept west across America drawing back the primordial virgin lands like a carpet whilst traders and adventurers swept in to Africa and Asia in the wake of the Christian missionaries, spreading their own gospel of distorted humanism and returning with plunder and tales of far off lands. In Europe, towns and cities grew like cancerous tumours sending their communication and transport systems like tentacles through the woods, heaths and fields of old Europe. Technology, population, economics and our relationship with the land were all on the move. But where there is a wasteland there is always a wounded king at its heart, and there too are always green shoots ready to burst through its desolate soil.

The 1850s seemed to be something of a fulcrum in this age of change. Whilst the wheels of industry turned, the Romantic movement sought to re-establish our relationship with the pre-industrial landscape and our inner worlds, and Spiritualism emerged as an international movement striking at the newly formed but seemingly immovable edifice of rationalism and materialism. Within a window of a few years, Darwin published his radical new theories on the evolution of species, breaking the church's stranglehold on the place of our own species in the universe. Karl Marx published his critique of capitalism, striking at the very roots of the *dark satanic mills* of Europe. In the West of England Andrew Crosse the 'wizard of the Quantock Hills' was declared evil as he harnessed the powers of the newly discovered phenomena of electricity to create life, and declared mad when he prophesised that one day that same electricity would allow us to communicate around the world. The great white whale Moby Dick breached the face of the flood and Herman Melville wrote the greatest Gnostic gospel of our age, whilst in the Western Seas the admirality received official reports on the sighting of a giant sea serpent by a naval patrol in the Atlantic.

From the Reformation up until this point there had emerged a breed of workers and weavers of magic known variously as white witches, conjurers or cunning folk. They perceived themselves to be quite separate from the charmers of the rural communities who specialised in forms of hands-on healing, or the gentleman ghost-layers or the shadowy figure of the witch on the heath. They were a professional class. They seemed to have been both men and women, though Robert Hunt with a hint of irony and humour states that in the case of malefic magic, the former tended to break the spells whilst the latter made them! Although they had a precarious relationship with the law, far from being peripheral figures they lived and worked very much at the heart of the community, some like Thomasine Blight (whom we will be visiting later) even had a practice on the main street of a busy well-to-do market town. They seem to have been widely respected and were patronised by a wide sweep of society. Rather than being one trick ponies like many of their counterparts, they had a wide repertoire of magical practices up their sleeves; including divination, healing, the making or breaking of spells and the manufacture of charms. Though some made great claims as to the supernatural origin of their magical skills generally they openly relied on the use of grimoires and magical texts and good hard study as their source of power. The idea of magic being practiced primarily by uneducated women on the edge of society seems to be something of a myth. It is a mistake in many ways to think of the general populous in the early-modern period as being uneducated and illiterate. In the 18th to 19th centuries with the growth of the non-conformist churches, domestic reading of the scriptures became widespread; consequently literacy spread in rural communities. In fact Britain in the 17th century had a very high level of schooling that was not matched until the 1940s.

This seems to be reflected in the magical practice of the times. Without a doubt, the wave of transformation that took place in the mid 19th century made its mark upon the world of magic.

Certain places in the land seemed to be well-heads from whence this shadow of change gushed forth. Cornwall, the most South-westerly extremity of Britain, reaching out in to the Atlantic like a crooked finger, was one such place. As once Cornwall had supplied the tin that facilitated the cultural revolution of the Bronze Age, so now from her fathomless depths she gave forth her bounty to provide much of the knowhow and raw materials to fuel the new industrial revolution. For one brief period the now desolate ridge from Camborne down to St. Just was the wealthiest area in the world. The Cornish however were not only limited to their engineering prowess, other luminaries also emerged. In the far West, Humphrey Davey (who was reputed to have been of witch blood) whilst embarking on a career of invention and discovery which laid the foundations for what we now know as chemistry and physics also wrote a body of poetry extolling the magic of the land. He wondered at the incomprehensible unmanifest forces that formed the material world and communed with shadowy beings on the moors of West Penwith. Upon the craggy cliffs of the north coast, the poet and mystic Reverend Hawker fished shipwrecked sailors from the deep, sung to the mermaids and invoked the Sangraal whilst inland on the remote wastes of Bodmin Moor another luminary emerged, John Couch Adams, who later became president of the Royal Astronomical society. In 1846 in a feat of mathematical complexity (which even today in our age of computer technology is hard to replicate) he discovered Neptune. This newly found heavenly orb heralded a crashing wave from the great bitter oceans of creation to baptise this new age of dreamers and visionaries. Some, like old Captain Ahab, were consumed by the vastness of the unseen oceans and were lost to the deep, whilst others drew deep of its waters and manifested their dreams. It was at this time the cult of the Pellar was first recorded in Cornwall.

Cornwall in the mid 19th century throbbed with the sound of the beam engines throughout her hills and valleys and from her shores her boats sailed out across the seven seas. It was here from the lineage of witches and cunning folk of an earlier age that the cult of the Pellar emerged. The term first appears in print in 1849 in a Cornish dialect story in the New Monthly Magazine. In 1863, *pellar* appears again in an article in the 'West

Briton' reporting a scandal concerning the Cunning man James Thomas the Husband of the Helston Pellar Thomasine Blight. It appears again in the 1865 publication of Robert Hunt's *Romances of the West of England* and in 1870 in William Bottrell's *Traditions and Hearthside Stories of West Penwith*. (Hunt based much of his work on Bottrell's previous writings, but both men were probably collecting their material around the 1850s. Hunt and Bottrell provide most of the source material for the Cornish folklore we now know today.) From then on it begins to appear in Cornish dialect dictionaries and glossaries and seems to enter in to general usage. The roots of the word are uncertain. The Cornish term for witch most used are *wragh* or *pystry*. Some have speculated that it is a dialect contraction of *expeller* or *repeller*, referring to the Pellar's function as a curse breaker and exorcist or even possibly *peddler* owing to their supposedly itinerant and peripatetic habits. Robert Morton-Nance, pioneer of the Cornish Gorsedd and the Cornish language revival traced the word to its Cornish root of *pellhe* – the verb *to cast away*. Its origin, however, remains obscure.

In Hunt's work the word *peller* (the spellings *pellar* and *peller* seem to be arbitrary and interchangeable, which seems to suggest that the word is drawn from an oral rather than literary tradition) is used on several occasions to denote a professional magical practitioner. The client would invariably go to visit the Peller. The Peller would use some form of divination to diagnose the problem, which would invariably be as a result of 'ill-wishing' or 'the evil eye.' If the culprit was a spirit then they would be banished to some far place or chained under a rock (those that proved to be immovable were given an impossible task to keep them out of trouble!), or if the malefactor was a human then a charm could be constructed to protect the recipient or to return the curse to its sender. Here the Pellar's role is not only social and economic but also shamanic, as they stand as intermediaries between the world of humans and the world of spirits. For this reason the Pellar is cognate with the wayside-witch or the hedge-witch, for they truly stand between the worlds. The Pellar becomes as the old stone stile, where spirit force may pass from one side to the other. Bottrell, in his work (with his greater use of narrative) expands the concept of the Pellar. He tells the tale of the *Old man of Cury*, in which the Lutey family on the Lizard peninsula become a hereditary family of Pellars by making a pact with Morwena – a spirit of the sea. Whereas the witches of Europe draw their power from the Sabbat and the witches of England draw theirs from their familiar spirits, the Pellars of Cornwall draw their virtue from the primordial forces of the living rocks and the fathomless ocean.

Apart from the fact that the term *pellar* only seems to have been used in a relatively localised area, two other factors make it significantly different to other cunning traditions. In Bottrell's account, in defending her magical status Thomasine Blight stated that *the Virtue was in her,* and that she was of *real pellar blood*. Firstly, the concept of Virtue was central to the concept of pellar. Virtue is the essence that inhabits the being of the pellar which facilitates the working of magic and defines them as a magical entity. It is the spirit force that links the pellar to the spirit world – their source of power, and the catalyst by which the spirit world may operate within the world of matter. Virtue is described as a kind of energy that could be transferred from person to person (usually contrasexually) or to and from magically charged objects such as charms, talisman and magical tools. The greatest of these is the mysterious Milpreve or Adder stone, charm par excellence and Holy Grail of the Pellar, which as well as offering protection could bestow the gift of virtue upon its bearer. Secondly, the concept of Pellar blood implies some kind of otherness and heredity in the Pellar. As those versed in the artes are aware, this does not necessarily mean a genetic lineage – it may also refer to an initiatic lineage, passed on either from pellar to pellar, or directly from the spirit world. Whichever way it may be, the implication is that both the definition of the Pellar and the modus operandi of their work is of supernatural origin.

With the advent of the 20th century, the Pellar cult, along with many of our other indigenous magical traditions seems to fade away. The bard, folklorist and *searcher out of witches* William Paynter claimed that the last Cornish cunning man died in 1932, but in retrospect this was a pessimistic and unwarranted final curtain for the Old Craft. Partly this is due to the fact that the social structures that created and supported it were no longer in place, and partly because our thirst for the spirit world was being quenched by the new more articulate and popularist magical currents of Spiritualism, Theosophy, the growing Western Mystery traditions (which sprung from the ashes of the Hermetic order of the Golden Dawn) and finally Wicca and its associated Neo-Pagan traditions. Ironically however it was from these camps that also came the revival of the Pellar tradition. In the early 1960s self-styled traditional witch Robert Cochrane in describing his magical tradition wrote:

> I come from the country of the oak, ash and thorn ... I describe myself as a 'Pellar' ... The people are formed in clans and families and describe themselves by the local name of the deity.

Cochrane began a movement amongst occultists of orientation towards their traditional roots. But above all he made the salient point that it is not so much the magical practice inherent in a magical tradition that defines its nature, but the deity that overshadows it, for that is the point from which your tradition emanates. In the early 1980s, researcher Robin Ellis made contact with the remnants of a Pellar cult on the Lizard peninsula in Cornwall (of which Surrealist poet Peter Redgrove was involved). From his conversations he wrote a series of articles for the Meyn Mamvro Journal in the early 1990s. He describes the Pellars as 'the nature mystics and shaman of Cornwall.' Like Cochrane he saw the role of the Pellar as both magical and mystical. He describes their task as being to manifest the serpent virtue of the land within the being of the Pellar by unifying its light and shadow aspects, thus developing a transpersonal superconsciousness:

> The aim of the Pellar is to finish the task started many thousands of years ago by their predecessors in Lyonesse.

Lyonesse being the Cornish 'Atlantis,' the mythical source of the lore and the virtue of the Pellar now sunk beneath the waves. As I write these words I sit in an old disused granite quarry in West Cornwall. Beyond there broods a hill once crowned with cairns, in times gone by known as the Pellarstone. Still further West lays the Lizard peninsula and a blood red sunset over a sea where once the forests of the southern shores of Lyonesse stretched out to its holy western mountain. Looking out one cannot help but ask the question: Who indeed is the deity who lies in the heart of Pellar?

Bottrell recounts the following tale entitled *A legend of Tolcarn*. One day in 1592 some of the fishermen of Mousehole (Mowzle) were out mending their nets when the devil passed by. The devil took it into his head that he wanted to go fishing, so he snatched up their nets and tried to make a getaway. Unfortunately for him the fishermen also happened to be members of Paul church choir. They lost no time in following in hot pursuit chanting the Apostle's Creed, the Lord's Prayer and any other prayers that came to hand. The Devil left Tredavoe road and in one giant leap from Captain Tonkin's orchard crossed the valley to the blue elvan crag of Tolcarn. His mighty hoof sank into the rock leaving its imprint to this day. The devil however was still within the influence of those cursed psalms and prayers, so realising that he could not escape with his booty he raised himself up to his full height belching sulphurous smoke from his mouth, fiercely uttered three times *Buckah, Buckah, Buckah,* and dropped his nets upon the rock. This strange cry Bottrell interprets as a prophesy of the forthcoming Spanish attack in 1595, in which Paul, Newlyn and Mousehole were razed to the ground. The call however appears to be of an infinitely more arcane origin.

This story appears again recorded by the folklorist R. A. Courtney in her 1886 book *Cornish Feasts and Folklore.* As told to her by Rev. Lach-Szryma:

> The summit of the rock is reticulated with curious veins of elvan, about which a quaint Cornish legend relates that the BUCCA-boo, or storm god of the old Cornish, once stole the fisherman's nets. Being pursued by Paul choir, who sang the creed, he flew to the top of Paul Hill and thence over the coomb to Tolcarn, where he turned the nets to stone.

In the *Old Cornwall Journal* (no.3, 1926) Rev. G. H. Doble recounts, 'At Newlyn, near Penzance, a spirit called 'Bucka' is believed to come down from Paul Hill, by 'Bucka's pass' and haunt the road to Penzance.' Thus the legend of the Bucca enters in to the cannon of Cornish folklore. Another intriguing tale relating to the Bucca was collected from a Mr Hennery Maddern of Penzance by W. Y. Evans Wentz, who travelled through Cornwall at the turn of the century gathering first-hand accounts of færy lore (*The Fairy-faith in Celtic countries* of 1911) in which he relates a strange story of a being said to inhabit Tolcarn, 'The fairy of Tolcarn was in some way like Puck of the English Midlands but this fairy or troll was supposed to date back to the time of the Phœnicians.' He relates as to how he lived within the rock but sometimes he chose to make himself visible. He also added that if one pronounced the appropriate incantation whilst on Tolcarn, he would appear in the form in which you existed in a former life, 'You only had to name the period or age, and you could live your past life their in over again.' It was said that he assisted in the building of Solomon's temple and came to these shores in search of tin; he was sometimes called *the wandering one* or *Odin the wanderer*. With this epithet, one is put in mind of that archetypal wanderer beloved of the 3rd century Gnostics and contemporary Sabbatic witches alike – Cain, who is described in the old Cornish creation plays (*The Creation of the World*, William Jordan, 1611, the earliest reference to the Bucca recorded) as *Bucca Nos*, Bucca of the Night. Maddern also adds that one could call him up by standing on the carn with three dried leaves of oak, ash and thorn in your hand whilst speaking the appropriate incantation. The charm could only be passed on contrasexually and to a believer. The informant however was a sceptic so sadly never learned the incantation.

This is a classic example of a legend directly relating to a feature in the landscape, a theme that betrays an ancient origin. Tales recounting the mythical creation of the land are far more than just idle entertainment, or even a means of explaining a natural feature. From the dreamtime myths of the Australian aboriginal song lines to the Dindsenchas of the Celts, they are an embodiment of our relationship with the soul of the land. Their form changing over time; giants becoming saints, kings and devils, but their essence remains the same. Two notable features appear upon Tolcarn. Firstly the Bucca's footprint. This is a common mythological motif; others appear at the Devil's doorway cave at Polperro (near to the evocatively named Polbucky – Bucca's pool), on Tintagel castle or on the Giant's rock adjacent to the Boscawen-un stone circle for example. The mythopoeic significance of this could relate to the mark signifying the presence of, or ownership by, a spiritual entity. One must not forget the significance of such markings in relation to rituals of kingship or initiation. Secondly the veins of quartz in the blue elvan rock are of notable significance (the Net-Of-Bucca is one of his most profound mysteries). The beauty of such a feature can be quite breathtaking. I have seen that same glowing web of crystal etched into the beach pebbles below the cliffs of the Helford overlooking the haunt of the sea beast Morgawr, and at a natural serpent altar in a cave on the beach on the north coast of Cornwall below the brooding hill of Buccator, and upon the great standing stone of Men Gurta on St. Breock's Down ... a lightning flash frozen in stone – like the merry maidens who danced on the Sabbath.

Evans Wentz described Tolcarn thus:

This is a natural outcropping of greenstone on a commanding hill just above the vicarage in Newlyn, and concerning it many weird legends survive. In pre-Christian times it was probably one of the Cornish sacred spots for the celebration of ancient rites – probably in honour of the sun – and for divination.

Some years past, when I first went in search of the sacred shrine of Tolcarn, I recall being at something of a loss. All I had to go on was an obscure 100 year old folkloric reference. After finding the likely location on the edge of Newlyn I noticed, hidden behind a row of houses, a huge and imposing inland cliff. Seeing someone in the garden I politely enquired as to whether they had heard of Tolcarn or the said hoof print. I was met with taciturn and hostile response. I was put in mind of an account of the frosty reception surrealist, folklorist and occultist Ithell Colquhoun (who had once lived in nearby Lamorna) received when looking for a holy well near Germoe. She explains, 'Country people are sometimes ashamed of having forgotten or neglected their holy places. I rather feel, though, that their reluctance is due to diffidence in showing them to a stranger, who may not sympathise with the age-long cult.' A request to have a closer look at the end of their garden however magically broke her amnesia and she directed us to a road at the top of the cliff. Dutifully we climbed the hill to a small housing estate. There between two garden fences I found a narrow entrance leading in the direction of the top of the cliff. I picked my way through the garden waste and brambles and in the path before me saw a flat slab bearing a distinctly phallic form. As to whether this was of human art or a simulacra of nature it was impossible to tell. (I have seen a similar image to this, but in negative on the cliffs above Boscastle.). Stepping beyond the slab the alley opened out to a numinous elvan crag high above the valley. There I stood like the Bucca in this lost acre bathed in the virtue of the dreamtime, whilst only a few yards away families cooked, cleaned and watched the television in a suburban world which could have been a thousand miles away.

This tantalising tale begs the question: Who indeed is the Bucca? Robert Hunt in his taxonomy of the world of faery defines Buccas as being cognate with the *Knockers*, the subterranean spirits haunting the old tin mines. This interpretation of the Buccas as being one of the faery tribes is a thread which continues throughout Cornish folklore. In the Museum of Witchcraft in Boscastle an inscription on the wall quotes Katherine Briggs' *Dictionary of Faeries* and describes them as, 'Goblins of the wind who foretold shipwrecks.' Looking at the legend of Tolcarn one cannot help but feel that this identification of the Bucca with some kind of faery or non-individuated nature spirit is on the wrong track. Possibly this is an example of de-deification. The gods of the old religion can become the ghosts and demons of the new. As Arthur Machen states, 'The Fairies are the gods of the heathen come down in to the world: Diana becomes Titania'; or as Rudyard Kipling in *Puck of Pooks Hill* (1906) put it, 'First they were the gods, then they were the people of the hills, and then they flitted to other places because they couldn't get on with the English for one reason or another!'

William Bottrell, however, sees the Bucca of a very different mythological lineage to that of Hunt; he quotes from an article in the journal 'One and All' (1868):

> 'Bucca' was once a divinity, but, being older than English Christianity, it became degraded from that high rank as the new religion came westwards. Nevertheless the Bucca did not die. Within easy memory every boat in Newlyn always set aside a portion of its catch, and left it in a collected heap on the beach to propitiate the Bucca; and every fisherman noted, with superstitious awe, the remarkable regularity with which 'Bucca' fetched away his offerings, after dark.

The writer then goes on to describe as to how the term 'Bucca' was once used as a term of pride to denote an inhabitant of Newlyn, but as with the deity to which the name pertains, it has degenerated into a form of derision. He also goes on to describe how to denote the supreme deity the term *deus* is used amongst the Latins and *Gott* amongst the Teutons, whereas it is *Bog* (from which 'Bucca' Bogy, Puck, Pwka etc. is derived) is only used amongst the Slavs; these last manifestations of the divine 'having fallen amongst Teutonic thieves, were robbed of their divinity and cast adrift as disreputable devils.' This seems to be leading us to look at the Bucca as being a quite distinct entity in his own right. In an intriguing pamphlet by Cornish folklorist Charles Thomas (*The Taboo*, 1951) also puts forward the hypothesis that, 'The Sea has always been regarded under the protection of its own deities – Poseidon, Neptune, Dagon and all the fishlike anthropomorphic sea-gods.' Therefore one must have been present in a seafaring nation like Cornwall.

There is ample evidence to suggest that on the western shores of Mounts Bay he was known as the Bucca. This god or sprite (properly speaking there is only one Bucca) can be equated with Puck, Brownie or Robin Goodfellow of English folklore ... at Newlyn, Bucca has been transferred to the sea. He was controller of the fishes, and three fishes would be thrown in to the harbour, or left on the beach for him to ensure a plentiful catch. He is Bucca-Gwidn, the good spirit as opposed to Buccaboo, or Bucca-dhu, the storm god who stole fisherman's nets and raised the wind and whose name still survives in the name for a scarecrow. The bucca of Newlyn was a benevolent god.

He recalls the tradition that was said that if the sea was *moaning* it was the Bucca calling for rain, suggesting that the Bucca presided not only over the catch but also over the weather. He speculates that a kind of dual faith observance grew up amongst the fisher folk, 'Bucca on weekdays and God on Sunday'; the Newlyn fishermen would never fish on Sunday.

One cannot help but think that the Tom Bawcock festival held in Mousehole in between Christmas and the winter solstice, in which torchlight processions in the streets celebrate the mythical Tom Bawcock, who saved the village from famine by braving the storm and returning with 'seven sorts of fish,' is possibly a relic of the rites of veneration to the old Bucca ... and when Cecil Williamson described the old Cornish witches on the sea cliffs ecstatically dancing with the wind ... maybe it was old Bucca with whom they danced. From these tales it is clear that the old Bucca has two faces: Bucca-Gwidn, the white bucca, the bringer of peace and plenty; and Bucca-Dhu, the black Bucca, the storm that flattens crops and smashes ships and houses. Like the sea, the one can transform into the other in an instant, but the irony is that it is the darkness of the storm that turns the wheel of the seasons and brings fertility to the land and sea. As sure as day follows night, so Bucca-Gwidn emerges from Bucca-Dhu and only through Bucca-Dhu may Bucca-Gwidn be known.

Let us for a moment look at the derivation of Bucca and return to Evans Wentz:

> Bucca, who properly is but one, is a deity and not a fairy, and it is said that at Newlyn, the great seat of his worship, offerings of fish are left out on the beach for him. His name is the Welsh Pwca, which is

probably 'Puck,' though Shakespeare's Puck was just a Pisky, and it may be connected with the general Slavonic word 'Bog,' God; so that if, as some say, Buccaboo is really meant for Bucca-dhu, black bucca, this may be an equivalent of Czernbog, the black God, who was the Ahriman of Slavonic dualism, and Bucca-Widn (White Bucca) which is rarer , though the expression does come in to a St Levan story, may be the corresponding 'Bielobog.'

Nigel Jackson (*Masks of Misrule*, 1996) expands upon the etymology of the name:

The Indo-European word BHUG denotes a horned beast, goat, ram, stag and in ancestor of the modern English 'Buck.' From this root word are derived terms: Sanskrit 'Bukka' – 'He goat.' Anglo-Saxon 'Bucca' – 'He goat', Middle High German 'Bock' – 'Goat,' Gaelic 'Boc' – 'Goat,' Icelandic 'Bukkr' and Latin 'Boquena' – 'Goatskin.'

And of course one must not forget the Cornish dialect word *bucca* meaning scarecrow, fool, ghost or goblin.

Charles Thomas suggests that the name Bucca may be just an epithet, or as the Saxons called it a *kenning*. That is to say, the actual name of the deity is taboo, and cannot be spoken in the ordinary way, thus a descriptive title (which may equally obscure or elucidate the nature of the being to which it pertains) is used in its place. This theme emerges in the tale of *Duffy and the Devil* in which the Bucca rears his head in a different guise. The tale is a kind of Cornish Rumplestiltskin story in which the protagonist has to guess the name of the shadowy Devil figure. One also suspects that it is the Bucca who emerges in the tale of St Mawes (The old Cornish saint stories being a rich reliquary of folkloric material). The story goes that one day the pious St Mawes was preaching on a rocky promontory looking out to sea at the mouth of the Carrick roads. The seals however, having no appreciation of the word of god just continued to bark and call to one another across the waves. Such was the good saint's anger at this unwanted distraction that he picked up a boulder and pitched it at the offending seals, thus scattering them and inadvertently forming the treacherous rock, known as Black Rock, that now lies at the mouth of the harbour. Canon G. H. Doble, in the 1920s, collected a Breton version of this tale in which the fiend disturbing the peace was not a mere noisy seal, but was the demon and 'sea-monster horrible to behold' Teus/Tuthe. This name appears to be related to the Gaulish/Celtic name Tutates which in turn appears to be a kenning applied to a number of Celtic Gods. (In the same way that the term Baal, or Lord, was used to denote a number of Near Eastern gods), but from its context, the finger points towards the Bucca. The stretch of sea where the action takes place has been called Morgawr's mile, for it is the haunt of the mythical Cornish sea monster Morgawr (a name coined by surrealist Tony 'Doc' Sheils in the 1970s, meaning sea giant). Little is known of the monster except for a string of sightings dating back to the turn of the last century, but like the pellar it seems to straddle the worlds. 'Doc' Shiels famously embarked on a series of cryptozoological magical experiments with a group of Pellar-witches around Mawnan woods in an attempt to conjure the beast; in the old tongue of the Cornish they chanted *Morgawr cref yn nerth ef*. With the Bucca's blessing the beast arose from the depths and entered not only into our waters, but into our consciousness once again. I too once saw Morgawr on a bright moonlight night in the mid 1990s, when the Hale-Bop comet was high in the sky and the sea was as calm as a millpond. There she was, off Trefusis Point, heading from the old oil rig towards the shore ... but that is another story. One cannot, however, underestimate the profundity of the feeling one gets when one glances through the 'gap in the hedge' and for one brief moment one touches the spirit world. It is moments like that which are known amongst the Pellars as the Bucca's benediction.

One must not forget that the realm of the Bucca is not entirely limited to the sea; the Bucca is of a chthonic nature too. The spirits that inhabited the old mines were known as *knockers* or *the Buccas*. The term knockers was used to describe the sound they made in order to warn the miners of impending danger or to guide them towards rich lodes, the name Bucca being more akin to a proper name. Their origin is said to be traced to the Phonecians or the spirits of Jews sent to work in the mines in days gone by. One can only assume that the term Bucca, however, suffered the same process below the ground as it did above ground and upon the shore.
Did that same antediluvian god serve the dark recesses of the caves as he did upon the waves? The belief in the knockers in the mines was by no means limited to the dim and distant past. Their presence continued into the 1980s until the last mine, South Crofty, was closed. Contemporary

witnesses have reported that areas of the mine had to be abandoned due to unwanted knocker activity, and a votive cairn was still in use on one of the lower levels. In the tale of *Tom and the Knackers* collected by William Bottrell around St. Just he describes how precarious our relationship with the spirits of the mines could be. Whilst working in the depths of Ballowal mine he heard the spirits calling in the darkness, to which he discourteously replied with a curse and a hand full of gravel. To which they replied with the chant *Tom Trevurrow! Tom Trevurrow! Leave some of thy fuggan for the Bucca or bad luck to thee tomorrow!* requesting him to leave an offering of a morsel of his food, as was customary amongst the miners. Of course the curmudgeonly old Tom Trevurrow refused and ill luck sure enough befell him.

So too, it would seem, that the Bucca was also known in the fields. Charles Thomas in his 1952 pamphlet *The Sacrifice in Cornwall* suggests that the ubiquitous habit of country folk leaving offerings of their produce to the Piskys is in fact directed towards the Bucca. The term Bucca was also used as a dialect term for Scarecrow. To the mind of an animist, the bundle of rags upon a wooden cross can become far more than just a bird scarer, it becomes the spirit of the land itself. In many traditions, the witch and the hedge are synonymous, and so, here too the essence of the Bucca is made manifest. Bucca-Dhu is the hedge that ever seeks to encroach over the field and the Crow that pecks away the newly sown seed, in an eternal quest to return the land to its primordial state. Whilst Bucca-Gwidn is the Hedge cutter and the scarecrow, turning around the darkness of the land that it may feed our bellies. In his paper, Charles Thomas connects the Bucca to the enigmatic scattering of small uncultivated areas of land often present amidst cultivated farmland known as No man's land, Jack's land or the Devil's acre. These lost acres, often enclosing prehistoric features, are left as a refuge for the spirits and the old gods. He recounts a tale told by John Harris of Camborne in 1825 in which as a child he became lost in the fields. This phenomenon of being unaccountably disoriented and lost in a small and familiar piece of land was known as being *Pisky-led* or *Pisky-laden*. In the parish of Constantine in the early 1990s, I was in all earnestness warned of this, and I did indeed subsequently fall victim to it! Anyway, back to the story – the young boy Harris eventually returned home, sobbing 'There is nobody here but I and the BUCKAW.'

The Bucca seems to exist on many levels. Far from being only an embodiment of the landscape, he lives just as comfortably within the sphere of human life. In his guise as an intermediary between the worlds he can be Mercurial in aspect. A cycle of stories collected by Bottrell from the St. Just area describe him as a trickster, somewhat reminiscent of Mullah Nasrudin of the Sufi tales, the divine fool, shifting our consciousness by turning the world on its head. One story relates that one day Bucca strolled into a tavern in St. Just, and there sitting in the window seat sat two gentlemen. Looking at the slovenly Bucca standing there 'rough as the hair on a badger's arse,' they exclaimed, 'Which art thee, Bucca, a fool or a rogue?' As quick as a flash, he seated himself between the two and replied, 'I'm between both, I believe!' From this retort is derived the expression 'Between both, as the Bucca said'; and this expression, like the Sufi tales, may be read on many different levels.

As his goat-like name suggests, the Bucca can sweep from the Mercurial to the realm of the Saturnian. But however, as Bottrell observes:

> In a great number of our legends, the devil is a prominent personage; yet the mythical demon of 'Bucca-Boo' of our drolls has few of the malicious traits of our satanic Majesty.

Like Bucca the trickster, Bucca the Devil changes our consciousness, but in a different way. He comes to us as an initiator. In a cycle of tales entitled the *Legends of Ladock*, Bottrell tells the tale of John Trevail the prize wrestler of the parish. Wrestling is a well-respected traditional Cornish sport, tracing its pedigree back to the mythical fight between Brutus's commander Coreneus and the old giant Watcher-king Gogmagog, which resulted in the Celtic occupation of Cornwall. The protagonist, also known as Cousin Jacky, one midsummer day, in a fine bout, threw the neighbouring parish's champion. In a fit of rash pride he announced that he 'wouldn't mind having a hitch with the devil himself, if he would venture.' Sure enough, on his way home across the heath, in the dead of night, he was approached by the Old One himself in the guise of a man of the cloth who offered to 'try a bout' with him the following midnight. Jacky accepted and the stranger was gone. In the cold light of day realising what he had done he approached the Rev. Wood, the rector of Ladock Parish, who was well versed in the magical arts. Under the good reverend's tutelage young Jacky was furnished with a magical charm, with which, after a fierce bout, he managed to overcome his otherworldly opponent, emerging as a wiser and more worldly fellow. In another story collected by Bottrell entitled *Uter Bosence and the Pisky* he relates another initiatory tale of a wrestler called Uter Bosence returning home from a Midsummer Day of wrestling and revelry in St Just. Midsummer Day was not only a traditional fair day, but it was said that this was the time the Cornish witches gathered upon the moors, lit their ceremonial fires and renewed their vows to the Old One. In this tale he inadvertently encroaches upon one such taboo time and place. He found himself in an old ruined chapel near Botrea. Before he knew it he was amidst a morass of serpent headed beings and was caught up in a wild frenzied dance, then as he tried to get away, before him stood 'a being much like a black buck goat, with horns and beard more than a yard in length; but the goat was of such a size, with such flaming balls of eyes and such a length of tale behind, was never seen on hills and mores before.' The creature grasped Uter with its great hairy hands it had in place of hooves. In a panic Uter took a swing at the great black Bucca with his blackthorn staff, to find himself pitched up in the air, spinning over the valley and left for dead on a rock at the foot of Beacon Hill. He eventually recovered and from that moment forth, rather than continually attempting to prove himself, 'He paid more attention to his farm and family; so perhaps the rolling did him good, on the whole.' As in many cultures, martial arts, dance, labour and spiritual practice are all inextricably entwined. So as Jacob wrestled with the angel, so must the Pellar wrestle with the Bucca. There are three things that will allow the Pellar to prevail, that is, hard training, magic and fair play, and when the struggle is done they must learn to walk away or be caught in a cycle of eternal conflict.

Another tale we have already touched upon is *Duffy and the Devil*, in which the Bucca appears again in the guise of the Devil. There he appears as the lord of the Sabbat amidst a circle of dancing witches within a cavern at the head of Lamorna Valley. In a ceremony of ritually revealing his name the witches chant, *By night and day, we will dance and play, with our noble captain – Tarraway! Tarraway!* (*Taran* being the Cornish for thunder, thus linking him to Bucca the storm god.). Charles Thomas suggests:

> The earth Goddess was displaced by a male hunting-and-woodlands deity, who seems to have been connected with witchcraft rather than agriculture. This entity – Dr. Murray's god of the witches – has had

many names, but in Cornwall he still clings tenuously to the soubriquet of Bucca.

Let us not however fall into the trap of over-anthropomorphisation. The Bucca is far more than just a god of agriculture and fishing, or even a mysterious folkloric Devil. The Bucca is an embodiment of the primordial forces of the land and the sea; an exposure to the storm, a rending of the soul. Arthur Machen in *The Great God Pan* (1894) describes the experience of encountering such a being:

> There is a real world, but it is beyond this glamour and this vision, beyond these chases in Arras, dreams in a career, beyond them all as beyond a veil. You may find this all strange nonsense; it may be strange but it is true, and the ancients knew what lifting the veil means. They called it seeing the god Pan.

It is from the word *Pan* that the word panic is derived, so in this sense Bucca is cognate with Pan in that he is not so much an entity but a state of being. The Bucca is experienced not through reason, but through the sense of the numinous, that is to say, the direct super-sensory experience of the divine made manifest within the realm of nature. This however is not just an inward experience of the mind. Mystic and Surrealist Ithell Colquhoun, whilst living in Paul (Bucca's heartland), described this experience as that which brings forth:

> A 'fountain of Hecate,' an uprush of force from a macro-cosmic underworld which focused by ceremony may coincide at precise times with the microcosmic unconscious.

There is a Cornish dialect word – mazed – which on one level can mean intoxicated, but on another can mean being carried away by a consciousness-altering ecstasy of the spirit. This is the true mystery of Neptune, immersion in the seas of our subconscious, and in the soul of the world.

Another writer well versed in the magical arts, Dion Fortune in *The Goat Foot God* (1936), describes how her protagonist develops a magical relationship with the landscape in order to invoke the wild pagan forces of Pan. The paradox is that once Pan is made manifest:

It was not the Goat-god, crude and earthy. It was the sun! But not the sun of sophisticated Apollo, but an older earlier primordial sun, the sun of Helios the Titan.

Once again Bucca-Dhu is transformed into Bucca-Gwidn. Although these are both fictional accounts, the work of both Machen and Fortune are firmly based in actual magical knowledge and experience. To the Pellar, the gnosis of the Bucca, far from being destructive, is an awakening of the soul to its true divine nature, as Plato's prayer to Pan in *Phaedrus* tells us, 'Beloved Pan, and ye other gods who haunt this place, give me beauty in my inward soul, and may the outward and inward man be one.' Several years ago I delivered a folklore lecture in West Cornwall in which I had touched upon the subject of place names connected with the Bucca. I had mentioned Chybucca, near Truro, which had commonly interpreted as meaning 'haunted house.' Afterwards I was approached by a wily old Cornishman who insisted that it meant 'house of the spirit.' He went on to explain, 'and that's what we are… A house of the spirit … and that's what we can become.'

So this indeed begs the question, where would a multi-faceted deity who brings forth both fish for our bellies and rapture for the soul hale from? The gnostic element of the Bucca in addition to his elemental, magical, tutelary, metallurgical, nautical and fertility aspects suggest that rather than being of a purely singular and indigenous origin (a Cornish version of Manannan mac lyr of the Gael or Wade of the northern folk) he is indeed of a syncretic nature and of a composite origin. Cornwall has never been an isolated land, since prehistory it has always been a seafaring nation. There has been a persistent belief in Cornwall that the Phoenecians once came to our shores in search of tin. The Phoenecians were a seafaring people who ruled the sea-roads of the Mediterranean from the second millennium BCE to the end of the last Punic war in the 5th century BCE. Their culture was a melting pot of the Near-Eastern, Egyptian and the Classical worlds. We have already looked at two direct references to the Phoenecians in relation to the Bucca. Cecil Williamson (the old proprietor of the Museum of Witchcraft in Boscastle Cornwall 1909–1999) spoke of a tradition he knew of that told of the *Troy People*, whom he describes as 'the wandering 'Charmers' of the Mediterranean seaboard,' who he claims settled in the South-West of Britain establishing a Phoenecian cult of

Tannit. The Phoenecians were in the habit of establishing a composite tutelary deity in the places they settled, composed of a fusion of the local god's and their own. These were given the epithet Ba'al (meaning Lord) plus the local gods name. It is interesting to note that many near-Eastern tongues have no phonetic *p,* so it is often replaced with *b*. An example of this within the Phoenecian homeland on the Syrian-Israeli border is the spring dedicated to Pan, which has mutated from Panyas to Banyas, thus in the same way the Pucka of the Britain's could mutate to Bucca. As to the question of who is the most likely candidate for the Bucca's ancestor, the Phoenecian god Kusor seems to loom out of the mist. In the first century, in his treatise on the mythology of the Phoenecians, Philo relates:

> Kusor practiced the arts of magical formulas, incantation and divination ...he invented the fish-hook and bait, the fishing line and the fishing boat, and he was the first to learn how to navigate.

Earlier legends describe him as the originator of smithcraft, the controller of the rains and the turner of the seasons. Is this not an almost perfect description of the Bucca's areas of jurisdiction?

Again I think it is misleading to think of a folkloric phenomenon as having a pristine original (and by implication correct) form that existed at some indeterminate point in the past, which has been periodically 'polluted' as it travels down through time. Our concept of the gods is in no way separate to any other cultural phenomenon. It is syncretic and dynamic, growing and changing all the time. And so too does the Bucca as he strides down through history, like the serpent shedding his skin each time he is called forth from the sea. From God of the seas, to Pisky, Devil and scarecrow, and now within the modern 'Traditional Craft' revival the Bucca has emerged once again.

In an underground form, the Cunning magical traditions seem to have survived into the 20th century. In the 1950s there emerged a popular revival of Witchcraft instigated by Gerald Gardner (1884–1964). For a while, on the Isle of Man, he and Cecil Williamson resided together, sharing a dream of founding a Witchcraft Museum. Gardner's interest however was in creating a mass popular pagan religion; its adherence to any traditional forms of magic was of secondary importance to its utility, whereas Cecil Williamson devoted his life to studying and practicing the lore of the traditional witch. Gardner with his populist Wicca entered the popular consciousness, whilst Williamson faded into obscurity. Meanwhile, in a strange twist of fate Wicca became the prevailing paradigm and the old craft was pushed even further into the shadows. Robert Cochrane (whom we have already visited) was one of the few voices of dissention, but on his passing, his own tradition (under the guise of the Regency Coven and the work of Doreen Valiente) cross-pollinated with Wicca and the two became virtually indistinguishable.

The first stirrings of interest in the indigenous magic of Cornwall came from the Folklore camp; with William Paynter, Charles Thomas and B. C. Spooner and of course Cecil Williamson, who had arrived in Cornwall in the 1950s and there quietly practiced and researched the ways of the old Cornish Crafter in the Museum of Witchcraft until his death. Apart from Williamson, surprisingly it was from the Surrealist art camp that the first wave of the revival of the actual practice of traditional Cornish methods of magic emerged with Ithell Colquhoun, Peter Redgrove and Tony 'Doc' Sheils. All this emerged against a backdrop of a growing interest in Celticism and Romanticism and 'Earth mysteries' in Cornwall. It was not however until the 1990s that a revival of a wider interest in the 'Old Craft' seemed to really get under way. Nigel Jackson, Mike Howard and Nigel Pennick emerged with a vision of a reformed Old Craft, but it was Andrew D. Chumbley, Essex cunningman and Magister of the Cultus Sabbati (1967–2004) who set the template for the Traditional Craft revival. In a sense he did for the Old Craft what Gardner had done for Wicca, only rather than establish a homogeneous universal system, he was passionate about the 'reification and enfleshment' of the regional manifestations of the traditional craft – in all their idiosyncratic glory! It was to this end that he devoted the final years of his life. He envisioned, in the West, a revival of the Pellar cult under the tutelage of the Bucca. On one of his many visits to Cornwall he spoke this charm:

Come Bucca Come, noble Captain of our Sabbath,
Come forth our good and faithful king.
Come dancing over the mound to stand upon the stone of truth,
Here to plant the tree of Bucca; the goat horned stang of Pellar.

About this same time Oxford based occultist Jack Daw (Paul Ratcliffe) was envisioning his own re-emergent form of the Pellar craft, which he in turn had inherited from his Devonshire grandmother. He disseminated a list of aphorisms, terminology, spell recipes and the following prayer:

> Horned Bucca, both dark and fair, divine androgyny, be in all hearts and on the tip of every tongue. For your time has come again as it does with the beginning of every moment.

With the revival of the Midsummer festivity of Golowan/Mazey day and the Midwinter festival of Montol in Penzance, the Bucca (under the guidance of Cassandra Latham the Village Witch of St Buryan) has become a key part of the town procession. The Bucca became the Teaser that guides the Penglaze (the horseskull-bearing Hobby Horse that appears as a key focus of the processions) in an eternal dance of death and resurrection. It is from this image that within the neo-Pellar revival, that the horses skull has become synonymous with the Bucca. History relates that when the Spanish raided Mounts Bay in the 16th century they claim to have found a horse-headed idol in Paul church. The line from the Indian Upanishads, 'the horse's head is the gate of god,' is brought to mind, or the verse from the *Rig Veda*:

> The horse has come to the slaughter, pondering with his heart turned towards the Gods, the goat (Bukka), his kin, is led in front; behind come the poets, the singers.

In 2008 Gemma Gary produced *Traditional Witchcraft: A Cornish Book of Ways*. Drawing from Jack Daw, Jackson, Williamson and her own Craft experiences, she created a complete cycle of Pellar praxis under the auspices of the Bucca. Thus the Bucca enters into the cannon of the modern traditional magic revival.

Of course the internet has spawned a plethora of folks peddling their own vision of the traditional Cornish craft. Most of which is at best derivative and at worst a show of fancy dress, adolescent images of blood and skulls and other foppish neo-gothic excesses. But the Bucca still lives on, in the howl of the wind and the crashing of the waves. It is here the Bucca is to be found, in the stories in our hearts and the labyrinths of the land. With the emergence of the great orb of Neptune into our group consciousness in the mid 19th century, there came a re-emergence of the Mysteries in the form of the Pellar cult and a re-remembering of the Bucca that once blessed our shores. But still there are those who would say that the Bucca is but a fancy picture woven from the warp of folklore and the weft of the romantic imagination. All I can suggest is that you go to the shoreline at twilight and call three times to the waves, *BUCCA! BUCCA! BUCCA!* Then walk away and don't look over your shoulder till dawn, and there you will find your answer. To this very day rumours persist of a Bucca cult in the woods and fields of West Penwith, the valleys and moors of Central Cornwall, in the estuaries and the old disused granite quarries of West Cornwall and on the rocky crags of the north Cornish coast. As Cecil Williamson once said, 'it still goes on today!'

> *Bucca above and Bucca below,*
> *Bucca fore and Bucca aft,*
> *Bucca-Gwidn hag Bucca-dhu,*
> *Bucca cref yn nerth ef.*
> *Bucca, Bucca, Bucca!*

WILLIAMSON, CECIL. Despite his huge influence on the world of Witchcraft and Cunning traditions very little of his work has been published. The Author is currently working on a book on Mr Williamson incorporating much unpublished magical material.

CHUMBLEY, ANDREW. His work with the regional witchcraft traditions was very much a work in progress, which was sadly cut short by his untimely passing. Consequently nothing was published directly relating to this, but many of the ideas inherent in it are implicit in his earlier work, but also I feel that paradoxically it also made much of his earlier work redundant.

BIBLIOGRAPHY

COLQUHOUN, ITHELL, *The Living Stones of Cornwall*. Peter Owen, 1957.
DAVIES, OWEN, *Popular Magic*. Hambledon Continuum, 2003.
DOBLE, GILBERT H., *The Saints of Cornwall, Vol. 3: Saints of the Fal*. Llanerch Press, 1930.
GARY, GEMMA, *Traditional Witchcraft: A Cornish Book of Ways*. Troy Books, 2008.
HOWARD, MIKE (ED.), *The Roebuck in the Thicket: An Anthology of the Robert Cochrane Witchcraft Tradition*. Capall Bann, 2003.
LATHAM JONES, CASSANDRA, *Village Witch*. Troy Books, 2011.
NANCE, MORTON, *Folklore in the Cornish Language*. Francis Boutle, 1925.
SEMMENS, JASON, *The Witch of the West*. Privately printed, Plymouth, 2004.
——— *Bucca Redivivus: Folklore and the Construction of Ethnic Identity within Modern Pagan Witchcraft in Cornwall*, Cornish Studies 18, 2010.
——— *On the Origin of the Peller*, Old Cornwall Society Journal. Autumn 2009.
——— *The Cornish Witch-finder: William Henry Paynter and the Witchery, Ghosts, Charms and Folklore of Cornwall*. Federation of Old Cornwall Societies, 2008.
SHEILS, TONY 'DOC,' *Monstrum*. CFZ, 1990.
THOMAS, KEITH, *Religion and the Decline of Magic*. Weidenfeld & Nicolson, 1971.

Exorcists, Conjurors and Cunning Men in Post Reformation England

RICHARD PARKINSON

HAT ARE THE LINKS BETWEEN the medieval minor clerical order of exorcist and the cunning men or conjurors of later centuries? This is one of the missing pieces of cunning craft history, and as such is written from an English perspective and with particular reference to the county of Lancashire. There is a demonstrable continuity of practice from the church sanctioned professional exorcists to the profusion of freelance quack doctors, cunning folk and expellers. We will also witness the creation of the Witch bottle, the breaking of a hangman's rope, authentic rituals of exorcism and sundry other marvels in our tale.

To the medieval European mind the universe was created by God. Everything in Heaven and Earth was ordained by God and every event from the Creation to the Last judgement was predestined. In such a universe nothing simply happened, every event had a place and purpose.

The universe was envisaged as being essentially Aristotelian or geocentric in character. In other words the Earth sat at the centre of a neatly stacked series of concentric spheres. This model of the universe comes down to us in the form described by the celebrated astronomer Claudius Ptolemaeus in the 2nd century CE. Besides the earthly sphere there were seven ascending planetary spheres each containing one of the planetary bodies, an eighth containing the fixed stars and a ninth containing the mind of God. The planetary spheres were the Moon which was closest to the Earth followed by Mercury, Venus, Sun, Mars, Jupiter and Saturn.

Students of the Qabala will recognise that this arrangement corresponds with the Sephiroth on the Qabalistic tree of life and with the Platonic and Mithraic planetary ladder to enlightenment. This concept is seen in its most elaborate form in Dante Alighieri's visions of seven heavens expanding outwards from the Earth and the nine circles of hell descending down into the Earth's core.

Linked to the geocentric worldview was the concept of a great Chain of Being. According to the Chain of Being all created things could be ranked in a hierarchy according to their level of development. Living beings could be ranked in the following way: God/Angels/Saints/Clean Souls/the good Longaevi[1] – Humans/Animals/Plants – the wicked Longævi – Unclean Souls/Demons/Fallen Angels – the Devil.

According to this theory humans were the only living creatures in the Chain of Being who could ascend to heaven. This was because God had breathed his Holy Word (or breath) into the clay from which Adam was made, giving to him and his heirs a soul derived from God.

Aristotle saw the sphere of the Moon as lying between the material and spiritual worlds, 'Aristotle made a sharp distinction between the world above and below the moon. In the ethereal region above, celestial laws hold, while below earthly bodies are subject to mutability, the force of time. All matter seeks its proper place in the divine hierarchy: heavy bodies fall; light bodies rise.'[2]

---

1 The Longaevi was a term used by C. S. Lewis to refer to that group of beings which rank between humans and angels, known by some as Fairies and referred to by Virgil as Fauns and Nymphs in the 1st century BCE and by Robert Kirk in his *The Secret Commonwealth* in 1691 as Elves, Fauns and Fairies.
2 From *An Introduction to Chaucer, Chaucer and the Medieval World View*, Jamie Spraggins, 2002, published by Gilman School, Maryland.

This separation could be seen throughout the created world. Within man himself there was a separation between the higher spiritual nature and the lower animal nature ruled by carnal appetites. The same division of the chain of being was envisaged within human society. The king was placed at the apex, below him were the clergy; the princes; the nobility and gentry; the craftsmen, burgesses and yeomen farmers; and lowest of all the unfree peasants or *villeins*.

The same hierarchy could be found in the ecclesiastical structure in each feudal territory. The church hierarchy incorporated nine ascending orders or grades split between the three major holy orders and the five minor holy orders. The major holy orders are still familiar to all Christians and comprise the originally celibate orders of Deacon, Priest and Bishop with the Primate (senior Bishop) at the top of the pyramid. The minor orders are now much less familiar. In all but the Eastern Churches the Minor Holy Orders (*Ordines Minores*) have long since been abolished or converted into lay offices, or grades for priests in training.

The situation was quite different during the Middle Ages. Each of the five minor orders had a clear and important function within the Parish. Members of the minor orders carried out most of the routine and administrative work within parishes. Membership of the minor orders was by admission rather than ordination and was usually granted in person by the local ordinary, generally a bishop but sometimes an exempt abbot and, occasionally a lesser prelate.

Minor orders were conferred by the presentation to the candidate of the appropriate instruments, a key for a Door Keeper; a lectionary for a Lector; the book of exorcism for the Exorcist; and a candlestick for an Acolyte. Members of the minor orders were not required to be celibate and most lived normal married lives. Surprisingly many members of the minor orders became the Rectors of Parishes, but being unable to celebrate the Mass would retain a poor Priest to perform the Holy Office or 'Serve the Cure' as it was known on their behalf. Such poor Priests hired on an annual stipend were known as perpetual curates and performed Mass where the Rector was either absent or a man in minor orders. In other cases a tenured deputy with the right to collect the lesser tithe was appointed; these were known as vicars (from *vicarius*, a deputy or lieutenant). This situation although frowned upon officially became so commonplace in many rural areas of England as to become unremarkable despite many attempts to eradicate the practice. There are two celebrated instances of hereditary clerical offices in Lancashire; these are the Rectors of Standish and the Deans of Whalley. In parts of Ireland and Scotland the occupation of church offices on an hereditary basis became almost the norm and a whole class of churchmen known as Erenachs developed who though having received only the first tonsure were both clan chiefs and lay abbots. The first grade of the minor orders – though strictly speaking not an order – was the first tonsure.

> The first tonsure, although it was reckoned to confer upon its recipient clerkly status (*Ordo Clericalis*) and the duty of singing in church, was not regarded as an order or as a sacrament itself, but merely as a pious intention [...] The tonsure made a boy or man a clerk, but it separated him from the lay world only by a presumed mental state of intention.[3]

This was simply an undertaking to follow a religious life within the church. The first tonsure distinguished a cleric from a layman and entitled a man to the benefit of clergy. Benefit of clergy exempted one from the jurisdiction of secular courts including criminal courts. Admission to the clergy could be abused in order to avoid criminal prosecution. Prosecutions could still be brought in church courts, but church courts had a reputation for their leniency towards clerics.

The first true minor order was that of Doorkeeper (*Ostiarius* or *Custos*). The Doorkeeper was the keeper of the church keys and was responsible for the maintenance of the fabric of the church and the church grounds. They supervised the burial of the dead and were responsible for the church plate, vestments and any relics the church possessed. In England after the Reformation most of the functions of the Doorkeeper were divided between the lay offices of verger and sexton (formerly Sacristan or Custos).

The second minor order was that of Lector or reader. The main responsibility of the Lector was to read the lesson in church. They could also be used for a wide range of administrative duties. In the Church of England (or World Wide Anglican Communion) Lectors have been replaced by lay readers. Lectors were frequently also the Parish Clerk.

3 *The English Parish Clergy on the Eve of the Reformation,* Peter Heath, 1969, Routledge & Kegan Paul, University of Toronto Press.

The third minor order was the Exorcist. As their title implies the main functions of the Exorcist were exorcism and the care and welfare of those possessed by demons.

The seventh canon of the fourth Council of Carthage in 398 CE describes the ritual by which the minor order of Exorcist was conferred, 'The bishop is to give him the book containing the formulæ of exorcism, saying, "Receive, and commit to memory, and possess the power of imposing hands on energumens (demoniacs), whether baptized or catechumens (people receiving teaching prior to baptism)."'

The minor order of Exorcist was abolished at the time of the Reformation and unlike the other orders was not replaced by a lay office. Exorcism is still carried out by Anglican Priests in the present day, but the wider functions of the Exorcist effectively ceased to be carried out in England from the time of the Reformation in the 16th century.

The final minor order was the Acolyte, an altar server and assistant to the Priest performing the Mass. This office though no longer an order is still performed by lay people within Anglican Parishes.

From the earliest times until as recently as the 18th century a wide variety of diseases were believed to be the result of possession by fairies, spirits and demons or caused by elf-shot. Such diseases included fevers, ague or the quakes, worms, frenzy, seizures, stroke and many forms of mental illness including schizophrenia and dementia. It was widely believed that in deserted places elves would shoot invisible arrows at people and animals causing fever, lethargy, wasting or madness. The only cure for such conditions was believed to be the expulsion of the disease-causing agent be it dart, unclean spirit or infernal worm.

> In early modern England both ordinary and learned people believed that certain kinds of illness might be the result of maleficium (harmful magic) or demonic possession. While belief in witchcraft and demons may have declined somewhat during the course of the seventeenth century, it remained acceptable to attribute certain forms of disease to the Devil, particularly certain types of mental illness.[4]

4 *The Medical Diagnosis of Demonic Possession in an Early Modern English Community*, Judith Bonzol, Parergon, 2009, volume 26, no. 1, Australian and New Zealand Association of Medieval and Early Modern Studies.

Charles Singer in his British Academy lecture on *Early English Magic and Medicine* states that:

> A large amount of disease was attributed ... to the action of supernatural beings, elves, Æsir, smiths or witches whose shafts fired at the sufferer produced his torments. Anglo-Saxon and even Middle English literature is replete with the notion of disease caused by the arrows of mischievous supernatural beings. This theory of disease we shall, for brevity, speak of as the doctrine of the elf-shot. The Anglo-Saxon tribes placed these malicious elves everywhere, but especially in the wild uncultivated wastes where they loved to shoot at the passer-by.[5]

Beside their obvious and ostensible function of exorcism the Pre-Reformation Exorcists primary functions were to feed and care for demoniacs (those who are possessed), and to care for anyone afflicted by the wide range of diseases believed to be caused by supernatural agencies. The Exorcist would additionally take on a veterinary role caring particularly for cattle afflicted by murrain (an umbrella term for a range of diseases including rinderpest, erysipelas, foot-and-mouth disease, anthrax, and streptococcus infections). Sick people and animals would be brought to the church for treatment but the Exorcist would also tour the outlying parts of the Parish to minister to the sick and possessed. To our modern eyes the Exorcist in a rural Parish would combine at least some of the functions of a range of modern health professionals including mental health nurse, counsellor, vet and general practitioner.

Whilst exorcism was their main stock in trade they would also have used simple herbal medicines and general nursing care to help their human and animal patients. Though we may dispute the efficacy of exorcism for some of the conditions treated, its placebo effect should not be underestimated. The healing effects of simple kindness combined with good food, safe fluids and hygiene are undoubted particularly when given to those members of society who, being feared, were often ostracised and neglected.
In rural areas where the services of surgeons and physicians were either inaccessible or far too expensive for the majority of people, the Exorcist

5 *Anglo-Saxon Magic and Medicine Illustrated Specially from the Semi-Pagan Text Lacnunga.* J. H. C. Grattan, and C. Singer. 1952. Publications of the Wellcome Historical Medical Museum, new series 3, London: Oxford University Press.

was a valued member of society. The abolition of the exorcist left a huge gap in rural society, a vital function had been removed; in addition a large number of relatively educated and specialist health professionals were now unemployed.

The crossover between the clerical function of the Exorcist and sorcery becomes apparent when one considers the following example:

> In 1531, John Cousell, of Cambridge, and John Clarke, of Oxford, two learned clerks (indicating membership of a minor order), applied for and obtained from Henry VIII, a formal license to practise sorcery, and to build churches, a quaint combination of evil and antidote. They professed power to summon 'the sprytes of the ayre' and to make use of them generally, and particularly in the discovery of treasure and stolen property. The seventh petition is to build churches, bridges and chapels, and to have cognizance of all sciences. One of their petitions refers to a 'noyntment' to see sprytes and to speak with them dayly. Strange that Henry VIII should have granted this license, seeing that a statute was passed in his reign, making 'Witchcraft and sorcery felony without benefit of clergy.'[6]

The methods used for exorcism in the Judeo-Christian cultures have changed surprisingly little during the period covered by the historical record. The earliest contemporary record of such an exorcism was recorded by Flavius Josephus in the 1st century CE:

> I have seen a certain man of my own country, whose name was Eleazar, releasing people that were demoniacal, in the presence of Vespasian and his sons and his captains and the whole multitude of his soldiers. The manner of the cure was this: He put a ring that had a root of one of those sorts mentioned by Solomon to the nostrils of the demoniac, after which he drew out the demon through his nostrils; and when the man fell down, immediately he adjured him to return into him no more, still making mention of Solomon, and reciting the incantations which he composed. And when Eleazar would persuade and demonstrate to the spectators that he had such a power, he set a little way off a cup or

---

6 *Lancashire Folk-lore*, Harland and Wilkinson, 1867, Frederick Warne, London.

basin full of water, and commanded the demon, as he went out of the man, to overturn it, and thereby let the spectators know that he had left the man; and when this was done the skill and wisdom of Solomon were shown very manifestly.[7]

This exorcism is very redolent of the *Book of Solomon* and will be familiar to any student of the *Goetia*. Verse five of the *Testament of Solomon* explains how King Solomon also used a ring to compel the demons to build the Temple of Jerusalem. Adjuring the demon to depart using words of power and the Names of God is a constant element in all exorcisms. Compelling the demon to perform a task to prove it has complied is a less common element in exorcisms but recurs frequently.

The *Testament of Solomon*, which is contemporary with or perhaps a little earlier than Josephus, follows this theme.

> Now when I Solomon heard this, I entered the Temple of God, and prayed with all my soul, night and day, that the demon might be delivered into my hands, and that I might gain authority over him. And it came about through my prayer that grace was given to me from the Lord Sabaoth by Michael his archangel. [He brought me] a little ring, having a seal consisting of an engraved stone, and said to me: 'Take, O Solomon, king, son of David, the gift which the Lord God has sent thee, the highest Sabaoth. With it thou shalt lock up all demons of the earth, male and female; and with their help thou shalt build up Jerusalem. [But] thou [must] wear this seal of God. And this engraving of the seal of the ring sent thee is a Pentalpha.'[8]

Modern Jewish exorcisms like this one described by Geoffrey Dennis contain the same familiar elements:

> Many possessing spirits are evidently quite forthcoming and loquacious. At times cooperation was coerced from the demon by 'fumigation,' exposing it to smoke and sulfur, a sympathetic invocation of the infernal

---

7 *Antiquities of the Jews,* Josephus, edited by William Whiston, 1867, published by William P. Nimmo.
8 Translated from the codex of the Paris Library, after the edition of Fleck, Wissensch. Reise, bd. ii. abth. 3

realms (Igrot ha-Ramaz). The goal of the interview is to eventually learn the name of the evil spirit [...] The exorcist then uses the power of the demonic spirit's own name to 'overpower' it, by round after round of scripted ritual actions involving threats and rebukes, getting more intense and invasive with each effort. A few ceremonies on record reached the point of actually 'beating' the demon out, but most simply involved verbal coercion.

Jewish exorcisms are usually 'liturgical,' using protective passages from the Psalms and other sacred texts. Antidemonic Psalms have been found among the Dead Sea Scrolls, though whether they were used in actual exorcism is impossible to know [...] The primary sign of a successful exorcism was a bloody fingernail or toenail, the point by which the dybbuk enters and leaves the body. Occasionally there are reports of spirits violently leaving through the throat, vagina, or rectum. A sudden and dramatic change in the victim's behavior is also a sure sign of recovery.[9]

The Christian version of exorcism is clearly derived from now familiar Jewish methodology. The early Christian theologian Origen recorded Christian exorcisms in the 3rd century CE, 'that he saw people cured of dangerous diseases – of possession, madness, and other ills – simply by calling on the names of God and Jesus, and that otherwise neither men nor demons could cure them. Christianity has preserved this belief up to the present day, for exorcism still forms a part of the rite of baptism.'[10]

The Roman Catholic and Anglican Rituals of Exorcism are essentially identical. Since the two faiths parted company in 1538 it is reasonable to assume that the ritual in its present form dates from before this. The original medieval version must have been very similar. There are three main exorcisms within the text, each progressively more intense. The text itself is easy to obtain for those so inclined. I have included below a portion of the second exorcism just to provide a flavour of the ritual and to provide a comparison with the charms used for exorcism by the Cunning Men of later centuries.

---

9 Igrot ha-Ramaz *The Encyclopedia of Jewish Myth, Magic and Mysticism*, Geoffrey W. Dennis, 2007, Llewellyn, 2007.
10 *Contra Celsum*, III. 24.

A PORTION OF THE SECOND EXORCISM

I adjure thee, thou old serpent, by the judge of the quick and the dead, by thy maker and the maker of the world, by him who has power to send thee to hell, that thou depart quickly from this servant of God, N. (name of the possessed), who returns to the bosom of the Church, with fear and the affliction of thy terror. I adjure thee again († on his forehead), not in my infirmity, but by the virtue of the Holy Ghost, that thou depart from this servant of God, N., whom Almighty God hath made in his own image.

Yield therefore; yield not to me, but to the minister of Christ. For his power urges thee, who subjugated thee to his cross. Tremble at his arm, who led the souls to light after the lamentations of hell had been subdued. May the body of man be a terror to thee († on his chest), let the image of God be terrible to thee († on his forehead). Resist not, neither delay to flee from this man, since it has pleased Christ to dwell in this body. And, although thou knowest me to be none the less a sinner, do not think me contemptible.

For it is God who commands thee †.
The majesty of Christ commands thee †.
God the Father commands thee †.
God the Son commands thee †.
God the Holy Ghost commands thee †.
The sacred cross commands thee †.
The faith of the holy apostles Peter and Paul
and of all other saints commands thee †.
The blood of the martyrs commands thee †.
The constancy of the confessors commands thee †.
The devout intercession of all saints commands thee †.
The virtue of the mysteries of the Christian faith commands thee †.

Apart from the Ritual of Exorcism itself Exorcists used the Holy Relics of Saints to drive out demons. Demoniacs were frequently taken to the shrines of major saints where they were left overnight and sometimes for days or even weeks at a time in order to affect a cure. Whilst at the shrine the demoniacs would be cared for by the resident Exorcist(s). At major Cathedral shrines there would often be a large number of Exorcists under the authority of a shrine keeper or Feretrar such was the demand for their services.

> Demoniacs were tied up and taken to medieval shrines and kept there for days or even weeks, until their rage subsided, though it was difficult to carry on the liturgy with much decorum during their screaming 'fits.'[11]

When it was impractical to bring a demoniac to a local shrine a standard exorcism would often be combined with the use of a portable saint's relic.

> Considering the condition of the demoniac, as it often excluded the taking of the victim to the relics of a saint, the evil spirits were sometimes chased off with portable relics. The idea was to direct the demon out of the possessed body, which, as mentioned above, often turned into the scene of hunting the demon within the body. The most common practice was to place the relics at the victim's head or mouth, sometimes also in the mouth cavity.[12]

The English Reformation began in the 1530s during the reign of Henry VIII and may be considered to have been completed by the 1560s early in the reign of Elizabeth I. The Reformation swept the minor orders away. Where they were considered to be necessary the roles were secularised, but the exorcist's role was considered unnecessary and was abolished altogether.

In the more remote areas of England Exorcists had performed a vital social and medical function and they would have been sorely missed. The population was no healthier after the Reformation than before and belief that supernatural agencies were a major cause of disease had in no sense diminished. In fact the bitter Civil War of 1642–51, and the outbreaks of plague which followed it, resulted in the death of perhaps a quarter of the population of England. The inevitable social disruption this caused re-

11 *Miracles and Pilgrims: Popular Beliefs in Medieval England*, Ronald C. Finucane, 1977, J. M. Dent & Sons.
12 Marek Tamm, Saints and the Demoniacs: Exorcistic Rites in Medieval Europe (11th–13th century), in *Folklore* 23, (July 2003) edited by Mare Kõiva and Andres Kuperjanov.

sulted in outbreaks of hysteria and an upsurge in superstitious beliefs the like of which had not been seen since the early Middle Ages. The need for a professional to fill the role previously fulfilled by the Exorcist was now greater than ever before.

Many of the men who had formerly been Exorcists but now found themselves unemployed took a natural course of action. They offered their skills to the public in the capacity of private practitioners. In this way a new profession was born. Throughout the rural areas of England former Exorcists and ex-monks set up business as private practitioners specialising in the expelling of unclean spirits and other forms of healing.

One such man Thomas Pavil said, 'I have no other means left for my maintenance but to turn physician. And concluded mournfully: God knows how many men's lives it will cost.'[13]

One of the commonest names for such rustic medical practitioners was Quack Doctor. Others included Cunning Men and Conjuror from their ability to conjure spirits, Dispossessor and Dispeller from their ability to exorcise the disease-causing spirit. This last is one possible explanation for the name of one form of Cornish cunning man or cunning woman, the Pellar. This point is however a matter of contention, particularly amongst modern Cornish cunning men.

One explanation for the name of Quack Doctor is given by Robert Means Lawrence, M.D:

> It has also been maintained that quack is a corruption of quake, and that quack-doctors were so called because, in marshy districts, patients affected with intermittent fever, sometimes vulgarly known as the quakes, were wont to be treated by ignorant persons, who professed to charm away the disease, and hence were styled quake-doctors.[14]

Ague was the name given to the severe fevers prevalent in marshy districts and in Lancashire, '"Casting out the Devil" was also known as "casting out the Ague," since he caused his victims to shiver and shake.'[15]

A celebrated example of the cunning men who began to practice in

13 *Magic, Medicine and Quackery*, Eric Maple, 1968, Scientific Book Club.
14 *Primitive Psycho-Therapy and Quackery*, Robert Means Lawrence MD, 1910, self published.
15 *The Devil in Lancashire*, Vera Winterbottom, 1962, The Cloister Press.

Lancashire during the reign of Elizabeth I was Edmund Hartlay, a conjuror called in to dispossess the children of Nicholas Starkie of Huntroyd who was living at Cleworth Hall in the parish of Leigh in 1594. A full account was set down in 1600 by William Darrell in *A True Narration of the Strange and Grievous Vexation by the Devil of Seven Persons in Lancashire, by John Darrell, Minister of the Word of God*. This can be found in full in chapter VII of *The Devil in Britain and America*, by John Ashton, published in 1896 by Ward and Downey.

The children of Nicholas Starkie had been suffering from convulsions and Nicholas employed physicians at the exorbitant fee of £200 (an enormous sum at the time when a yeoman might expect to earn £5 a year and a Lancashire gentleman perhaps £20)to affect a cure. However no cure was forthcoming. At his wit's end, Nicholas Starkie employed the conjuror Edmund Hartlay to dispossess his children of the evil spirits who tormented them. Edmund Hartlay was retained for a fee of £2 a year. Hartlay was able to help the children; to achieve this he went with Nicholas Starkie to the Starkie's main house at Huntroyd near Whalley in North Lancashire:

> On a certaine time Hartlay went with M. Starchie to his father's house in Whally parishe, where he was tormented sore all night. The next day, beinge recouered, he went into a little wood, not farr from the house, where he maide a circle about a yarde and halfe wyde, deviding it into 4 partes, making a crosse at euery Diuision; and when he had finished his worke, he came to M. Starchie, and desiered him to go and tread out the circle, saying I may not treade it out my selfe; and further, I will meete with them that went about my death.
>
> When M. Starchie saw this wreched dealing of his, and his children still molested, he waxed wearie of him, howbeit he sought other helpe for his children. Then he tooke his sonnes water to a phisitian in Manchester, who sawe no signe of sicknes; after, he went to Doctor Dee, the warden of Manchester, whose helpe he requested, but he utterly refused, sayinge he would not meddle, and aduised him that, settinge aside all other helpe, he should call for some godlye preachers, with whom he should consult concerning a Publicke or Privat fast. He also procured Hartlay to come before him, whom he so sharply reproved, and straitly examined, that the children had more ease for 3 weekes space after; and this was upon the 8 of December.

After being rebuked by Dr Dee, Hartlay was enraged and embarked upon a campaign of sorcery and harassment of the Starkie household which created pandemonium at Cleworth Hall.

> But Hartlay withstood them, and, because they went to his house, notwithstanding his prohibition, he told them, with an angri loke, that it had bene better for them not to haue chaunged an old frend for a new, with other menacinge speaches, and so went before them in a rage, and neuer came neare them all the way home.
>
> Upon the Tuesday after new yeares day Ianuarie 4. Iohn Starchie was readinge, somethinge gave him such a blowe on the necke, that he was soddenlye stricken downe with an horrible scryke, saying that Satan had broken his necke and laye tormented pitifully for the space of two howres. The same day, at night, being in bed, he lept out on the sudden, with a terrible outcry, that amased all the familye. Then was he tossed and tumbled a long tyme, was very feirce like a mad-man, or a mad dogge, snacted at and bite euery one that he layde hold on, with his teethe, not spareing his mother, smiting the next, and hurling Bed-staues, Pillowes, or whatsoeuer at them, and into the fire. From this day forwarde he had no great ease until the day of his deliverance.

Eventually seven members of the Cleworth Hall household whom Hartlay had kissed and *breathed the Devil into* became possessed by evil spirits. The victims were haunted by spectral black dogs and cats, taunted by unseen spirits who shouted at them, causing them to bark like dogs and became the subjects of violent fits and seizures. In 1597 Hartlay was examined and tried by the magistrates of Lancaster.

> At the assises at Lancaster, was Hartlay condemned and hanged. The making of his circle was chiefly his ouerthrowe, which he denyed; but breaking the rope, he, after, confessed it.

Hartlay was sentenced to hang and in March 1597 and he was duly hanged outside Lancaster Castle. The rope broke but, undaunted, the hangman fetched another rope and finished the job.

This example shows how this new breed of cunning men could aid the afflicted; but also demonstrates how easy it was for such a man to cross the line and use his skills for evil. It becomes apparent that a man capable of dispelling a spirit could just as easily conjure evil spirits to do harm if he chose to.

No longer under the authority of the Church, the conjurors could incorporate new and un-canonical methods into their practice. Apart from the more usual forms of exorcism to which we will return in the next section, one of the most widely used and persistent tools used by cunning men to counteract witches was the Witch bottle. One of the best descriptions of the use of a Witch bottle was set down by Joseph Blagrave in 1671.

Joseph Blagrave, a 17th century polymath, was one of the closest friends of Elias Ashmole and a brother of the Regicide Daniel Blagrave (one of the commissioners who sentenced King Charles I to death in 1649); he wrote on subjects as diverse as farm management, astrology, medicine, herbs and alchemy. One of his most famous texts was the *Astrological Practice of Physick* in which he describes in detail the uses of witch bottles.

> Here followeth some experimental Rules, whereby to afflict the Witch, causing the evil to return back upon them. Another way is to stop the urine of the Patient, close up in a bottle, and put into it three nails, pins, or needles, with a little white Salt, keeping the urine always warm: if you let it remain long in the bottle it will endanger the witches life: for I have found by experience that they will be grievously tormented making their water with great difficulty, if any at all, and themore if the Moon be in Scorpio in Square or Opposition to his Significator when it's done [...] The reason why the Witch is tormented when the urine of the patient is burned, is because there is part of the vital spirit of the Witch in it, for such is the subtlety of the Devil, that he will not suffer the Witch to infuse any poysonous matter into the body of man or beast, without some of the Witches blood mingled with it as appeareth by the whey mentioned. For 'tis the Devils policy either by this way to detect them or otherwise by torment to bring them unto their ends. For the devil well knoweth that when the blood or urine of the patient is burned, that the witch will be afflicted, and then they will desire to come to the place, for to get ease, for by the smell thereof, their pain is mitigated by sympathy, when the blood or urine is burning, they are tormented, yet sometimes they will rather indure the misery of it than

appear, by reason country people oft times will fall upon them, and scratch and abuse them shrewdly.[16]

Cunning men and of course cunning women continued to practice in the English countryside until at least the end of the 18th century.

James Cunning Murrell of Hadleigh in Essex is perhaps the most celebrated cunning man of all. Like Joseph Blagrave he was a great proponent of the witch bottle.

> He often travelled great distances, always at night. Frequently his mission was to exorcize an evil spirit from a house and occasionally from a human being. Epilepsy was as little understood in the Hadleigh of the last century as it had been three hundred years earlier, and hysteria and attacks of fits were often ascribed to witchcraft. In the following legend may be seen the methods used by the Cunning Man in combating a witch.

Some time in the 1850s a young woman went into a barn where the harvesters had left their beer. She discovered an old gipsy there and roughly ordered her out. The gipsy trudged off, muttering, 'You'll be sorry for this, my girl.' Almost immediately the girl was attacked by a series of fits. She ran on all fours, mewed like a cat, barked like a dog and was uncontrollable.

Suspecting witchcraft, her family called in Cunning Murrell, who at once confirmed their suspicions. The wizard then prepared a concoction comprising the urine of the bewitched girl, together with blood, herbs and pins. These were put into a bottle and heated on the fire. The room was darkened, the doors locked and the family instructed to maintain a strict silence or the counter-spell would be broken.

Presently footsteps were heard outside the door. This was followed by a furious knocking, while the voice of an old woman cried out: *For God's sake, stop. You're killing me.*

At that moment the bottle exploded and the voice outside gradually died away. From then on the sick girl recovered. In the morning the body of an old gipsy woman covered with dreadful burns was discovered in the road three miles away.

16 *Astrological Practice of Physick*, 1671, Joseph Blagrave, London.

This legend indicates how little the traditional form of witch belief had altered since the 17th century in a district which was less than forty miles from London.

> Towards the end of 1860 Murrell was taken ill. He called for a pen and paper, and calculated that he would die on the 16th of December and calmly awaited the end. His last hours were disturbed by the frantic efforts of the Curate to administer religious consolation. At last Murrell could stand it no longer, and fixing his piercing eyes on him, he roared 'I am the Devil's master' and the Curate fled in terror from the room.[17]

Unlike the diabolical Edmund Hartlay it was James Cunning Murrell's proudest boast that, 'I never put on, but only put off,' by which he meant that he never put a spell on anyone but used his talents only for good, putting off the spells of others and dispelling unclean spirits.

Very many examples of the Ritual of Exorcism used by cunning men have survived. They range from the incredibly simple, such as the charm below, which was found at Madeley in Shropshire in 1882, 'I charge all Witches and Ghosts to depart from this house, in the great name of Jehovah and Alpha and Omega.'[18] Others are very complex such as a charm found by Jeremiah Garnett esq. of Roefield Clitheroe in Lancashire during the early 19th century which was deciphered by his brother the Reverend Richard Garnett, an historian at the British Museum in 1825. The charm included magic number squares, kabalistic symbols, astrological sigils and an angelic seal of St Michael. The charm also included a fairly standard exorcism text in Latin, the legible portions of which are reproduced below.

> *ut dicitur decimo septimo capitulo Sancti Matthaei a vigesimo carmine*
> *fide demoveatis montes, fiat secundum fidem, si sit, vel fuerit*
> *ut cunque fascinum vel daemon habitat vel perturbat hanc*
> *personam, vel hunc locum, vel hanc bestiam, adjuro te, abire*
> *Sine perturbatione, molestia, vel tumultu minime, nomine*
> *Patris, et Filii, et Spiritus Sanctu. Amen. Pater noster qui es*
> *in ccelis, sanctificetur nomentuum, veniat regnum tuum, fiat voluntas*

---

17 *The Dark World of Witches*, Eric Maple, 1962, The Chaucer Press.
18 *Charms, Charming and the Charmed*, G.S.Nottingham, 2007, Verdelet Press.

tuo, sicut in coelo etiam in terra, panem nostrum quotidianum da nobis in diem, et remitte nobis peccata nostra, etenim ipsi remittimus omnibus qui nobis debent; et ne nos inducas in tentationem, sed libera nos a malo. Fiat.

A translation for this is supplied by Harland and Wilkinson in *Lancashire Folk-lore*:

> It will be seen that the first three lines of this charm are a sort of gibberish, with an admixture of Greek and Latin words, constituting in itself a charm, supposed to be efficacious in expelling or restraining evil spirits. With the fourth line, then, we begin our translation.
>
> As it is said in the seventeenth chapter of St. Matthew, at the twentieth verse, 'By faith ye may remove mountains: be it according to [my] faith,' [19] if there is, or ever shall be, witchcraft [or enchantment] or evil spirit, that haunts or troubles this person, or this place, or this beast [or these cattle], I adjure thee to depart, without disturbance, molestation, or trouble in the least, in the name of the Father, and of the Son, and of the Holy Ghost.

Robert Kirk's *A Short Treatise of the Scottish-Irish Charms and Spells*, provides us with several good examples of exorcisms dating to the late 17th century from Perthshire in Scotland. Below is a charm against the palsy and falling sickness.

> *In nomine patris et fili et spiritus sancti amen. Dirupisti Domine vincula mea, tibi sacrificabo Hostium Laudis sed nomen Domini invocabo, nomen Jesus Nazarenus Rex Judeorum, Titulus Triumphalis, Defendas nos ab omnibus malis, Sancte Deus, Sancte Fortis, Sante et immortalis, Miserere nobis Heloj, Heloj atha, Messias, Eother, Immanuel, Pathone, Saboath, Tetragrammaton, on. eon, athonay, alma, avala, Thone, Emanuel.*

---

[19] 'This is not a literal quotation. The verse runs thus in the ordinary version: *If ye have faith as a grain of mustard-seed, ye shall say to this mountain, Remove hence to yonder place, and it shall remove; and nothing shall be impossible to you. Amen.* [Then follows the Lord's Prayer in Latin, ending with the word *Fiat* (be it done), instead of Amen.]' – *Lancashire Folk-lore*, Harland & Wilkinson, 1867, F. Warne, London.

Which translates roughly as:

> In the name of the Father and of the son, and the holy spirit, amen. Thou hast broken my bonds, O Lord, to thee we offer the sacrifice of praise, but will call upon the name of the Lord, the name of Jesus of Nazareth the King of the Jews, Called Victorious, Defend us from all evils, God the Holy One, Holy and Mighty One, Holy and immortal one, Have mercy on us Heloj, Heloj atha, the Messiah, Eother, Immanuel Pathone, hosts, the Tetragrammaton, the on. Eon, athonay, alma, avala, Thone, Emanuel.[20]

This is followed in Kirk's text by a spell to expel the *unbeast*:

> Come out thou piercing worm as my King appointed, either die or flit thy lodging as Jesus Christ commanded. God and the King omnipotent either chase you alive or slay you within.
> These words the charmer speaks holding his two thumbs to his mouth still spitting on them, and then with both thumbs strokes the sore, which daily mends thereafter. They use spitting as an antidote against all that is poisonous or diabolical.[21]

The exorcist continues to practice today, even in our secular age, using rituals such as those related here. Thus we can see that cunning craft and the Church cannot be seen as separate, but often share the same root.

---

20 My translation – R.P.
21 *The Secret Commonwealth*, Robert Kirk, 2007, New York Review Books.

The Liturgy of Taboo

FRANCIS ASHWOOD

Seek ye inspiration among the thorns, briars, bramble and berries;
in the nectar of flowers, fruit and blood.

N THE WAY OF OUR HOUSE, the family gathers at the hearth, reigniting the holy fire gifted to us by our patron spirits, and releasing within the aroma of sacred herbs and woods the breath of the hidden. Like the wind, this breath transcends all boundaries; it flows softly, speaking words to the soul in a tongue we know as the Language of Night, conveying the knowledge of elders both human and fey. In this choreography of ritual, emotion and surrender we remember and learn the songs of the old folk whose strength proved vital for the survival of our families. This contemplation provides the location where both our personal and spiritual power resides.

Power is activated through will; this is what allows us to shape our reality in accordance to our perception, and this determines the type of relationships we develop with our surroundings. Power-bonds among people are manifested through respect, kinship, imposition or denial. The same is true within our community, our family and also within the animal and plant kingdoms and the world of spirits. In order to properly exercise the gift of our own will, and to direct power correctly, respect and kinship must be at the forefront of our relationship with the world around us.

Being cordial or making fair pacts with spirits will attract those who may aid us. In order for power to manifest there must be at least one entity which projects it, and another who is receptive to it. In our belief, it is incorrect to assume that our power is subjectively created and that it exceeds the powers of other entities. What is more, if this belief were in fact true, the source of human power is not a capability honed by humans at all. The manifestation of our will is directed by powers beyond the control of most people in our world, and it is this which makes human beings what they are.

The same happens within the animal and plant kingdoms, which are equally subject to the manifestation of will, in this case through certain spiritual intelligences which awaken them. These intelligences are the reason why the world of spirits or more precisely the world of fairy is so intimately connected to them. This force of will directs power as well; it is a comprehensive intelligence which affects the destiny of these physical entities called plants and animals. But their will, unlike that of humans, is beyond the control of these beings.

Using power-bonds as the way to understand the evolution of humankind and their environment, it is possible to discover a secret history which speaks of the relationship people have shared with the world of spirits. The reality of the otherworld has always been present in the lives of our antecessors, and even in those cases where there wasn't conscious interaction, it still impacted the subconscious minds of the people and shaped their world. However, with time's passage this subconscious imprint of the otherworld reality has become blurred, and it is our belief that as a result of this the problems of our modern world have arisen.

The consequences of not realising this loss of connection becomes all too obvious if we consider the increasing number of fears which permeate our civilization. Some of the most apparent to us are the exaggerated fear of darkness and the tendency to isolate ourselves and our homes from all contact with the natural world. We as practitioners stand against such a mundane way of perceiving reality. It is the secret history of the dealings between humans and fairies which nurtures our myths, our songs and our knowledge, as recounted by the breath of our patrons.

Witches are said to be people of special pedigree; we have inherited a particular kind of will, different from that of other people. This willpower was once aligned with that of the fey, entities which inhabit the otherworld in communities we refer to as courts, or *fatara*. Our myths, knowledge and inspiration recount the common lineage we share with those of the fairy race. It is also said that the occult bonds of kinship with these hidden people were once present in the worldview of the old folk, and that there are some who were born with an awakened sight who could recognize the nature of those bonds.

The folklore of every era is full of stories about the meetings between humans and fairies, and how these encounters sometimes bring death to the human or instead unleash the power to heal, grant seership, make predictions, shapeshift, or walk between the worlds. But in order for these gifts to be bestowed ordeals must be suffered, taboos must be observed and obeisance to ruling entities must be rendered. This is mandatory even for those who are born with an awakened sight. The reason for this is that we would otherwise become something that we are not; a witch is a witch because he or she is human in part. If a witch loses its human nature, then they are no longer a witch and will die, only to become a spirit of the land. Taboo exists to prevent this occurring.

Taboo defines what a human being is, and the reality to which they belong, according to the standards of their specific culture. Taboo prevents human beings from becoming 'other' and conventionally serves to set the unspoken rules by which a community interacts with nature. Nevertheless in every community there is always someone with the capacity to travel between the worlds and commune with the spirits. The role of mediator between both sides of reality must be fulfilled by someone with that capacity. The other must manifest an entity of its own in order for the community to be definable in opposition to it. In primitive cultures the other is always related to the unknown, the world of spirits, or the different manifestations of its creatures. However, the witch doesn't neatly fit into this category.

The witch is a creature who always stands in-between, understanding itself as not belonging to a community at all, although s/he is often part of one. Half of its nature is bound to the world of man, but its spirit and soul belong to the other, the realm of darkness and the occult. If getting immersed in the other is inherent to the nature of the witch, what better way of fulfilling one's inclinations than by using taboos themselves as indicative of the other? This is the principle which defines the liturgy of our house. The understanding of taboo is vital in order to be able to learn the Language of Night and understand the way we work with the spirits. This particular form of language is articulated beyond the purely cognitive sphere, its expression being an art of subtlety involving the breath and the sight manifested at once; this has its source beyond the self.

We are taught that observing taboo is essential in avoiding the mirror trappings and dangers in dealing with the hidden people. But it is important to note that taboo does not equal 'the forbidden.' It simply means that there is a line which a human should not cross unless they wish to die, disappear and cease to be, or lose their identity within their community. But the witch is already beyond this line, so in our house we have been guided by the patronage of faerie entities towards overcoming these taboos as a means to reach the otherworld, and specifically the place where the courts dwell, not the other way around as folk stories warn. The bulk of our work relies on articulating those minute guiding principles in ritualistic and ecstatic experiences within the land. The virtue and purpose of this is based in the recognition of our ancestry and an understanding of who we are and where our rebellious spirits originate from.

The loss of connection to the otherworld which we have culturally inherited has meant the retarding of our evolution. But for us witches the careful analysis of this reversal reveals the way forward through themes that are all the more relevant to the discussion ahead. We can consider the previous examples, the fear for darkness and fear of nature, as potential sources of taboo, and thus also of power. The lack of power-bonds with the otherworld in our age has made our perceptions stagnate, diminished our capacity for survival, for exercising our will, and ultimately for connecting with reality. However, by approaching darkness and the wild with absolute surrender, we are able to find a huge amount of power. It flows between us and the spirits. This process transforms fear into physical, mental, and spiritual strength, and by working in this way we become purer beings and progressively recover the virtue we have been losing down the long road of the centuries. It is difficult to detach the concept of taboo from that of power, because taboo is in essence a form of power. Yet it cannot be forgotten that this is just a means by which we can reach a deeper understanding of our reality, and honor and evolve in our own way; not a manifestation of power for power's sake.

The nature of the witch is eternally bound to the other, we realise that no archetypal self identifies the witch; the witch transgresses the limits that define the self, making this transgression the liturgy by which he or she gains access to the world of spirits. At the same time, by becoming other the witch transcends the very concept of other, becoming something completely different, permeating all the worlds apprehended by men. By overcoming the duality between self and other we become the eternal one. This one is the center of our being, our spirit and the axis mundi.

The identification of the center of our being as equivalent to the center of the world is, in our opinion, fundamental to understanding the complex relationship witches maintain with the spirits. Cosmology was once intimately connected with features of the land. Sometimes a tree was considered the center of the world, at other times it was a stone, a mountain, a spring. Our approach is no different in our dealing with the blessed ones. There is a mountain inhabited by a company of spirits of diverse natures, which span from the most chthonic and primordially unruly forces to the highest essences of the angelic. At its core the source of our sacred fire issues forth.

Fire has a number of meanings here, the most important of which is that it is the power of creation; it was revealed at the beginning of time by a sacred union between heaven and earth. In this union the first fire bloomed, and from it came all the wonders of nature through a number of mysterious processes. It is this first fire which burns at the heart of the witch, which warms its blood, and raises its passion in the path of fulfilling its fate. This fiery seed is shared with the blessed ones of the mountain, which are our companions on the path of the night.

The quest of the witch according to the ways of our house is ultimately to reach the virtue necessary for gaining access to the center of the mountain, merging with the fire which burns within its depths. Some witches prefer to live a simple life and do not strive towards ultimately merging with the center, but are content to exist close to the mountain, revering their ancestry and living according to the old ways. The capacity for healing, magic, seership et al is sometimes all that is needed in order to fulfill one's fate, leaving the essentially mystical connotations of such occult knowledge for others to consider. What is important is to maintain respectful reverence and nurture our relationship with the patron spirits of our House. Even in those cases where the witch treads the old paths in a simple way, the inner passion towards the source never ceases to exist, as that is the nature (a curse according to the vulgar) of the witch.

This sublime love and attraction is what allows for the identification of the center of the world with the center of our being. The relationship the witch has with the entities which inhabit this world is defined by this identification. It is what indicates the patron spirits which are to lead our way; the transformations each one of us have to undergo in order to gain further knowledge, the ordeals we have to suffer, and the sacrifices to be made to prove our virtue. In the midst of these transactions power is derived and the spiritual currents which nurture our ways are kept alive.

The foundations of every cosmology are primarily spiritual, and in our modern world people are more prone to migration, but that doesn't mean that a connection with the land of one's birth, the center of our world, whatever it may be, is necessarily diminished. Indeed, the domicile of all things spiritual is the otherworld. By this natural identification almost instantly the realm of night is evoked, marking the moment where spirits roam the surface of the earth, and witches access the oneiric dominions from where they can tread the sacred land in the company of spirits.

The psyche of the witch is the same; their blood never loses its sympathies for their land, and passion does not wane during their sojourn. What happens in these instances is that the spiritual land of our cosmology conjoins with the physical land we currently inhabit. In these cases, the witch will look to identify the places of power where ingress is granted. These are the physical places that match the spiritual loci and power of the otherworldly land of our heritage. It would be ideal to find a location in which to live that completely meshes with the entire cosmology we have inherited. Needless to say, it is most powerful if the place we live in is native to the particular cosmology we embrace, but that is not a prerequisite for working with the land. There will be differences, tangible changes in the telluric forces and certain kinds of spirits attached to the physical land, but the core, the anchor, the retinue of patron spirits which sustain this perpetual passion for everyone in the family will always remain the same, no matter where we are. Virtue is what kindles this passion and nurtures it. The brighter the fire, the stronger the connection becomes.

There is a meeting point between the serpent of the territory, the fiery force which animates the earth below our feet, the courts of the blessed ones which inhabit this territory, and the entities native to our spiritual land. This is the crossroads where the different worlds merge together to form a conjunction of power wherein everything becomes one during ritual. One path is bound to the earth; the other path is bound to our blood. In the intersection of the two is our path cast, as iron fallen from the stars.

The blood, the mothers and patrons of our ancestry are related in our house to the powers of the moon. Whereas the serpent is common to all territories, and can be experienced by everyone regardless of their tradition, the path of the moon is specific to each house. It is the one which contains the keys to our centre, and the taboos which allow access to the knowledge of our antecessors, and the land where the source of our sacred fire, our power and our love exist. The crossing between the paths of the serpent and the moon opens the gates of understanding and transformation within us. But the liturgy of taboo must be strictly observed if profit is expected from this conjunction.

Heredity is first experienced in the flesh, the body from which we are born and to which our destiny is fixed by time, territory and the celestial bodies. It is through the unbroken chain of mothers that every one of us exists. This may be interpreted as meaning that we all come from the same mother; we are sons of an ancient female being who was the first of her kind, blessed with the gift of will, and the seed of fire in her blood. The reasons for this blessing are part of what we call the 'Pacts of Old,' which go far beyond the laws of taboo. The purpose of these is one of the mysteries which give an explanation of the origin of all beings including those of the fairy race. But this is beyond biological considerations and is inevitably connected with myth and symbols of power.

Darkness is one of these, it is the realm of the first Mother. The atavistic reaches of our psyche go back to that realm, the most hidden source of reality. Her dominions are of infinite extension; they are so vast that they cannot be expressed through words. There is no way to disclose its whole nature in common language, concept, image or feeling, and this forms the first of the taboos of men: fearful darkness which must be conquered before delving into the world of spirits, in order to reveal the many secrets of the unknown and our ancestry.

The wonder of infinity can be contemplated beneath a starry sky, but night raises terrors in people. The enchantment of the stars upon men in contemplation relieves them of the duty of keeping ward against the threat of predators; this is another taboo. Overcoming these terrors is a precondition for the contemplation of the vastness of our genealogy, its comprehension being mirrored by all the possible permutations among the stars. But how can one do so without perishing by the jaws of the wild beasts of the night? The only way is by giving yourself up to all the spirits, fair or foul, surrendering in love eternal, which means merging with them. This act is one of recognition of the pacts of old, of which the satyr and the nymph are representative. It is the everlasting persecution that eternally leads the lover towards the loved one, sexual pleasure, or the violent act of raping where harmony is absent. But the secret is that both acts belong to the same force, both are a manifestation of the same power. Both 'rape' and 'passion' in this instance are mythologems, and express a metaphor of how the nuclear forces behind this sublime form of Love are stronger than other opposing forces. This force can be experienced in the caves in mountains, penetrated by forces apparently milder than the strength of stones. It is the breath of the hidden. It is the manifestation of the void through the matrix of the first mother. It is the very same vast force that allows women to give birth to their children, beyond pain and pleasure. The source of that power is a form of awe-inspiring fire, which reaches back to the first mother every time a child is born. Thus the cave in the mountain, the night (both mirroring darkness and fear of the unknown) become a necessary referent in pursuing the path against the laws of taboo.

The understanding of the path towards the one is learned through ordeal and trial as put forward by our fellow men during the day as well as our spiritual benefactors and malefactors at night, and we mean that literally. The messages from the spirits flow throughout all layers of reality, including dreams and vigil. Indeed, we receive them before we are aware of them. An omen is produced when our attention is fixed to a synchronic event happening within or without us at the same time. All images of the sacred, symbols and icons are portals for the manifestation of these messages. There is no single way for divine or spiritual messages to manifest: the choices are limitless. These events occur most often during moments of tranquility and contemplation, many of which are empowered during the night, dreaming, or during liminal occurrences of iconic beauty or significance for the witch.

Awakening the Sight and the understanding of the merging of the world of matter and the world of spirits is the basis of all our work, and we all strive for it through different rituals involving the application of the formulae of taboo; pushing against all preconceived notions we have, exposing oneself to the wild that the way might be shown by our tutelary spirits. There is no moment that defines the witch more than the surrender to the unknown in the path of spirit, because by this act the psychological barriers that keep us ignorant of our true nature are dissolved. Fear lets pure love emerge, causing pain to succumb to ecstasy.

These are the ways of our blood. It is this incredible force of ecstasy, the breath of the hidden and the fire, which will eventually cause our merging with the centre of our land. It is in the direct, unmediated union of the empyrean with the earthly that the fall of the starry fire occurs, the curse is cast, and the otherworldly nature of faeries is manifested once again in the flesh. In the old lore, the mating of one of the fairy realm and a human marks the beginning of the witch's race. In becoming one, according to the ways of our house, we become our own creators, we reenact the primal union of heaven and earth and we become one with the source of our power and heritage.

It is through the Language of the Night, which contains the knowledge of what is sacred to our family, that we come to recognise and understand taboos. In the contemplation and application of the wisdom therein is the knowledge by which we learn the ways to overcome them. It is a tricky and dangerous path, but love and the favor of our mother, queen of the blessed ones, is what allows us to proceed through the ordeals and terrors of the way.

There is no straight path towards success in this endeavor, and the path is singularly one for every witch. Not many will understand, but we would be content if they at least bear in mind how important power and mastering the relationship we have with the spiritual world around us is, in order to exercise our will to its full potential for the benefit of all humankind.

How should we ride through the mists
if it is not riding the Serpent?
How are we to understand without
the intercession of the Blessed Ones?

How are we to see without the Fire of the Mother?
How are we to reach Her domains
and not be exterminated by the Dragon,
without the virtue of Love and Wisdom?

Beware, understanding Love is painful;
And Wisdom is gained through ordeal.
In our quest, this is what makes a hero.

Trolldom

JOHANNES GÅRDBÄCK

EW PEOPLE OUTSIDE SCANDINAVIA have ever heard about Trolldom or its practices. From the start of the process of urbanization at the end of the 1800s up until age of modernization in the late 1940s, most practitioners were weighed down by the social stigma of association with evil spiritual forces, or subject to ridicule for indulging in superstitious actions which implied a lack of education or intellect. The vocabulary of practitioners has changed, and the context of their methods and procedures has been kept under the lid of silence for the past sixty years or more. This description of a regular working day, with some historical context and an explanation of the traditional roots of the methods may help shed some light on the real nature of Trolldom.

I arrive at a small apartment block in a suburb just north of the city of Gothenburg on the Swedish west coast. The clients living here are a Serbian couple in their mid 30s. They are second generation Yugoslavian immigrants and, as with most people from rural or just recently urbanized cultures, their lives still include some folk magic concepts and experiences.

For more than a year the couple has experienced many kinds of difficulties and the woman claims that the reason behind all the trouble is that another female, envious of the stable income and happy marriage the couple enjoys, is using black magic to destroy their life, their income and their relationship.

The couple heard from a friend that I 'know a bit about these things' and 'is the one to call when things like this happen.' Like most urban people the couple is not at all familiar with the Swedish folk magic tradition of Trolldom.

The word *troll*, in this regards often used as a prefix, is a complex word. Since the age of the sagas it has been in use to describe something out of the ordinary, something spiritual moving in the air and also something slightly uncomfortable. The noun troll has also been in use as a collective word to describe spirits and deities of older cultural layers and beliefs that are now unwanted and dangerous for the contemporary culture. In the popular culture of today it is used to describe a form of North European nature spirits. Those dealing with these powers and spirits are usually described as *trollkunnig*, that is, able to perform magic, or knowledgeable in magic. My grandmother's generation did not use socially loaded terms like this at all. They usually described people who were *trollkunninga* as those who 'know a bit more than others' or 'someone who knows a bit more than his Our Father.' In her parent's days and before, the term *klok*, that is wise, or cunning was more common. That generation also used specific terms like *Signare*, someone who reads charms and incantations, and *blygumma*, a woman who uses the method of melting lead to divine and to cure. They might have even used terms like *kuckelgubbe*, originally derived from the eerie sound people thought to come from ancient grave mounds when the spirits awoke; or *kyrkogårdsgångare*, a person who walks in cemeteries. Every generation has used the terms *trollgubbe*, an old man practicing Trolldom, and *trollgumma*, for an old woman practicing Trolldom, but the word was usually too socially loaded and they preferred other terms.

Like most people this couple would never use the term *häxa*, a witch, or speak outright about magic. They just wanted help and they heard I could provide it.

I did not inherit all my troll formulae but I have the gift of *synskhet*, seership and *varma hander*, warm hands, which is the old term for a person with natural healing abilities. These gifts run very strongly through my family and I am not the only one who does odd things for a living. When it comes to the traditional practices, a lot were taught by my grandmother and others, who constantly denied knowing anything at all about magic. In my early days I too had no idea that these things were magical at all. They were simply the things which were done when you were having trouble, when you were sick, that only happened when someone in the family was upset and, sometimes, things were done just for fun. It was not until later in my life that I found out that my grandmother, and others of her generation, usually became curt and looked away in a slightly shameful way if asked whether they knew any Trolldom or things associated with these ideas. When talking or demonstrating the very techniques they usually gave the short introduction that this was what they used to do 'in the old days' or what once 'was done out on the countryside' if this or that problem occurred. Such a frame is a nice way to avoid the social drama attached to loaded words and is what I also use, as it allows me to focus on actually solving the problems I am confronted with.

Referring to the past is a long standing tradition when talking about Trolldom. 'This is how they used to do it in the old days' has been said about acts of magic since the days of the Sagas. In fact one of the other old words for trolldom used in the saga Age is *siðr*, custom. It is often referred to as *forni siðr*, the old custom, and one of the more popular names for a trolldom practitioner was *forneskja*, meaning one that knows (or practices) the customs of the past. In time the negative associations of this falls away, while framing contemporary practice in the past remains a customary way of talking about trolldom.

What my grandmother and others did not teach me about Trolldom I learned through old-fashioned Svartkonst books, books of the black art or Black Books as they are called by people who study them in the academy. These are usually handwritten books that contain a collection of spells, remedies and procedures to cure, harm and increase income. The oldest preserved one, the Norwegian *Vinjeboka* has been dated to 1480. In fact, most of the material in these books first came from the almanacs published all over Europe. One of the most influential books in the second half of the past millenia was published in Stockholm in 1650. It was a translation of *Magia Naturalis Libri Quatuor* by the German Wolfgangi Hildebrandi, first published in Leipzig in 1610. It contains everything from how to dye hair and keep bees, to making love talismans and removing spiritual problems. From this many methods were copied into local black art books and these were complemented with orally transmitted material. In time more orally transmitted and local material was incorporated and the books were marketed with claims of having been authored by historical figures such as Moses, Faust and Cyprianus or associated with the legendary German town of Wittenberg, in which most Nordic priests received their education and from where much magic was said to have come into the Nordic countries. That is, of course, not literally true and rather belongs to the drama of Trolldom and the Black Arts than the actual folk practice, much of which had been around since before Christ was born.

Just having a black book, or the reputation of having one was previously enough to be counted as someone knowledgeable in magic. It did not matter that most of the material in these books would not be counted as magic at all by modern standards. They provided a person with *tydor* and knowledge stronger than most. Since folklore began to be studied in the late 18th century, the books of magic in Scandinavia changed radically. The collections of handwritten, printed and orally transmitted information gathered in these are something that Trolldom practitioners of old could only dream of. More than 50, 000 verbal charms have been collected since the beginning of folklore in Sweden alone. Not that one would ever need more than a handful, but this changed the books of the black arts forever.

My current clients know nothing about this and they probably do not care at all.

Once we are introduced and they have given me some background and information about their troubles it is time for me to make a diagnosis. This process involves divination, or rather triggering *seeing* through various means of divination in order to diagnose what the origins of the problem might be. We call this process *spådom*. The word is as old as Trolldom and it is often used as a synonym for it, or at least it used to be. Nowadays it usually means to see the future, even though what can be seen through this is much more than just possible futures. A qualified guess is that they used it as a synonym because the ability to see the future is very closely tied to being able to change it as well. Many Swedish words bear witness to this: *förutspå*, to predict the future, *förutse*, to see ahead, and *förgöra*, to destroy; the most common term for the act of destructive Trolldom is *förbanna*, curse: all imply spiritual acts and the ability to place something in a future that has not yet taken place. This is why tieing knots on a thread was such a common method in the old days, since threads and bonds were strongly connected to the thread of life and time itself.

In Trolldom the meaning contained in an event, a material, a person etc. is a power that is always in action. This meaning is called *tyda*. The word also means a sign, so when doing spådom one is taking *tydor*, which means both collecting various signs and accessing the power behind them. Spådom and Trolldom in this regard become very connected and once you have the *tyda* you can use it to perform Trolldom. The *tydor* (pl.) is usually defined and enhanced by the use of the spoken word and/or by actions. The spoken words increase the power of the tyda, which means that speaking out loud about what is seen during *spådom* is a risky process. It can become an *ofärdsspådom,* the old word *ofärd* means bad fate, something that enhances the wrong tydor and negatively affects the future. It was a common way to curse people in the old days and as such it often appears on old rune stones as a curse against anyone damaging the stone. Nowadays such curses are not usually that deliberate, but in everyday life they are tremendously common.

The first thing to look for in spådom is the state of the relationship the people have to the spirits around them. How do the local spirits feel about these people? Why were they not protected? It is a pretty predictable thing these days, since most people neither know nor care about the spirits that surround them. But nevertheless, it may pay to check this. My version is not like most people used to do it; whether melting lead or wax through the hole in a bread cake held above the heads of the persons, by pouring egg white into a glass of water or by laying cards. My version of it is simply calling the spirits and asking them about their opinion of the clients in a low tone of voice.

The first, and often regarded as the most important spirit, is the *tomte* or *bo-vätte,* who is responsible for all the luck in the house, the *tomtebolycka.* In Trolldom the *tomte* is usually regarded as more of a title and a function and it is often said that the first person who dies in a house becomes the tomte or that he arrives the first time fire is made in a house. As a spirit of the dead, the tomte, by being dead, has power over the general luck in a place and can draw in or remove luck depending on how he is treated by the living inhabitants. If offended they can wreak havoc, or leave, which is considered very bad luck. In that case the person who is trollkunnig can remove or even sell the tomte and hire another one.

Most of these things are culturally forgotten today, but most people out in the countryside still pay their tomte on Christmas eve, unknowingly continuing the most widespread and unbroken spiritual tradition in Swedish history. Of course few know that this practice is actually necromancy and prefer the cute and socially acceptable tomte form created by the poet Viktor Rydberg and the artist Jenny Nyström in the late 1800s. Feed the *tomte* with one hand and call the spiritual mediums to remove any signs of a *spöke* (shining spirit of the dead) with the other and expect the *tomtebolycka* to prosper? A rather odd behavior, in my opinion, but there you go.

My *spådom* reveals that there used to be a *tomte* in the house of my clients but he left, apparently angered by the laziness of the woman. It is hard to blame him, considering he seems to have been a working man at one of the local shipyards and the morals of his generation are usually that everyone should be hard-working to earn their living and all else is moral decay. The fact that the couple often used a language the tomte found ugly and offensive is not a good thing to verbalize either. Racist spirits are unheard of in today's literature on the subject and defy most of the common spiritual assumptions, so wording any of that will probably be counterproductive in this case. I will try to get a new tomte into their house later on. Time to talk to their *vards*.

Today the *vards* are usually referred to as *skyddsänglar*, guardian angels. In the old days the *vard* was not really an angel as most people would define it, but a spirit of the dead. Or, more accurately, a term used both to define a spiritual part of a living being as well as describing something remaining after the death of the physical body which is able to serve as a protector. When it appears to humans it is often called a *vålne* or *vålnad*. The soul and spirit concepts of the old days are intellectually complicated due to local variations, exchange and intermingling of terms so it is best understood through the function and context rather than from the modern perspective of coherent systems.

The couple have no *vard* tree around, which is more common in the countryside, otherwise I would have gone there to talk instead of sitting in the kitchen. Spiritual residences such as the *vard* trees are greatly underestimated nowadays.

At first I had some trouble understanding her *vard* since it seemed to speak in some language that was probably Serbian. But after a while it switched to sending other impressions that were more easily understood. The *vard* of the female client seems fairly uninterested in protecting her protégé and it seems like anyone can do anything to her as far as the *vard* is concerned. A bit of a surprising attitude, but there you go. Telling the clients about this does not seem to be a good idea.

People have so many ideas about spirits and there is no time to explain to this couple that not all spirits are godly light beings. The *vard* of the man stays silent and I cannot get it to talk at all. Either it has been put to rest, or removed completely, or it has some other agenda. At least it did not seem like stopping others from doing magical harm to the man's life was a priority to this *vard*. It all paints a pretty good picture of the client's spiritual relations and it is time to proceed with the next steps of the *spådom*.

In Trolldom the second most important thing to find out during a *spådom* diagnosis is usually the location where the problem first began. It can be very useful if there is something hidden or buried on the property. In Trolldom, a very common saying is that one should *ta boten där man fick soten*, meaning that one should take the cure where one contracted the problem in the first place. For example, problems originating with an offended water spirit are best cured through water or ritual remains should be disposed of in the source location to restore proper order.

I bring out a small glass, a bottle of grain alcohol and fill the glass up. Then the woman is instructed to take a drink without swallowing and instead spit it back into the glass.

Occasionally this is accompanied by speaking a trollformel in order to start the process of removing any problem. It is a nice way of weaving in the very act of doing something about the problem during the diagnostic process. Since it is believed that formulae lose their power when taught – and I tend to be one of those who share this belief, a very similar formula from 1860 reads as follows:

Ture stod på berget,	Thor stood on the mountain,
talte till sin moder Helena:	Spoke to Helen, his mother:
«Skott I munn, ur munn,	'Shot in mouth, out of mouth,
Bot i samma stund!»	Cure in the same moment!'

The procedure is repeated three times. Then I sit down with the glass and look into it. The procedure is not really necessary if one is *synsk*, but the closeness to her personal trace – the spittle – makes it a bit easier and I kind of like the procedure. It is a good introduction to the procedure which follows and the clients usually like it.

Looking at the formations made by the spittle in the glass a fairly descriptive picture of an older woman and a younger one doing something on the ground can be seen. The location where this took place is unclear but it does not appear to be anywhere nearby, so there is no use in finding out where it is. A closer, inner look reveals a cemetery and the two women are apparently casting some sort of spell. A nasty spell by the look and feel of it.

It is unnecessary to add power to these *tydor* by telling the clients about it and they do not need to know just how strong the thing put on them appears to be. The issue now is to find something that has stronger *tydor* and use it to counteract what has been done to the client. My belief is strong, so that will greatly enhance whatever material and procedure is used but the tydor of the material must be strong as well, in order to efficiently remove and counter the spell cast on the clients. I need to seek help from the trolls and the powers of the dead.

So I bring out two small pouches of graveyard dirt bought from two separate graves at the cemetery on a waning moon between 23:30 and 00:30 on a Thursday night.

This is a classic ingredient used in Trolldom for almost every conceivable purpose. Some say the reason why most Trolldom is done on Thursdays is because in the older calendar the week used to have five days instead of seven. The fifth day was Helg, a word meaning sacred time, a time when peace should be observed and no work should occur. This is a time when spirits are considered to be more active and interacting with the dealings of the living. Long ago this was the time of the Ting, when the deities and ancestors were present to receive gifts in exchange for luck, and to assist in solving conflicts through ordeals. Later, when these spiritual forces came to be considered as Trolls, the day for interacting with these forces remained the same.

As customary I paid the *kyrkogårdsrå* and asked him to find two spirits willing and able to do the work at hand. The *kyrkogårdsrå*, also occasionally called *kyrkogrimmen*, is the spiritual keeper of the cemetery and the dead residing there. Folklore says that the first one buried in a place will become its caretaker. In some places they used to say that to get a Rå into a newly built cemetery they killed a living rooster or a calf and buried it in order for it to become the Rå of that place.

This did not seem to have been the case at the cemetery that was visited when collecting the dirt. When calling the *kyrkogårdsrå* at the gates of the cemetery a male spirit came along and I told him my purpose was to find a spirit willing to draw bad stuff into the grave and a spirit able to work as a protector. It did not take long to find the graves. Once there I walk around the graves backwards and counterclockwise three times and called their spirits up. The procedure of walking like this used to be called *begå* to be forbidden at one point in Swedish history because it was so closely related to the practice of Trolldom and the old religion's methods of medicine and cures. Some called this *carrying water to the Devil* and it was regarded as both sinful and dangerous. It is still a common method used to enter the realm of the dead and is in use in many spells involving the dead or in the summoning of the *vålne* (spirit) of a living person.

Once the walking is done and a brief explanation of just what kind of help is expected the spirits agree and are paid by placing a few coins in exchange for the removed dirt. I paid the Rå on the way out as well; not all people do this, but to me it feels appropriate.

In addition to the pouches of graveyard dirt I pull out a small wooden box containing a mixture of dried and powdered leaves taken from nine fruit bearing trees. These were also collected on Thursday, with a waning moon, with circumambulation, from trees growing on or near old grave mounds and ancient stone circles. In this case the spirits that I turn to are females. Some say they are the old Völvas, Norns or priestesses of old that have taken up their abode in trees; some approach them under various names as Hyllemor (for the spirit of Elder trees), Askefrun (for the spirit of an Ash tree) and so forth. It is rarely necessary to know who these spirits were and what they used to do and sometimes they are offended by being called by the old names. That's why I mostly call them without any name and then respectfully tell them what is going to be done with the leaves. If there is no resistance or if they happily agree, the leaves are collected from the tree. The trees are always paid, either by pouring out some milk or placing some coins amongst the roots.

Finally a bottle of water is brought out from the bag. It is slightly murky since it was collected with an upstream motion from a stream that runs towards the north. Northwards and down is the direction to the realm of the dead and the sprits and that is where all disturbing things belong. At least that is the general idea and it has been empowered for a substantial amount of time in these lands, so it has some pretty strong and useful *tydor*. Usually strong enough to persuade most things to leave, so I settle for that.

Sometimes I use well water which is another common ingredient that has at least a few thousand years of tradition to it. But the *tydor* of the wells too often seems to have become so weak that they hardly enhance my own powers of belief. This may be due to the fact that many were so exploited in the 1800s and early 1900s by the trend of *dricka brunn* (well drinking). Once the upper class embraced this health trend, people stopped paying the Källrå (Spirit and caretaker of the well) and companies started to exploit the sacred wells for their mineral water. So people say that the wells lost most of their power. Others, at least the most popular, had their visitor's interest taken over by the Church, which often, but not always, led away from the practices that give strength to their *tydor*. Amusingly enough, many wells can be found in the middle of industrial areas, on hospital grounds, by big churches in the center of cities and in the middle of dense forests where they appear forgotten. Fortunately some of them are still quite powerful and others seem to burst into an odd cascade of power when approached and treated according to the old customs.

I explain to the couple a little about what is going to happen and then instruct them to turn off their phones, close all the windows and doors, and tell them that once they are all closed no one must enter or exit though them but me until it is all over. It seems not to be a problem. They are not expecting any visitors. Then they are told that once a sign is given not a single word should be said until it is all over. No matter what happens. Not to me, not to each other, until I am completely finished and give the sign again. Furthermore, they should not speak of what happened until they have had a good night's sleep. Not to anyone. By the look in their eyes the drama of these instructions has been conveyed. These rules are fundamental in Trolldom and perhaps were even more so in the past. Silence is crucial in order to control *tydor*. In modern terms one could say that the dramatic effect and traditional and cultural value of silence serves to focus the power of belief, emotion, concentration and all other useful components that makes procedures like this work. Plus the fact that the *trollkunnig* do not have to put up with the giggling and chitchat of people who think it is entertaining and exciting, or the nervous, analytical people who feel that verbalized rationalisation needs to take place to calm their emotions. These are good rules.

I mix the alcohol and the water by stirring it with my left ring finger (it is sometimes called the Nameless Finger), counterclockwise. Some use a knife made of nine pieces of steel to stir it, but the process of gathering the ingredients and the ritual involved is so comprehensive that I have not got around to making one. Whilst the liquid is being mixed another *trollformel* is spoken with my mouth close to the bowl, so that the breath touches the mixture. A similar one to the one used for the couple reads:

Förr då Frälsaren kom gångandes	When the Saviour came walking
Mötte honom de ondas skott	He was met by shots from the evil ones
Ståndandes sju Guds andar emot	Standing against were 7 spirits of God
Men sju heliga Guds änglar	But seven holy angels of God
Lopp till bot	Rushed to cure
I den treenige Gudens	In the name of the threefold God
Fodrens, Sonens o. D. H. A-s namn.	The Father, Son and the Holy Spirit.

I read it three times and blow into the water after each reading. Some say this should be read with one's teeth closely bitten together and each formula should be read in a single breath. But that does not make much difference to me, so I just stick to the simple stuff. To add some extra *tydor* the process is repeated using another formula which is similar to this one used in the north of Sweden and documented in 1820:

Det gick en finne på hafsstran,	A Finn walked on the seashore
han kunde jära	he could remedy
för alla skott	for all kinds of shots
som i världen var	that are in the world
han kunde göra	for finnshots
för finnskott	for bloodshots
för blodskott	for trollshots
för trollskott	for evil from water
för ont av vatten	for evil from earth
för ont av jorden	for evil of the weather
för ont av väder	for hate and envy
för hat, för avund,	for aches and pains
för värk och plågor	he could remedy
han kunde göra	for all kinds of shots
för allt slags skott som i världen var.	that are in the world.

Then I let the clients have a small sip. This time they must swallow it. In the old days it was said that this was done to prevent the bad stuff from going inwards. I don't know about that but to me it is a very good way to make things come out and stay out. Now it is time to wash them down.

As previously instructed the couple have now stripped down to their undergarments. People tend to be quite uncomfortable and feel vulnerable with this and that works to make their subconscious add to the impact of the work. The couple is looking down and the man has his hands covering his privates, which is a good sign that they feel vulnerable. I start with him, so he feels more comfortable when doing the same for her later on. She will also feel more comfortable since her protective male will undergo the process first and she will see his acceptance. It will make her subconscious more passive.

I dip the pouch containing the dirt from the spirit that promised removal in the water/alcohol mix and begin the washing. The procedure is usually called *smörjning*, which means anointing, and the term covers both procedures of washing someone down with liquids and anointing with ointments, salves and moist things.

Starting from the left side of his head going crosswise down to his right foot, then from his right side down to the left foot. Then the same is done on his back. Once that is done it goes three times counterclockwise around each limb downwards; his neck, his elbows, his wrists, his hips, his knees and finally his feet. The pouch of graveyard dirt is dipped in the water afresh for each limb. All the while he is being washed another trollformel is spoken. Some speak it out loud, but I prefer to keep it in a low toned voice and let the voice rise and fall on its own, depending on whether it hits resistance and needs added power. A quite similar formula to the one used in this part of the procedure was used by Hanna Isachs in Malmö, Sweden who, for this practice faced a court sentence in 1706:

För min ande	*Before my spirit*
To händer	*Two hands*
Och 10 fingrar	*And ten fingers*
12 Gudz englar	*12 angels of God*
Skall sky	*Shall shun*
Och fly	*And flee*
Allt ondt!	*All evil!*
I nampn ...	*In the names ...*

Once the washing is done the man is asked to spit into the bowl three times and I then spit into it myself to fix whatever nastiness is in it.

The *smörjning* is finished by making the sign of the cross on his head, his chest, hands and feet with my left nameless finger. The whole procedure is then repeated on the woman.

After the spitting is done the bowl is placed outside the threshold of the house and I spit once more into it, whilst standing inside the house. That should keep any nastiness outside until it is time to dispose of it. Then it is time for the process of *röka* (smoking) the clients.

A small brass incense holder is brought out from the bag and charcoal is lit and placed on it. When it is glowing red I add the powdered leaf-mix of the fruit bearing trees and smoke the couple using the same procedure as I did with the liquid and the graveyard dirt previously. Sometimes the remaining ashes are then used to anoint the clients, but the idea of walking around with their faces smeared with ash might be a bit much for these urban folks so the incense holder is just put aside to cool off. If any of these procedures had been used alone, I would have repeated the whole process of *smörja* or *röka* three times. Or even nine times if necessary.

Once the smoking was complete my next step was to send back the evil and teach the person on the other end of this problem a little lesson. I rarely tell my clients that the procedure is about sending things back and hitting the people who sent it, unless they are experienced practitioners themselves.

There are so many assumptions carried by regular folks when it comes to punishing someone through the use of Trolldom. They get afraid that the other person will be hurt and they don't want to be responsible. Sometimes they think the culprit will die in agony and leave the client with a harsh judgment from God that may cast them out of heaven when they die. In fact it usually does not harm the person on the receiving end very much at all; at least not physically. People are rarely that sensitive and have an intellectual agenda to try to rationalise things within their own worldview, so whilst the real reason why they fall and hit their head is clear to their spirit, they usually think it was an accident and do not pursue it further. But since their spirit knows, they tend to avoid the behavior causing the fall and thus they usually leave my clients alone or behave better in the future. But I don't have time to explain all this, so I avoid telling the clients what this part of the work is for.

Sometimes I draw blood from the left little finger of the client afflicted by a curse and twitch the hand over an open fire so the blood gets into the fire in order to send shit back, but even though it can be done on an electric stove the *tyda* does not have the strength of an open fire and new clients usually respond pretty dramatically when someone cuts them with a sharp knife even if it is explained beforehand. So, no cutting and blood staunching in their kitchen. Instead I bring out a small wooden ring made of birch and place it on the threshold. A few strands of hair taken from the nape of the necks of my clients, a coin for the broken economy and three pieces of glowing charcoal. I use incense charcoal again and put it on their electric stove and heat them up until they are glowing. It isn't the heart fire of the living fire stoves of the old days, but this tyda will have to do. I use very small coals, since this place is located in a city and we do not want to trigger a fire alarm.

I place it all inside the birch ring and bring out my small hand axe. The names of the persons suspected and anyone else who might be a culprit is mentioned as a recipient of what is about to be reversed is addressed out loud and another trollformel is spoken. A milder and less controversial one from Dalarna, Sweden in 1717 reads as follows:

Jag skall binda en biörnrahm
Och ulftand för troll källingen
I Faderns, Sonens och Den Helige Andes Namn!

I shall bind a Bears frame
And wolf's tooth for [around] the Troll-bitch [sorceress]
In the names of Father, Son and Holy Spirit!

Then I smack the backside of the axe in the middle of the ring. It should be done hard and it is usually only repeated once, but I always wait a bit to get an indication as to whether it worked or not. If not, I repeat the blow up to nine times. This time it seemed sufficient with just one blow. The blow left a fairly deep black mark in their threshold, but I doubt they minded it much.

In the old days this procedure was often said to kill the guilty party. This has never happened for me, but it tends to put an end to things and I settle for that. I remove the ring, brush off the coals and the hair outwards and return the coin to the couple. Now it is time to dispose of the stuff.

I make a gesture to the couple to sit down and go out to put on my shoes and jacket and grab my bag of tricks. I pick up the bowl outside and head down to a nearby three way crossroad I spotted on the way here. Three way crossroads also play a major role in Trolldom. This is where people go to dispose of ritual remains, diseases, problems and nasty spirits. This is where one goes to meet with spirits and deities, to do yearly divinations and so on. The place where three roads meet (or where three borders meet) is where the Ting was often held, judgments were settled by the deities and ancestors through ordeals and so on.

This suburban crossroad does not have a slightest trace of something that could be associated with fantasies of Viking kings, Blot-priests, all powerful Völvas proclaiming the destinies of men, bloody ordeal duels or the kind of majestic greenery associated with the ancient power of the Old Norse. Not at all. Shabby looking red brick walls surround it and the ground is covered with a tarnished and worn down grey tarmac. An empty coke bottle and a bunch of cigarette butts add to the vapid impression. But the road seems fairly old and people have traveled here for quite a few years which mean that so do the spirits of the dead and god knows what other unseen things. Good enough for me.

I call upon the spirits nearby with a short whistle and a prayer. It is a rough neighborhood, so many of the dead around here are too young and lack the working morals that would keep them more or less self-powered. But then an older man approaches. I silently tell him about the situation and he agrees to serve the couple as a Tomte. I bring out a small stone, taken from a cemetery, place it on the ground and ask him to hold onto the stone in order for me to bring him back to their house. After waiting a moment I put the stone back in my bag. Then I grab the bowl, turn my back to the middle of the crossroad and toss the contents over my left shoulder. Sometimes I speak a formula when doing this, but this time I skip that part and just walk away, not looking back.

On my way back I walk around the apartment building and pick up dirt from each corner. In its place I put some small hazel sticks. These used to be called *hassla* and were used to set up a sacred place. Way back when, the sticks were connected by bonds, *ve-bonds*, and breaking these bonds and the peace within them was a very serious crime.

The same kind of hazel enclosures were used to set up the spots for ordeals like the famous *envig* (duel). Setting one foot outside these bonds meant you lost and were severely punished both economically and socially. In later times the hazel was used to mark borders and declare ownership of land. With that in mind it is quite easy to understand why hazel became the most popular tree to use when making magical circles to keep spirits in or out.

While placing the branches and collecting the dirt from the corners I also sprinkle some of the graveyard dirt from the other bag. This procedure is called *ställa* (to make someone stand) and is usually done in order to keep thieves in or out and to protect whatever is inside the circle. Like all the other procedures, this is often accompanied by a spoken formula, in order to enhance the tydor. The one I used is very similar to this one:

Nio voro de Nockunden söner	Nine were the sons of Nockunden
Som noren förde	Who brought the Norn
Som buro deras moder döder	Who carried their dead mother
Vi bar de henne så döder?	Why did they carry her so dead?
För hon skulle alla mål hölja och dölja	So that she all targets cloak and hide
Som hon gjorde så skall och jag göra	As she did, so shall I do
Jag ska binda elden, där han brann	I will bind the fire where he burned
Jag ska binda kitteln, där han vann	I will bind the kettle where he runs
Jag ska binda mannen, där han red	I will bind the man where he rode
Jag ska binda skeppet, där han skred	I will bind the ship where it strode
Jag ska binda järngårdar	I will bind iron gates
Så de gråta blodstårar.	So it will shed tears of blood.

This particular version of the formula belonged to woman named Elin who was condemned to death, tortured and executed in a trial in the village of Ronneby in Sweden in 1679. The formula also occurs in Denmark and has been in use to bind enemies, dampen anger, put out fires and more. Its origin may be more than 1000 years old and may refer to the old tradition of carrying around dead ancestors (who were regarded as having become one of the gods after death). In this case the woman called Noren may refer to her being as a Norn, which as anyone familiar with the later mythology of the Norse, means that she was a weaver of fates and a Trollkvinna.

I mumble my formula until the whole block is surrounded, dirt is collected from every corner and the hazel sticks are in place. Then it is time to yell. After a little searching I find the closest earthbound rock. It is a stone about 80 cm tall that seems to have survived the bulldozers at the time this complex was built and was left as some sort of decorative element. It will have to do.

The concept of binding through the earth goes back into the mists of Scandinavian history. The power of earthbound rock does as well. In the old days they were called *Unlausan* (Not loose) or *Stupan* (Steady). Their tyda is one of stability over long periods of time, of something meant to last, of something having more power over a certain place than any moving thing on the surface. It gives authority over all mobile things. The Unlausan are as important as the concept of the crossroad and the burial places in Trolldom practice. The lands of Scandinavia are filled with Unlausan rocks. Some were raised by men, some were moved by the Great Ice during the last Ice Age and scattered across the landscape as if thrown there by *Jotnar* (giants), some are just little peaks of solid rock sticking up in an otherwise grass covered landscape. They all count as earthbound rocks in the history of Trolldom. Since they have the *tyda* of being able to affect the land over time it is said that judges used to sit on them when proclaiming verdicts at local Ting, kings were elected on top of some and vows of various sorts were proclaimed on them. There are many stone circles like this around Sweden and they are called *domarringar* (Judges' Rings). One famous Black Book even says that, 'all Trolldom should take place on a Thursday on an earthbound rock' (Heurgren, 1918), again indicating the close ties between old law and the magical tradition.

So, that is why I am climbing up on this grey block. I want to make an imprint on this little piece of land, where my clients live. The procedure I am about to perform can also be labeled *stämma*. The term originally (and still) means to be called to the Ting. Not obeying the call meant being exiled or certain death, so it was a pretty strong call. Knowing this, *stämma* has and is still being used in Trolldom as a description of the process to stop or move people, animals, blood in the veins and so on. People often used this in the days of my great grandmother to keep out wolves or bears or even wandering criminals. The same process is often used to draw in luck and other desired things, but then it is not called *stämma*. I will use it to keep out the bad influences sent towards my clients. The point is that everything that comes within hearing distance should be affected.

Some shout out a *trollformel* in plain words but I usually tend to make it sound a bit like an attempt to sing in a very high pitched tone, and project it as far as possible. It is the tyda that I want to put into this piece of land. The technique is occasionally called Galdra and a nice old example of it can be found in *Grógaldra* in the Older Poetic Edda in where the dead Trollkvinna, Groa, having been summoned by her son to give him advice and protection states:

... á jarðföstum steini	... on an earthbound rock
stóð ek innan dura	I stood indoors
meðan ek þér galdra gó.	while I sang the Galder for you.

In more recent times this way of singing or shouting is called *kula* and has been in use by herders as a way to communicate over long distances. So I climb up the Unlausan rock, make my usual simple statement:

Så långt som dessa skrik hörs, så långt bort ska allt ont stanna och stå.
As far as these cries are heard, as far away shall all evil stay and remain.

Then I unleash my Galder scream in each direction three times. My screaming seems to have scared the shit out of a dog who barks like crazy in one of the apartments nearby, as well as a Chinese lady carrying grocery bags walking across the small street. She looks at me like she thought I was a skinhead on meth and hurries along. Somehow I always find that a bit amusing.

I re-enter the apartment of my clients and add the dirt taken from the four corners inside their threshold. Similar to the many other techniques, this traditional method of protection goes back to the old legal procedures. Dirt from all corners of the house was used as a token of ownership. The importance of the threshold or doorpost has similar roots. If there was no Ting to be held, all vows and legal transactions took place while holding the doorpost and standing on the threshold. When called to the Ting the issue at hand was first proclaimed by the bedpost, then the threshold then at the Ting itself (held at a crossroad, by Unlausan stones etc.), so these places occur in many Trolldom procedures and works.

Once the dirt is in place the door to the apartment is closed and the couple is given the signal that the silence can now be broken. The small stone, that their new tomte attached itself to, is placed behind the stove in their kitchen and the couple are told that they now have someone protecting the house and themselves in the spirit realm. They must give him some beer and porridge once a year, at Christmas, and it is very important that they do not forget to do so if they don't want even more trouble in the house. If they move, they should say this out loud and ask if their protector wants to follow. He may or may not and they should not force him. I am well aware that merely 'protector' is not really the right description for the functions of the Tomte, but I figured it will assist in making the couple serious about their promise and the payment. I could tell them to give a little something to their Vards, who are actually more appropriate in terms of protection, on a regular basis as well, but I don't. They have got enough on their minds right now and what I did should be more than enough to keep that envious woman and most other crap away from this couple. So I take my fee, which is traditionally quite substantial in order to add to the value of what has been done and thus it will reinforce the strength of it all through the couple's beliefs as well as to keep people like me continuing our traditional practice, and we said our goodbyes.

Once outside I thank the spirits and the creator for allowing me to do all this and then I leave. Another day is at its end and it is time for dinner. On my way out I see that Chinese lady looking at me from a window on the second floor. Her eyes still look scared, but they have that look of knowing that something else took place here today that she somehow recognizes but can't consciously place. I reward her with a confirming smile. Now she knows. The question is if she dares to incorporate it into her reality? This is after all Sweden. Swedes do not do these kinds of things. Or at least she might have thought so. Until now.

LITERATURE

FINLANDS SVENSKA FOLKDIKTNING. VII. *Folktro och Trolldom. 5. Magisk Folkmedicin.* (Vol. 7). Helsingfors: Valter W. Forsblom, 1927.

GAMBO, R., *Norske Trollformler & Magiske Ritualer.* Oslo: Universitetsforlaget, 1979.

HELLQUIST, M. (Red.), *Folklivet i Åkers och Rekarne Härader – Av Gust: Ericsson, Metallarbetare.* Uppsala: Dialekt och Folkminnesarkivet i Uppsala, 1992.

HEURGREN, P. (Red.), *Salomoniska Magiska Konster; Utdrag ur en Westboprests Svartkonstböcker.* Meddelanden från Örebro Läns Museum, 1918.

HYLTÉN-CAVALLIUS, G. O., *Wärend och Wirdarne, ett Försök i Svensk Ethnologi.* 2 deler. P.A. Nordstedt & Söner, 1863.

LINDERHOLM, E.,*Signerier ock Besvärjelser Från Medeltid ock Nytid.* Serie: Svenska landsmål och svenskt folkliv, 1940.

R.L., *Rättsliga Symboler af R.L. Litteraturblad för Allmän Medborgelig Bildning XII,* 202–216, 1859.

The Bogomilian and Byzantine Influences on Traditional Witchcraft

RADOMIR RISTIC

N THE SOUTHEASTERN PART of Europe we find the Balkan Peninsula. This old territory was a land of hills, mountains and rivers in which many nations thrived and disappeared. Empires were born and found their destruction here. It was here that the East Roman Empire was formed and developed into the powerful Byzantine Empire which played a significant role in the formation of coven structures in the Southeast of Europe. Today the Balkan peninsula is divided into many countries, including Serbia, Croatia, Bosnia and Herzegovina, Monte Negro, Macedonia, Romania, Bulgaria, Albania, Greece and Turkey. Traditional witchcraft in this region is a product of the cultural heritage of various nations. Those nations were Illyrians, Thracians, Dacians, Paeones and later Celts, Romans, Slavs and Turks. Wars, migrations and trade resulted in a mixing of genes and cultures, with Greece being of predominant importance.

Arriving in the 6th century, the South Slavs became the dominant nation. When they came to the Balkans they did not have a polytheistic pantheon or a developed paganism, but something that anthropologists call a *developed demonology*. This is understood to be a system of folk beliefs which anteceded paganism and polytheism. The South Slavs settled only shortly before Christianity overshadowed the region. Because of this, they never had the opportunity to develop their pagan beliefs onto another level. Their religious system was an amalgam of animism and the cult of ancestors. They believed in spirits of nature, spirits of fate and death, superior forces, demons, et al. Their basic methodology and religious practices were based on folk magic and shamanistic rites. However, traditional witchcraft took shape during the Middle Ages under the influence of the Balkan Gnostic sect known as the Bogomils. The system itself had become a mixture of old folk magic, demonology, traditional medicine, herbal knowledge and heretical Christianity with shamanic methodology informing their ritual practice.

We can divide the Gnostics into three basic groups, those who lived before Christ, those who lived during the first centuries after Christ, and the third group who coalesced in the Middle Ages. It is important to note that this third group was formed upon European soil, and would spread their teachings through large parts of Europe. They became a rival to the nascent European Churches. However, the political structures of states helped them to be victorious when confronted with the Gnostic sects. The most well known Gnostics groups from this period were the Bogomils, the Paulicians and the Cathars.

For my story, the most interesting group is the Bogomils. By official reckoning, they surfaced in Bulgaria somewhere between 927 and 970. But this is incorrect. At that time many of the Balkan countries were parts of the Bulgarian Empire. The truth is that the Bogomils were formed in the country known today as the Former Yugoslavian Republic of Macedonia. The founder of the movement was a priest by the name of Bogomil who started preaching around 950 somewhere between the towns Veles and Prilep. Whether he was an historical person or a mythical one we will never know for certain.

The teachings of Bogomil spread quickly, in two directions. It spread over Bulgaria, Serbia, Bosnia and the region of Dalmatia in present day Croatia. From here it would move East and enter Russia, and West into Europe. Once in Western Europe Bogomilism would yet again fork. One faction went through East-Bulgaria, Serbia, Bosnia, Dalmatia, Italy and France. The other faction spread through West-Bulgaria, Serbia, Hungary and on to France. From France the movement spread to Southern Spain and upwards to the British Isles.

The teachings of Bogomil were a mixture of Indo-European beliefs fused with pagan, Christian and Gnostics ideas. They were local patriots and did not wish to speak Latin or Greek, nor adopt Christian Byzantine names, instead insisting on preserving the old names and terms native to them. Because of their patriotism they preserved folk beliefs, magic, rituals and folk festivals. Their accusers give a sense of this, Sinodic of Borila writing that the Bogomils were:

> Those who in month in June on 21th day, the day when St. John the Baptist was born, do magic and pick plants; and on that night do mysteries like Hellenic rites, say that Satan created all things, and those who with kumirs call up rain and greet all things that come from the Earth.

The historian P. Kemp has concluded that Bogomilian doctrine has influenced people in dramatic ways, and in particular all the beliefs and doctrines in the Balkans. In the Balkans at that time shamanistic practice was very much alive. Shamans were in every village. Their most important obligation was to give their community medicine and magical help. They were healers, herbalists, clairvoyants and fighters against unnatural creatures, demons and the weather. Besides that, they were keepers of folk beliefs, myths, knowledge and wisdom. However, the state, motivated by the Church, would come to call them warlocks and witches.

Bogomils would incorporate all forms of useful beliefs in their own teachings, and many of their books and texts are preserved for us, even today. In the Balkans these books are known as *knjige starostavne*, the ancient books. They are full of magical formulæ and rituals, exorcisms, healing rites, prayers, divination methods, astrology and so forth. Furthermore, we know that Bogomils didn't pay taxes and refused labour. Instead they worked as healers, herbalists, clairvoyants and witchdoctors. They traded their services for food, animals, clothes or what they needed.

In the Balkans the medieval Byzantine government and Church started to call them *babajci*, which means *people who follow grandmother's religion*; this was simply another term for witchcraft. In the Balkans it was mainly old women who were shamans and it was these old wise-women who were keepers of the treasure of folk beliefs and magic.

Roughly a third of the Balkan population would come to accept the Bogomil doctrine, since it did not conflict with their old beliefs, but rather continued them. The Bogomil doctrine did not result in accusations or hunts for heretics; they did not impose obedience, slavery or enormous taxes. Folk shamans, witchdoctors, healers and herbalists would find in it what they always searched for, namely, safety; a religious system that didn't deviate from their own, but offered easily incorporable novelties.

Bogomilism was ultimately a path to freedom, a way of surviving by working with what they knew best, without the Tsar, Church and Government dictating the shape of their lives.

Bogomils would gladly and willingly share their knowledge, techniques of healing, teachings about healing and magical herbs, and many methods of working, that were based on pure shamanism. Shamanism was present in Europe for many centuries, especially in the Mediterranean. The good part of this Gnostic shamanism is what was called witchcraft and it is still present in some rural parts of Southeast Europe and the Balkans. These people, mainly very old, still exist. The best examples can be found in Eastern Serbia, Western Bosnia and the littoral parts of Croatia. All of this is described in my book *The Last European Shaman*.

Shamanism cannot be summarized in a few words. The first problem is that most people think that it exclusively exists in Eastern lands, amongst Indians and Siberians, or is something found only in Africa or Latin America. The other problem is that the term largely refers to various techniques of entering trance and astral flight. However, shamanism is a part of the European cultural heritage and it also brings with it many other elements, including working with trance states, which help us to define the nature of shamanism more precisely and thus exclude what is not shamanism from the term. It is the focus on entering states of trance with the help of dance, herbs and mantras that would define the first stone on the path of traditional witchcraft in these regions. The elements that together form shamanistic practice are found in many traditions, and they are as follows:

- Performing rituals after midnight when the worlds of the living and the dead collide.
- Perfoming rituals at three and fourway crossroads, because they are the place where worlds meet.
- Performing rituals at holy places such as forges, mills, bridges and powerful places in nature.
- The use of special implements such as cauldrons, consecrated knives, magical wands, crystals and stones.
- The use of healing and magical herbs by oral consumption, the making of oils and the use of amulets.
- The use of masks and special vestments.
- Being possessed by animal forms during astral flights.

- The use of ritual nudity and orgiastic celebrations, something that originated with fertility cults and was continued amongst 'witches.'

The second stone of traditional witchcraft in these regions was lent by the Bogomils, and it would give to the Balkans something that would differentiate this witchcraft from other crafts: the influence of Gnostic Christianity and its doctrines.

It is necessary to understand that the Bogomils were not in any way a group that would blindly cling to dogma. Although they had a common basic doctrine, it differed from region to region, depending on how the groups lived and the influence of local beliefs and religious practices. However, as influence goes both ways, it is interesting to wonder what influence Bogomils had on folk shamans, and how they directly affected the formation of what we call traditional witchcraft in this part of Europe today.

Scholars define the Bogomils as dualists, but we cannot be sure that dualism is the right word for their central beliefs. To better understand what they believed, it is important to understand that they embraced Byzantine vocabulary in their speech. At their core was the belief in two worlds, the material world and the immaterial world. The world that was immaterial is the Heavenly kingdom that belongs to God, and the world they called the Earthly kingdom belonged to Sataniel, God's double in the world of matter and men. One day God became aware of his shadow. Feeling lonely, he made magical gestures with his fingers, crossing the shadow, and it came to life. That was how Sataniel was born. He was nothing other than God's shadow; in other words, another side of God. However, Sataniel grown bored in the heavenly kingdom, decided to usurp the power of God and sat upon his throne. God punished him by sending him to the Earthly kingdom, to rule on Earth and not in Heaven. It is important to understand here that the phrase *heavenly kingdom* describes the existence of an immaterial world, whereas the *earthly kingdom* implies all that is material in the universe. The Bogomils implied, using Byzantine terminology, that there are in fact two important kingdoms and two important rulers: the Tsar in Heaven and the Tsar on Earth. The people had no problem in accepting this, as it agreed almost entirely with their old beliefs. In Serbia, for example, Vid was the God of heaven and Dabog the God of matter, death and the underworld.

Bogomils believed that the God who ruled in Heaven could not have anything to do with the material world. Just like Buddhists, they upheld the thesis that life is suffering. They believed that there was no hell after death, but that hell was the material world and material existence. As a result, ruling that world, on his throne, sits Sataniel, the master of all occurrences, good and bad; while God in heaven, the immaterial world, has no influence on people, their lives or spiritual growth. He could be reached only through Sataniel, the guardian of the gate and master of death who would enable one to pass through.

This is why, to them, nothing was important; neither kings nor states, neither State nor Church laws, neither sexual restraint nor acquiring material goods. Following this logic, the Bogomils came to formulate the biggest heresy, the one which would eventually cause their tribulation. In their belief, Christ could not have been the son of God because he was in the material world, otherwise known as Hell, and by that logic he would have to have been Sataniel's son, or the Devil. This perspective on Christianity is present even today in Eastern Serbia, and I have encountered it myself around Majdanpek.

This view of the spiritual world, anarchism and sexual freedom also incorporated many folk beliefs and methods, which would bring the Bogomils to set the final stone in the path of traditional witchcraft in these regions. Bogomils refused to differentiate between men and women. Bodies were irrelevant to them, because they were made from matter, so gender was irrelevant. In their belief system all genders are in same position because all of them are in hell and hell is the material world. We don't need to emphasize how tremendous a sin this was in the Middle Ages and in the eyes of the Church. However, that didn't stop them from going one step further. They organized their groups by the old rules of 'one God and twelve members' or, one leader of a procession and twelve participants. Simply put, this basic coven structure has its roots in Christianity. Of course, the coven of thirteen members is one of the most usual formats and it has its origin in Christian mythology and the story of Jesus and his twelve apostles. Though coven structure has it origin in Christian mythology its roots run deeper into much older Gnosticism. In its early period, one group of Gnostics adopted the idea that Jehovah has thirteen virtues from the Hebrew's religion. We presume that this model was applied when a myth about God (or more properly his emanation on Earth) and twelve followers was created. Before Christ was born we had twelve signs of the Zodiac and the Sun in the middle of the system, which gives us the number thirteen again. This kind of organization of groups was nothing new. What was different with the Bogomils is that women were included in these groups. Women, furthermore, could lead certain rituals. So, imagine a group of thirteen people, men and women both, performing a ritual at the crossroads after midnight, perhaps naked and masked; it would look very much like a traditional coven, would it not?

Because of this, I believe there was a precise moment when the first coven structures of thirteen members was formed, as well as the basic systems of traditional witchcraft which we can still recognize today. Real traditional witchcraft is an amalgam of archaic shamanism, folk paganism and, crucially, Gnosticism. There was a moment when spiritual elements were incorporated into the craft as well as spiritual goals and this can only be due to the Gnostic influence. This for me is the moment when traditional witchcraft was born.

To make myself clear, there was not some central and dogmatic witch cult which would occupy the whole of Europe. That is what European 'Gnostic' groups would do, and they would be called witches' covens, firstly by people and then by Churches and governments. They would have many differences, but the basic structures are made from two pillars: folk magic and belief systems on one side, and Gnostic Christianity on the other which would give a final result, something that would come to be recognised as traditional witchcraft. I believe this medieval Gnosticism spread across Europe and brought with it the classical coven structure of thirteen members, with its other beliefs varying from one country to another.

The first groups to be persecuted were from Orleans in France in 1022 and Verona, Italy in 1175. During the reign of King Nemanja in Serbia, one third of the population was killed or banished from the country for being Bogomil heretics. Bogomils have not survived in history, though some of their proverbs, such as *when things go bad light one candle for God, but two for the Devil,* are still popular. However, traditional witchcraft which formed under their influence has survived, in rural regions of the Balkans. As an example I will use Serbia, because the most precise data we have is from that territory.

All witches in the Balkans are solitary. However, all of them are members of non-organized cults from specific regions of the country. There are several types of rituals that witches from one region of the country perform together. Some of those rituals are public and witches perform them together with other members of the community, while others are performed only in specific situations. On both these occasions, witches (male and female) form something like a coven which they call The Court. If the members of the court are only witches then they choose who will be the leader of the ritual. If that person is a man, he gets the title Tsar, if the leader is a woman she is titled Empress. Other men will be Kings and other women will be Queens. This is how the Byzantine Empire was arranged. One Tsar and one Empress ruled the whole empire, which included many smaller countries, each with their own Kings and Queens. In Bogomil thought there could be only one Tsar on Earth and one in Heaven. Rulers of the countries could be Kings and Queens only, nothing more.

The basic ritual structure would involve the Tsar and the Empress, followed by other witches, Kings and Queens, and finally the rest of the population, who would be Court Gentlemen or Court Ladies. For some specific rites there were additional roles and titles like Sabre man, Bagpipe man or Singer. To illustrate this further I will give an example. During the Christian holiday Duhovi, which overlaps with the holiday of the village Duboka, people gather in front of the deep cave at the source of the Duboka river to perform a ritual that includes the whole community. Here the witches fall into trance; these women are called *rusalje*, which means *the falling women*. The rite starts by parading to the wooden cross (most often made of oak) and offering a sacrifice of food and drink, after which rites dedicated to the dead are performed. People would start to dance *kolo* accompanied by deafening music, and the dance would last until complete exhaustion with the Rusalje fainting, shivering and falling with piercing cries. This marked the entry into the trance. They would clench, scream, sing and talk, which would show that spirits of the dead were in them and communicating to them, or that they were pulled out of their bodies by fairies who took them away. There were several ways to be brought back from the trance. One was to be sprinkled with chewed up artemisia absinthium mixed with garlic and vinegar, another was to be sprinkled with river water that was poured over a sabre. While a person was in trance there would be three girls in dresses named Queens, three men with sabres named Kings and a bagpiper dancing around them. This holy day is celebrated in the entire Balkan territory, but the ritual trance has only been preserved in this area of Eastern Serbia.

A slightly different ritual with the same name was enacted by Queens in other parts of Serbia, also performed during the Spirits' holiday, on Saint Nikolas' or Saint George's day. For that ritual people would chose one Queen, two Kings, one Court Lady and four female Singers. They would dance a lunar dance, turning to the left and singing, and they would visit all the houses in the village. Their intention was to bring fertility to people's homes.

Certain rituals are performed only in specific situations. In 1908 in the village of Veliki Izvor there was a great drought. Local residents thought that the drought was caused by the Dragon that resided in their area. They believed that their village was visited by the Dragon at night because of his liaisons with some of the women, and because of its flights clouds could not assemble over the village, and therefore no rain fell. In order to remedy this, some of the farmers suggested that the *vrzino kolo* (a frenetic dance of witches or fairies) must be danced to drive away the Dragon, as the most powerful ritual was needed to counter such a powerful creature.

The ritual was performed after midnight on the 21st of July. Around fifty villagers gathered at the graveyard and lit a big fire. The leader of the rite was elected, named as the Tsar and he took off his clothes, while other people followed him. Then they joined their hands and began to dance around the fire. This frantic dance lasted until the dancers' exhaustion caused them to fall into a trance. During the dance there was no talking, so if someone wanted to say something he would communicate by mime or mumbling. When they determined that the dancing was complete, people ran through the village banging bells and pots. This race represented them chasing the Dragon towards the graveyard, to the big fire. When they drove the Dragon into the fire, they joined their hands and once more started to dance until the Tsar ruled that it was complete.

When Svetislav Prvanovic related this event in his article *Our Ancient Superstitions and Customs*, he did not mention if the man who was elected Tsar was a witch, but we know that he would have been. The reason is clear. The persons elected to be Tsar or Empress would be keepers of traditions, rituals and knowledge and the only ones who would know which ritual was the best for that occasion, and how it should be performed.

From all of this evidence we can describe what The Court would look like and explain who plays which role. Of course, in most cases the form of the Witches' Court depended upon the reason for its formation and the ritual being performed. As we have seen, all witches in Serbia are solitary. If they are female they are Queens and if they are male they are Kings. Only in group work was one particular witch elected as Empress or Tsar. The leader's obligation would be to choose the appropriate ritual for that occasion and to lead the ritual giving directions to the participants. Other witches were Queens and Kings. Their obligation would be to perform whatever tasks the Tsar or the Empress gave them. The common people would be Ladies or Gentlemen of the Court and would not usually perform ritual per se but would dance, sing or play on musical instruments. Sabre men could be participants in ritual and were usually guardians. If a witch is in trance they would stand over her brandishing a sabre over her body, so that some other entity could not possess it. Besides that, he could facilitate a ritual return of the witch into her body as I have already described, by pouring a macerated herbal or river water over the sabre's blade and onto her face. The bagpiper's obligation is to play music; when the trance is induced, this could last for hours. The singer would be one or more young girls. Their obligation would be to sing the ritual song.

What we know for certain is that the origin of this structure is not to be found in folk paganism or shamanism, although ethnologists point out that in most European countries nature spirits commonly had titles such as Queen and King. My opinion is that we should look for the origin at the time when Serbian traditional witchcraft was formed – the Middle Ages. At that time Serbia was part of the Byzantine Empire and the Empire had several kingdoms. So the ruler was Tsar but every kingdom had its own King. All of those kings were under the authority of the Tsar. That was very much like the Witches' Court – but this arrangement is just one aspect of the origin; the other lies with the Bogomils.

The Bogomils were using similar vocabulary for titles in their belief system and mythology. For them there is the Tsar in Heaven (God of the immaterial universe) and the Tsar on Earth (God of the material world and the underworld) and in many myths the Tsar on Earth was mentioned as a ruler of three kingdoms (underworld, water and the earth itself). We know through these myths that he granted hidden knowledge and magical power. His consort, Maria, is very similar in this respect.

Our conclusion might be that a witch who is appointed Tsar or Empress would actually take the role of God on Earth or his Lady. We presume that all who are under his or her command become Kings or Queens because he or his consort were forces that initiated those witches, gave them magical knowledge and the power to implement that knowledge. So, the Court of the Witches is actually a Court of God on the Earth (Sataniel), while titles represent the position in the Tsar's castle and the castle itself represents the material world – or Hell, if you prefer the Bogomil term.

But To Assist The Soul's Interior Revolution

The art of Andrew Chumbley, the cult of the divine artist, and aspects of Sabbatic Craft

ANNE MORRIS

Art is magic or there is no art.
— Louis Cattiaux

HE ART BORN OF MAGICAL PRACTICE expresses secret iconography. It is an opening to what we cannot quite see. It is this mysterious realm which underlies the drawings of Andrew Chumbley who expressed the concept of the Cult of the Divine Artist by conveying his gnostic intentions through creative artistic expression. He chose to access what he termed *Divine Imagination*, a place of space/time/intention similar to Henri Corbin's *Mundus Imaginalis*. Chumbley described his working group, the Cultus Sabbati as a representation of the Sabbatic tradition that expressed inner qualities of the tradition through artistic and textual expression using this Divine Imagination.

Creativity can be a form of magical soul making, or *aesthesis*. As explained by Plato, aesthesis may be viewed as a sort of imitation of imitation in that the artist's vision that is expressed through the creative act can be a personal expression of the original intent brought forth in order to express that intent to others. Veils are created indiscriminately through the artist's expression, though the images will have an effect upon the image-maker whether the intent is communicated to the viewer, or not. Plato's idea is best served when the sorcerer is representing an idea as a goal of the product, rather than simply representing his impression. The image may therefore represent spirit brought into matter, or Logos.

According to Gettings, breath and spirit is reflective of Logos. Logos is animate, and art derived from gnosis is representative of Alogos, or the pre-animate, arising from Other, wherein dwells the Divine Imagination. It is the imaginal space. We may then ask ourselves which is the most valuable image; the raw image that may be closer to the 'truth' or the refined image that represents a conclusion? Art has magical power: it is perception/ingress, experience/congress, and insight/egress, differentiation. As such the function of the divine artist is the representation of gnosis as egress and manifesting it symbolically within our realm.

There has always been a sense of the sacred in artistic creation where the *doing* is as important as the finished image. It matters not whether the image is naturalistic or immaterial; all images are symbols. If the image is a true representation of the essence, the numinous manifestation of the information imparted through ritual egress, the image, as the key expression of an idea, is a *numinosum*. The image sparks an enactment of magical interaction, whether conscious or not, creating a significant transformation. This is the magical circle of return wherein all who participate in the art, from sorcerer and spirit, to the viewer, form an indivisible circle in the magical process.

The quality of sacred art is set aside from the mundane through intention. Chumbley proposed through his art that art can bring forth catharsis when used as a tool of magical practice. It is a transformation or initiation. The artist is only the purveyor of beauty, not the master of beauty, which remains absolute and inviolate. Something may emerge that indicates further shaping within the sorcerer through Will, Desire and Belief but it is appertained through the artistic image that appears to express more than the accompanying text. The imagery demands that its needs be met through manifestation.

Chumbley's art depicted his sorcerous inquiry into the roots of Sabbatic Craft formulated by the sorcerers who preceded him, notably Austin Osman Spare and Robert Cochrane. He expressed a rhythmic cosmos outside the perceptions of the group he called *the clay*, the everyday people who lived mundane lives unaware of such sorcerous investigations. He delved artistically into a prehistoric, mythical consciousness with the mimetic conveyance of values and ideas. His was the metaphor of nature as primary ground, the incorporation of the past into the present, the future as now, gnostic angelic whispering, and the implementation of rituals of eternal return. Unlike some of the Sufi precepts gleaned from his reading of Henry Corbin and Idries Shah, his Gnostic intent did not participate in the dichotomy that divides experience into good and evil, eternal and temporal, rather, it belongs to a syncretic system that accepts multiple truths and meanings and attempts to reconcile them. For Chumbley gnosis was not achievable through a rational process. The mythic man, as John Cobb Jr. has explained, does not recognize the 'separateness of subject and object but instead sees a flow of subjective and objective contributions ... bound together where there is no clear consciousness of subject as subject or object as object.'

There is an innocence of form that belies the deeper meaning of Chumbley's images. While these images look like they are fractured forms or abstract art, they are meant to portray not only a concept, but are a representation of what was seen. They are rhetorical renderings rather than aesthetic renderings. They are maps of the reality within a gnostic context; pictures of accessed image systems drawn from spirit. What we see are symbolic structures of knowledge within symbol, which can't readily be seen as logos figures, but might be appertained as alogos figures, expressing knowledge gained through magical access through dreaming. Missing from these images is a key to the information gained, save only for the bare outline of practice.

Expressing a rare sacred geography that consists of a complex knowledge of place and sacred terrain, embedded in a phenology of seasonal cycles and expressed magical doctrine, Chumbley's art dances close to the earth an intricate configuration of sacred associations with the spirits of time and place within their particular landscape. Time and space as well as sorcerer, spirits, all life and non-living matter forms a continuum that relates to themes of fertility, death and rebirth, and the sacredness of all things.

Chumbley forged a practice with inspiration from early and mid-century occultists and from reading materials of traditional magical practice which he then termed 'Sabbatic Craft.' Though he took the traditional path of declaring that the term is only the outer shell of understanding of what he did, this has become the name by which his personal way of working sorcery has become known.

Breaking onto the magical scene with his self-published grimoire *Azoetia* in 1992, Chumbley reintroduced the idea of magical practitioner as divine artist to the occult community. Building on the work of Austin

Osman Spare whom he used as inspiration for his artistic style, Chumbley expressed through his art images of what he had encountered whilst in the midst of ritual, and later in dreams. Calling his dream images gnosis from ritual, Chumbley drew fantastic visions that seemed to defy markings of spatial continuity. He drew a representation of a mythic and supernatural world through his exploration of alternate consciousness that understood the sacred nature of this world. Not wish-fulfilling delusions, Chumbley's results would be repeated through his written grimoire work, and similar images might be attained by other sorcerers trailing behind, book in hand.

Chumbley expressed in *Azoetia* that although it may seem as though the sorcerer has little power over the trajectory of the gnosis, it is true that only the sorcerer is the source of creativity and has the transformative power necessary for the spirit to express gnosis. If the sorcerer wants to succeed in the work of sorcery, he participates in the necessary process of abandoning old programming. But how does this refer to art in a magical practice? Von Franz said, 'A civilization which has no creative people is doomed ... The person who is really in touch with the future is the creative personality.' In other words, sorcerers involved in the artistic process prepare the way for others to follow and lay the pathway for a fuller understanding than simple words can convey.

It is important to explain that the mapping of magical intent and gnostic expression within the sorcerer's personal paradigm has both a deconstructive and constructive dimension: not opposites or in tandem as a duality, but as components in the process that are ultimately complementary. The components in relationship are a key factor: one light and one dark without either being inevitable. What we believe we are viewing as objective reality, is discovered to be the subjective experience of spirit: the created is being created by being observed, and both are occurring simultaneously. Without a magical sense of perception, the sorcerer cannot enter the magical realm within the art. It is not a matter of trying to imitate an archaic spiritual practice or artistic style so much as fostering psychic mobility: the sorcerer opening himself to a range of visionary experience in a modern culture whose contemporary beliefs have made the very idea of other worlds almost unthinkable.

Chumbley's art was an expression of divine prototype, a metaphor for the divine, not a simile as is so often the case in contemporary occult art. A metaphor gives us a way to define our own interpretation, and a simile expresses only the form. The form of simile is the clothed form of metaphor. Chumbley made his art more than simply an artistic expression of his magical practice through his use of rites and incantation. He made the art more than anecdote as a substitute for meaning, by adding the mystery of his rites to the process.

Chumbley offers art with a strong talismanic quality that is not always a representation of something that may have meaning for others. This is why art taken from vision or expressing a gnostic understanding may appear obtuse to the viewer. How are we to know the difference between true and false, good and bad when viewing art born from vision that does not provide references that we recognise?

The imaginal quality of Chumbley's art expresses a fundamental expression of the other. It becomes an imitation, or mimesis of the imaginal world that bridges the liminal space, altering the imaginal so that we may in turn be transformed. Chumbley's art becomes a mute performance, or silence. It allows distance between that which exists and that which perceives. We don't consciously see, but we sense the meaning and character of the Imaginal. We experience aesthesis, or living in our senses.

His art demands that the viewer explore his understanding of meaning and space as the creative process is stirred, and whether meaning has been made or not, a response to the original expression is created; a reciprocity is expressed and a return made. The viewer then becomes a part of the loop, generating a continuum of devotion and gnosis.

DREAMING, GNOSIS AND SYMBOL

HUMBLEY studied many non-drug induced techniques for altering consciousness in order to access his visions, such as Jain meditation, Spare's fatigue techniques, the use of *mala* visualization, and practices from martial arts all aimed at accessing the gnosis from ritual, but the most success he found was within dream.

Chumbley explored the concept of dream as initiation in his essay 'Mysticism, Initiation and Dream,' writing: 'We might say that the dream transforms the dreamer, that it possesses the ability to "initiate."' He later stated that dreams dictate how they are to be interpreted, in that the dream itself may be the author and meaning-maker.

Many of Chumbley's art renderings were images from dream. The rational waking mind is likely to dismiss an apparition as a visitor from a sorcerous operation or as an hallucination or illusion but to sorcerous dream consciousness it is totally, terrifyingly real. Chumbley wrote:

> It is related by Corbin that Ibn 'Arabi (1165–1240 CE) considered the true ta'wil – the hidden meaning of dreams – not to lie in interpreting the forms and symbols of the Imaginal realm in terms of worldly events, not in 'reading' the dream with reference to 'the order of sensible things and events,' rather to accomplish the true ta'wil: 'one must carry sensible forms back to imaginative forms and then rise to still higher meanings.' For Ibn 'Arabi this ascent path connotes a restoration in which the material world, 'the visible temple,' becomes identified with 'the mystical temple,' and thus reified-translated to the spiritual order of perception.

Miricea Eliade said that it is not enough, as it was a century ago, to discover and admire the art of the primitives: we have to discover the sources of these arts in ourselves, so that we can become aware of what it is in a modern existence that might still have a part of what is mythical. Chumbley created this expression of spirit, bringing aspiration into the mix, which he expressed as an ascent to the stars after a descent into matter; a return. One of the hallmarks of Chumbley's method is that it views everything as being in process, either becoming or decaying, that even the unmoving center is moving in its silence, that all entities are in flux. This is all in keeping with the ideas of modern science, philosophy, and culture. In other words, anything that is real, whether known or unknown, is in process. He combines the Neoplatonic concept of oneness (that the ultimate principle of the universe is single and undivided) with the Trinity, and in his art shows the struggle to describe a perfect representation of Spirit through the imperfect medium of image and symbol. In *Azoetia* he expressed some measure of his process of reification of his dream work in publishing two versions of the web of possibilities. One version is explained *as dreamt* and the other as reified from dream. One is imitative, and the other inventive through the interpretation brought to the art by Chumbley. He lets us in on how he saw things as they are in themselves, bringing himself to the work of sorcery as more than simply expressing what he remembered from dream in his artwork. He showed in this how art may live in both the functional as well as the spiritual realm, both within and without the sorcerer. As William Blake wrote: 'He who does not see more vividly and clearly than this perishing mortal eye can see, does not see creatively at all.'

In dream myth is available to those who seek gnosis. Sorcerers access the magical and sacred dimension which contains the past, present, and future. Visionary dream is a response against the literal mind; it is a movement towards a larger timeless dimension that is all time at all times. When we invite the object of spirit in the other world to join us, the transformation of the personality becomes a living experience and we encounter something that cannot be received on a waking basis or controlled by theorizing. When accessing dream through sorcerous intent, ancient forms of consciousness begin to acquire an importance and meaning beyond the purely historical, as we discover them within our own psyche.

Whereas science is based on the objective weighing of detail as fact, essentially seeing without imagination or artistic expression, myth is not fully understood unless one enters into a circular, non-Cartesian state, such as dream. It is this melding with spirit, or dissolution into a more encompassing identity other than the rationalized ego self, much like Jung's collective unconscious, that makes the gnosis retrievable for artistic rendering. Rituals and rites, structured fatigue, monotonous chanting, drumming, and repetitive movements are no longer an integral part of contemporary life, but they are a way to make a direct hit on the dreaming aspect of the psyche.

This dying to the world of rationality in sleep and dream whilst awakening to powerful archetypal forces in the visionary world of dream can be a treacherous business. In dream when the ego-personality is temporarily displaced, the mind experiences another world; this is Chumbley's Divine Imaginal world, where inside is not separated from outside and spontaneous experiences of presences that do not belong to the ordinary world seem to occur. These are the images that Chumbley brought us as gnosis from his sorcerous workings.

IMAGE AS DOORWAY TO RITUAL

RTISTIC expression is a means through which the sorcerer may travel to other places. The sacred image can act as a lure for spirits and as a means to access alternate realities and states of consciousness, all of which may be transformative and used to obtain gnosis, leading to yet further transformations. The magical and mythological understandings of gnosis wrought from ritual that may be unacceptable to standard consciousness can be transcended via image. These other modes of reality-vision outside of the ego's control, visions that are essentially rooted in the soul that were abandoned by the rational and scientific logic of the enlightenment, may still be accessed via ritual.

Coomaraswamy wrote of how 'the invisible things of God' can be seen through art. In private correspondence, Chumbley wrote: 'I am able to enter the immense fertility of the spirit world directly through my art. In rite as well as in sleep I cross over into a land far older than my dreams, where I know ancestors and spirits of countless animals; all secreting, weaving, digging, beckoning,' expressing that the fundamental thesis of his art is the deliberate portrayal of divinity.

Chumbley expressed meaningful transformation through expression within line in his automatic drawings, as did the artist who inspired him, AOS. He appears to express the wish to banish from art everything that reminds us of the everyday creating a tension that transgresses reality, projecting the artist and the observer into new territory. Much like Spare's art, Chumbley's renderings reflect the *wonder* of what Aristotle saw as the origin of philosophy in an attempt through aesthetics to make the distance between what we know and what we don't know absolute, and pointed.

Chumbley and Spare ask us to step away from mimesis and identification of images to allow the stream to carry the intention in a purer form. Both discussed how automatic writing and automatic art-making can be useful in understanding magical gnosis and concepts. Both explained how the process is as important as the results, explaining that the process *trains the information* one wants to explore to express its full power.

Working outside of the logic of identity, we may see immediacy and distance from intention. We may then begin to see the image as a vehicle that operates between dualities allowing poesis as a form of knowing to express Chumbley's magical formula of Ingress, Congress and Egress.

GNOSIS IN THE ART PROCESS

RT BEGINS FORMLESS, much like the earth before it became shaped and populated; the time before time, or the time before meaning. As the artist begins, an impression is made on the material that creates art, and it then expresses its message as the intention of the artist. Much like the sacrificial rites of Sabbatic Craft, in which the sorcerer sacrifices the old to birth the new, more perfect man, art is the unformed becoming the newly formed, from rite to re-membrance. There is a delineation of form within art that mimics the de-lineation of the sorcerer's form within the rite: the sorcerer becomes other, the mimicry of a god or spirit, and returns with the gnosis as the resolved new man. The art from the rite is then a metaphor of the process; no longer a copy envisioned in a mirror as simile, but as a magically transformed act.

How can subjective meanings become known objective reality? Or how may we express ritual activity as things? How indeed, for we must inquire into meaning-making or the *reality sui generis*. Within the ritual process that envisions art as a resolution, something must happen to develop the metaphor from the simile, as Meister Eckhart says: 'all her forms must be shattered.' This idea is similar to that of Michelangelo claiming that the image was in the stone and all he did was release it.

Chumbley saw the definition of making meaning from gnosis gained through ritual much as Berger who wrote of meaning-making as 'a quality appertaining to phenomena that we recognise as having a being independent of our own volition.' Another level of meaning-making within culture is a theoretical expression that is informed by symbolic meaning, referring to realities that are other than those we live in every day. Here meaning-making is found within symbol that expresses a form of meaningful integration. In lower forms of legitimation only parts of the known construct of meaning in sorcerous inquiry is known, but at the higher level of meaning-making creating a specific all-encompassing cosmogony becomes the point, because when all vectors of meaning are included a space is created wherein everything happens within the sorcerer themself.

Cosmological meaning-making is inherent within Sabbatic Craft and cannot be left out of any study of Chumbley's artistic expressions. This world, this universe has time incorporated in it, with a past and future as well as a 'now.' Everything becomes an expression of the divine, including trespass against taboo and inanimate objects, allowing for them to be recognized and dealt with in a social manner. This provides an order to the hierarchy of the universe, keeping the darker and more terrifying aspects of insanity at bay. The use of art as a way of meaning-making within the context of metaphor and symbol as an expression of the 'rightness' of reality fits into a sorcerous practice that encompasses this kind of advanced cosmogony. A sorcerous artist lives within a whole world in his art that allows him to find his location in the symbolic universe.

Any idea of sanity and the sorcerer as a sane, stable member of a contiguous society is threatened by the 'surrealistic' congruence of dreams which finds the sorcerer as a member of the symbolic universe. Within many cultural myths, the sorcerer's real name is given by the spirits allowing the sorcerer to anchor himself both within the cosmic reality of everyday life and the malevolent transmutations of the places between everyday reality and cosmic reality. No matter what happens, he knows that the spirits know him. This incorporates a knowing that transcends every possible transmutation of the sorcerer within the symbolic cosmos. He may bring back images from that other place with impunity.

An important factor within the legitimized symbolic art cosmogony for sorcerers is as Chumbley wrote, *going to death*. This knowledge of seeing the death of others points to the liminal space in gnostic dream and in symbol wherein the sorcerer may incorporate death into life as part of their sorcery. The integration of death into life then becomes the most important symbolic expression within sorcery and is an often unacknowledged part of the artistic occult image. All death within sorcery must allow the sorcerer to continue on with life after its embrace to continue the routine of everyday life. This may only be attained by integrating death into a symbolic cosmogony. Slipping into death, and then returning, transcends the power of a symbolic universe. This symbolic cosmogony is expressed readily within Chumbley's art.

ART-MAKING

ITHIN a magical construct artistic creativity can be understood as a meaning-making vehicle to restore a form and balance to what we either wish to find and experience, or what we have experienced. The magical artisan looks for a way to shape the experience grounded in image with a sensible immediacy, and art-making can give intention or experience form as something meaningful. Without the image the experience can fade fragment and become lost.

The concept of making a mark to indicate an idea is an old one, and we may explore the aspect of image as a metaphor for gnosis within a magical practice by looking more closely at how the development and 'unfolding' of image might artistically express gnosis. When relating what we find and do in magical practice, how can we make sense of what we have experienced? Creating an image of what we have experienced is a way of giving form to what we know and shaping the world we know in a new way.

By experiencing what we see expressed through a magical act, and making meaning of it through art, we are allowing it to show itself within the meaning that we give it, as well as the meaning inferred. We have wonder that is made into meaning. Wonder draws us into art but meaning is what we express from that art. Art-making as a magical act aims to project the sorcerer into the world of Divine Imagination. We could then describe art making in a magical sense as a vehicle for restoring our connection to the Other.

Post-modernists argue that concept has always overshadowed image in philosophical thought. I would rather suggest that the image stands next to the concept, expressing the concept in a way that bypasses our defenses, speaking to our deepest knowing. When evocation creates an image the sorcerer is dealing with a symbol. The meaning of the symbol must be known to be understood by an observer, as something intrinsically known; known without explanation. The magical nature of the symbolic egress cannot be objective or objectifiable by its very nature, for objective art is exoteric, not esoteric. Esoteric art transcends the objective, for the nature of the art is synthesis. According to Heidegger: 'In *Being and Time* truth is understood not in the Platonic sense of mimesis, correspondence to a pre-existing reality, but as alethia, the remembering or uncovering of what is hidden and needs to be brought into the open to be seen.' Art does not represent gnosis and is not a copy of what we have experienced, instead it works to tease silence from logos and bring it forth into our meaning making and understanding.

Art arising from magical practice does not always imitate what is found in the mundane, but instead brings into being what has arisen from Other, revealing the truth of what is. In this way a world is made from image; the spirit gnosis is shared with the sorcerer as artist and when the gnosis that strives to be known takes form in image, the sorcerer is as far from those who see the art as he is close to their fate. The sorcerer exemplifies his original intent through his art. We are initiated through the image making and through viewing the image. Sharing the image within the mundane world is a practice of seeing and the seen. Each informs the other and within that dance is initiation. It is a recognition of a concept in historical time. It creates a re-vision of our spirit within a moment. Each moment is its own history, an utterance of the direct revelation of the numinosum.

Chumbley's art relies on axial existence within his sorcerous work. His threshold crossing within ritual towards the center of organization, Jasper's *ashsenzeit,* or axis at death, or what Cobb calls the *seat of existence,* moved from the unconscious images to his conscious mind, and a new autonomy in the reflective consciousness effected a connection to the mythical age, and by accessing mythical imagery he brought to fruition the metaphor of magical gnosis. A new individual understanding of the gnosis received arose from his artistic rendering. This enabled Chumbley to engage in artistic self-awareness, or awareness of the soul as an object of reflection, and to begin thinking about the nature of man, the purpose of life, and how to achieve the ideal embodiment of this soul.

Through gnostic artistic expression and in images gained through ritual, a new center emerged that transcended reason and passion, and assumed responsibility for both. This new awareness was expressed by Chumbley as I, and became the locus from which ritual and image were made and carried out. Chumbley called this the culmination of Will, Desire and Belief, but as Cobb pointed out, it can be identified as such only from a higher perspective that transcends but includes this axis of I.

Although Chumbley wrote of being possessed by spirits as in being *ridden by spirits* in creating some of his artwork, his emphasis was on a personally transforming encounter between the appertained spirit and the human personal spirit. Through his art and magical practice, Chumbley sought to transcend the personal I and realize the spiritual I in his artwork. By attempting this, Chumbley's art embodied and showed the way to radical self-transcendence. The possibilities expressed in Chumbley's art are the spiritual self and the self-transcending self wherein the possibilities for creative transformation are far from exhausted. In looking at Chumbey's art we may note how he conformed to the formal, traditional and historical pattern of transcendence through rite, but in referencing the art of his predecessors, such as Spare, he included their achievements. Chumbley interwove the notion of *self* with the axial impress of rite in his nod to the sorcerer artists who preceded him as an understanding of self as the unchanging object of change.

Can what we do as artistic sorcerers allow us to be reborn through the creative process? There is something in this work of sorcery that resists image even as we arrive at knowledge through image. The Divine Artist must discover how the image will become manifest. A necessary tension emerges within the initiated, the initiation and the image.

Art-making as a sorcerous activity can in and of itself be a transformative experience. Using the senses to see what has been brought forth creates a link between our world and the world of Divine Imagination by becoming available to us even as it reverts to the place from whence it came. The information is no longer with us, save for the representation, but the representation holds the seed of the gnostic intent. The world of Divine Imagination can therefore be revealed through a work of art by giving a new sense to what we have appertained within our own magical practice.

From a phenomenological perspective, all artistic expression must be known by its appearance. There must be a subject behind an object, even if not perceived. The object cannot exist without being appertained: the subject must be viewed in order to exist. It is through aesthesis that the image becomes manifest.

As an expression of the sacred, magicians and artists struggle to manifest concepts that defy mundane expression. Making art as a magical process can transform the artist as well as the viewer. The process of imitating that which resists imitation is the task of those drawn to the Cult of the Divine Artist, though the task remains fraught, we must attempt it.

BIBLIOGRAPHY

ARGUELLES, J. A., *The Transformative Vision: Reflections on the Nature and History of Human Expression*. London: Shamhala, 1975.

BERGER, P. L. & LUCKMANN, T., *The Social Construction of Reality: A Treatise on the Sociology of Knowledge*. New York: Anchor Books, 1967.

BLAKE, W., WITH KEYNES, G. (ED.), *Drawings of William Blake: 92 Pencil Studies*. New York: Dover Publications, 1970.

BLAKE, W., *The Complete Illuminated Books*. New York: Thames & Hudson, 2000.

CHUMBLEY, A., *The Azoetia*. London: Xoanon, 1992, 2002.

—— *Qutub: The Point*. Hercules, CA: Xoanon, 2008.

—— *The Satyr's Sermon*. Hercules, CA: Xoanon, 2009.

—— *Opuscula Magica*. (vol. I): Hercules, CA: Three Hands Press, 2010.

—— *Opuscula Magica: Essays on Witchcraft and Crooked Path Sorcery*. (vol. II): Hercules, CA: Three Hands Press, 2011.

—— *Mysticism, Initiation and Dream*. Hercules, CA: Three Hands Press, 2012.

COBB JR., J. B., *The Later Heidegger and Theology*. New York: Harper & Row, 1963.

COBB, J., *Spiritual Bankruptcy: A Prophetic Call to Action*. Nashville, TN: Abingdon Press, 2010.

COOMARAWAMY, A. K., *Christian and Oriental Philosophy of Art*. Mineola, New York: Dover, 1956.

—— *Figures of Speech or Figures of Thought? The Traditional View of Art*. Bloomington, IN: World Wiscom Inc., 2007.

CORBIN, H., *Spiritual Body and Celestial Earth*. Princeton, NJ: Princeton University Press, 1989.

ECKERT, M., *Selected Writings*. New York: Penguin Books, 1995.

ELIADE, M., *The Sacred and the Profane: The Nature of Religion*. Boston, MA: Harcourt Brace Jovanovich, 1987.

—— *Images and Symbols: Studies in Religious Symbolism*. Princeton, NJ: Princeton University Press, 1991.

GABLIK, S., *The Reenchantment of Art*. New York: Thames & Hudson, 1991.

GETTINGS, F., *The Occult in Art*. New York: Rizzoli International Publications Inc, 1979.

HEIDEGGER, M., *Being and Time*. Albany, NY: State University of New York Press, 2010.

HOWARD, M. & FITZGERALD, R., *An Interview With Andrew D. Chumbley*, in *The Cauldron*, 103 February 2002.

JACKSON, N., *Masks of Misrule*. Chieveley, UK: Capall Bann Publishing, 1996.

NEUMAN, E., *Art and the Creative Unconscious*. Princeton, NJ: Princeton University Press, 1959, 1974.

PLATO, *Timaeus*. Cambridge, MA: Hackett Publishing, 2000.

NOEGEL, S., WALKER, J. & WHEELER, B. (EDS.), *Prayer, Magic, and the Stars in the Ancient and Late Antique World*. University Park, PA: The Pennsylvania State University Press.

SCHULKE, D., *Ars Philtron: Codex Vasculum*. Hercules, CA: Xoanon, 2001, 2008.

——— *Viridarium Umbris*. Hercules, CA: Xoanon, 2005.

SCHNEIDAU, H. N., *Sacred Discontent: the Bible and Western Tradition*. Berkeley, CA: University of California Press, 1977.

SCHWALLER DE LUBICZ, R. A., *Symbol and the Symbolic*. Rochester, VT: Inner Traditions International, 1978.

SPARE, A. O. & CARTER, F., *Automatic Drawing*. Quebec: 93 Publishing, 1979.

WASSERMAN, J., *Art and Symbols of the Occult: Images of Power and Wisdom*. Rochester, VT: Destiny Books, 1993.

——— *The Mystery Traditions: Secret Symbols and Sacred Art*. Rochester, VT: Destiny Books, 2005.

Passers-by

Potential, Crossroads and Wayfaring on the Serpent Road

JESSE HATHAWAY DIAZ

Midway in the journey of our life I came to myself in a dark wood,
for the straight way was lost. Ah, how hard it is to tell the nature of that
wood, savage, dense and harsh – the very thought of it renews my fear!
– Dante Alighieri, *The Divine Comedy*

Stand at the crossroads and look; ask for the ancient paths, ask where
the good way is, and walk in it, and you will find rest for your souls.
– Jeremiah vi:16

HIDDEN IN THE DARK FOREST OF EACH BREATH, there is a serpent-tongued road that offers the keys to heaven or hell; yet as quickly as this stang of opportunity reveals itself, it is gone again – until the bottom of the next breath, wherein a new road presents itself, and another, and another. This is where we meet him, the Man in Black, the Devil at the crossroads, the eyes-on-the-road of each potential choice. And he is always here, keys in hand, whether we realize it or not. Revelation of his presence is only the beginning, for now that you know he is here, this horned St Peter, what now?

There is no offering of arguments towards a mutual acceptance of this potential – it is simply here, always and never, flashing the temptation of choice in the dark flitter of every blink. It is here that the witch assumes her true power, it is here the Magus takes of the fruit of the first tree, watering it with the tears of his self-betrayal. It is here where the Mother of Blood waits to bring us to ourselves. And it is here where, with humility and awe, I find myself returning, trying to capture its smoke in the bottle of my memory.

When the map fails, I must re-examine the landscape. The same door does not always lead to the same place. It is so easy to be led astray by the projection of desire and ignore, rather than explore my current state. Stop. Regroup. Where am I? I feel that my left eyelid is heavy, a slight tension in the neck, I can feel my pulse in my left big toe …. ah, yes. There he is. A double arrow of awareness is suspended between us; at first my attention divides, flashing between inner and outer, and with a relaxed but focused effort the division gives way to a unified multiple awareness, a clarity of two-headedness. I notice that I am holding my breath, and I let this go, and as breath floods in, a new effort in allowing these sensations to inform, but not supplant. And, exhale.

> It is impossible for a person to mount two horses and to stretch two bows. And it is impossible for a servant to serve two masters.
> Thomas 47:1–2

There is a criticism of those who walk more than one path that we are spread too thin, and that we have divided ourselves, our attention, to the point where it inhibits our ability to fully engage in any path, or that we contaminate the pure tradition by contact with others. This seems based on the mistaken assumption that we must, by necessity, solipsistically combine all things, or compartmentalise to avoid any dissonance. While the treading of multiple paths may not be right for some, for others, it can be used as a tool to re-center the witch and provide forward momentum. There is an intense need to keep these paths not only separate from each other, for the preservation of tradition and the knowledge thereby gained, but also to allow them to work as a unified whole upon the consciousness of the witch, with necessary doubt and the discipline of self-examination.

In our larger mother-culture in the West, there is an absolutist precedent in religion and spirituality, where one-way, usually 'our way,' is the sole means by which to access the truth of God. But there are also worlds of thought where agglutinating pragmatic and myriad approaches is a natural expression and exploration of divinity. This does not automatically allow for the immediate acceptance of falsehoods as legitimate, but rather allows for a plurality of expression and explorations of the self.

Walking paths must be more than the collection of traditions for the satiation of the ego. But, through discipline and the cultivation of attention, the mind can engage in this by forging links and and deeper understanding based in comparisons and contrasts. If we get too lost in the specific contradictions between paths, we are lost. But when we use those same contradictions as explorations of a greater truth, our comprehension can blossom and provide new insights. Imagine these paths meeting, like spokes on a wheel. If we walk the perimeter of the wheel, we will be engaging in each path, but the momentum of the whole will throw us out of balance. Yet, if we can find our center, become the axis, then each tradition can still be engaged, but all will serve the verticality of the witch.

For some, a plurality of languages is normal, and one does not preclude the other. The subtleties of speaking Spanish are different from those of English or Mandarin. Some seem to have an ability to master many languages, others struggle with one. It is a balance of hard work and something less definable; some call it a *gift*. It is the same with the languages of spiritual paths. When we engage in this work of centering, this does not mean that the nuances of traditions are blurred, nor are 'all gods one god, and all goddesses one goddess.'

Without the benefit of guidance from self or tutor, it becomes all too easy to indulge in whim and give in to momentary impulses that distract from potentialities that serve a greater trajectory. It becomes essential to weigh decisions, actions, and impulses against their own opposites. This is the murderous blood of Cain, for the blood betrays itself, turning on itself, expressing enough doubt in the current situation, suggesting that you may want something different. This divine restlessness is the poison chalice that propels us, drives us, and turns impulses into fruit, venom into the wine-blood of salvation. Over time, we more quickly apprehend these moments and we are able to hasten our progress.

Witchcraft is not a religion, it is an approach towards religion and belief, an impulse of rebellion born in desire for change. Witches can and will work within whatever religious traditions serve them, whether out of cultural affiliation or adoptive practice. The right-handed worship of deities and the veneration of saints and the dead has tremendous power, but it is not witchcraft. It is the work in tandem with the left-handed acquisition of the power of those same deities, saints and mighty dead for our own, where witchcraft lives. Do not let the right hand know what the left hand is doing – an appropriation and re-reading of Matthew vi:3.

The secrets of rebellion and murder in traditional craft suffer gross misinterpretation by the right-hand path. For the pious, to embrace the qualities of Lucifer and Cain is at best an uncomfortable heresy. Equally mistaken is seeing the glorification of the same as the capstone of achievement and communion. If we do not use these impulses, this co-mingling of revolt and murderous resolve known as witchblood, for catharsis and transformation, it is as indulgent as any other blind adherence to right hand practice. This cannot be counted as true witchcraft. For just as Cain accepted his punishment as the properties of his actions and became the father of blood, so too did the Christ accept his burden, assuming the role of sacrificial lamb for the sins of the world.

Dual observance is ultimately about the intersection of orthodox and heresy, the witch standing on the center-point of power. For such a witch, the right handed practice, grounded in more orthodox workings, revolves around using observances, prayers, and offerings as a point of ingress for harnessing the power that may be accessed in the heretical practice of the left hand.

Just as the blood calls for the sacrifice of all that hinders the becoming of the witch, the left hand seizes the power of gods, spirits, saints and the mighty dead for their aid and use. Intercessor becomes mentor, and saint and devil merge in the fires of communion, and the blood is vivified, reified, and strengthened. While not a universal aim, often such an accumulation of power is first sought as a means for the control of the mundanities of life; yet often it plants a seed of awareness, and all workings become subservient to the Nowl-Star of self-understanding, the latter not eclipsing the utility of the former.

There are examples of this mindset in many paths and disciplines. In traditional astrology, an astrologer may know the lay of the heavens on any given day and interpret its significance and influence, but it is the art of the talisman, the harnessing of auspicious stellar and planetary elections in corresponding and sympathetic media where a similar 'seizing of power' happens. While a person may supplicate the planetary angels through offerings of prayer and incense, an astrological talisman places the power of those same angels in the hands of the cunning one. This is a less stigmatized version and analogous practice to our own work-with-both-hands.

Consider the worship of saints. While many debate the use of saints in traditional craft, both right hand and left hand workings with saints are practiced everywhere Christianity, especially Roman Catholicism and Eastern Orthodoxy, is encountered. The history of many saints often reveals a State-authorized seizure of power from other local cults. But we are not merely discussing the masking of pagan god as saint, as we find in many Afro-Diasporic traditions. Dual-observance looks to the saints themselves as the vessel of all its manifestations, holding a mirror to the tradition their veneration asks: *who is the mirror, and who is the mask?* When the curandera prays to the Virgin of Guadalupe, calling her Tonantzin, the saint is just as much the Mother of God as She is the Mexican earth mother. This is true syncretism, where the dominant culture's spirits consume the less dominant, and fusion takes place. This is the serpent under the foot of the Virgin, the inclusion and command of the legion of spirits that are now collectively known as saint. The question to be asked is how do we harness this serpent power?

On December 13th, millions of Christians celebrate the Feast Day of Saint Lucy of Syracuse, a virgin and martyr associated with festivals of light and with healing, particularly of the eyes. Lucy, whose name is derived from *lux,* Latin for light, is patron of the blind, and gives the promise and hope of seeing the rise of the Sun of God as Solstice and Christmas follow close behind. She holds her own eyes on a platter in her hands, removed as a punishment for, or as devotion to, her faith. The faithful make offerings of flowers, candles, incense, and prayers seeking her intercession. With the right hand, this veneration is mostly benign, with possible links to pre-Christian Solstice celebrations in Scandinavia and Italy. In Mexico, she is depicted as a little girl dressed for her first communion, with a crown of thorns on her head, her eyes gouged out, blood dripping down her cheeks like tears. Many possess eyes on a small platter, held in their hands, that can be removed to 'work the Saint,' a form of folk-Catholic magic that uses bargaining and coercion to force a desired action. In this case, her eyes are hidden from her until one's request is fulfilled, or conversely, her eyes can be placed somewhere you need her to watch over.

There is something telling in this depiction and practice, for it echoes another side of the Saint. Lucy, when worked with the left hand is a highly mischievous saint. She is a a young girl who enters riding the head of the dragon into the long night; she is the dying of the light, and maybe she'll see us through to the coming of light on the other side in the promise of Candlemas, as Lucifera, crowned with a wreath of candles. On her feast day, the cunning can seize power with both hands – offer a rosary to her, flowers, candles, incense; and just as the astrologer makes the talisman to seat the celestial powers, the witch can create any number of vincula to seize the powers of the martyr Lucy for their own. Heating sympathetic herbs in oil while calling upon her, make an oil in her name, and while the oil is still boiling pour it over the idol of the Saint, capturing the adorations of the right into the menstruum of the left. Let the oil be made only on her feast day, being sure to place eyes – actual or in effigy – within it, to seize the sight. This oleum can be applied to the eyes for health, or used as an unguent to instill second sight and the eye of prophecy.

We work with the right to know the Saint, we work with the left to steal their power. This is not an act of aggression – we are talking about raising the power of the right by utilizing a feast and worship as a means of harnessing that power on the left. The difference between the two is often born of differing attitudes at the intersection of orthodoxy and heresy. Within this vein is the left hand celebration of Good Friday, where the faithful seize the power of the Christ in the Harrowing of Hell, a practice with kindred manifestations, from the legends of the Pendle witches of Lancashire, the Easter Witches of Sweden, the Palo sects of Cuba, and Quimbanda in Brazil, amongst many others. The fruits of such dual observance can manifest as a talisman, an oil, a statue, or even an empowerment from the spirit itself. And it is in this intersection of matter and spirit, and only here, that true initiation takes place.

Initiation, to be genuine, requires a specific meeting of spirit and matter, where whether solely by spirit, or through the mediation of one already initiated, the force of blood will impregnate the chosen candidate. This is to say that the stirring of the blood that is affected is itself a coagulation of spirit within the body that must then be nurtured by the newly initiated. There must be a course of ingress for the novice, which seems to be provided through two traditional means: either by time, trial and study before empowerment as preparation of the void field of reception, or by means of the same after empowerment as incubation for that-which-has-been-received. An argument could be made that both happen naturally when spirit guides.

Initiation is never a guarantee, and should never be held over another's head as a reward. It should be given when it should be given, and only then, and at the discretion of its secret-keepers. It should also be noted that although solitary initiation is possible at the hands of spirit, given this requirement, there is no form of self-initiation. One cannot pass on to oneself what was not originally there. The curdling of the blood can indeed happen in isolation, but it is always and only at the hands of spirit, and this, truth be told, is rare to find. When this happens there is no need for initiation in a group lest mutual affinity bring you to each other. What is given in recognition can never be demanded.

Initiation tends to manifest bonds of kinship tied in blood, and adoption into such families should not be given casually. For the blood that flows at this intersection of spirit and matter has a life and direction of its own. While we must all tread this serpent path for ourselves, true companionship should not be cast aside, indeed, cherish it, for this is a lonely road, an endless path through the night, where blood calls to blood, blood answers, and recognises its own.

> for the one who will gaze upon this bronze serpent, none will destroy him, and the one who will believe in this bronze serpent will be saved. For this is Christ; those who believed in him have received life. Those who did not believe will die.
> *Testimony of Truth*

> and your eyes shall be opened, and ye shall be as gods.
> Genesis 3:5

The serpent path that we walk is an eternal unfolding of the crossroad. Each moment becomes choice, and each choice leads us to the next intersection of what-needs-be with what-is. Here, in this fertile ground of opportunity, we find the scattered seeds of the forbidden tree. It is where we hear the hissing of the first serpent, that blind dragon, which offers us the poison chalice of our godhood.

The blind dragon comes to each of us, whether as the slant serpent or the tortuous, to whisper of the potential of our own becoming. And here, if we are ready, we may slough our skins and ascend the very same tree, seeking the balance of the Pole of verticality. Until we do so we are as beasts, like the serpent, with our bellies on the ground, confined by the gravity of the world and the siren song of the spreading earth.

This ever-expanding pull of the black earth that calls us to live and die by the land, toiling to dig our fields by day and our graves by night, calls us to lay down in submission to the natural order. While the same order nourishes us, it will destroy us, it is what we are made for. But in this submission, what do we sacrifice? Where is our humanity and the awareness of choice we have cultivated? This is the Mother of Lies. Do not get swallowed by her. While by the lie we live and die, in the lie we find proof of the incorruptible truth.

The ascent up the tree is the assuming of a new burden – for in our ascent, in our spiral climb, there is a new seduction, a new danger. It is the blood of the celestial serpents, those ancient angels, that again rebel within us. Here, where our ophidic nature meets once more with the eyes and ears of humanity, we are offered a new temptation. Strike out and claim the tree for ourselves, or sprout the wings of flight, just as the tortuous serpent becomes the owl in the night.

For high in the tree the serpent has transformed his axis, trading the horizon for the pull of zenith and nadir. It is at once the pole of the brazen serpent, the tree of Golgotha, and the gallows of Judas. It is a memory of the fall of the king, and radiates the lux smaragdina of the cunning-race. Here we may speak with angel and god, meeting eye to eye, as they walk through the garden in the cool of the day, but still we are bound to the tree, captive in its branches. We have traded a mistress for a master, and are still slaves.

To prevent this bondage from overtaking us, the witch, in time, must inevitably seek to balance horizontal and vertical, tempered by the vantage and perspective of flight. This is the gift and legacy of the blood mother, who in refusing to lay flat on the earth in submission, in weighing both the potential and the limitations of the erectness of the Pole, takes the power of creation into herself and leaves the bonds of both axes, taking to the sky in flight. Through her, the restlessness of the blood becomes the wings we need to understand our position and make our own fate. For the witch is not bound to the dragons of horizon and apex, but to their own power to decide for themselves.

In this fury of sabbatic flight, the crossroads crosses upon itself, multiplying, changing and shifting, opening worlds within worlds of possibility. This is the blood acre of our becoming, made manifest through an internalisation and awareness of the crossroads of each moment. Victory is fleeting and short won. It must be weighed against itself, like all our previous decisions. With every breath, we must renew the path. With every heartbeat, we must again assume the mantle of the first sorcerer; Cain must slay Abel, calling upon the fire in the blood to burn away the dross. And with the next moment, we start again. This is our benediction and execration.

> Come to know what is in front of you, and that which is hidden from you will become clear to you.
> Thomas 5:1

In the infinity of that crossroad of the Sabbat, we must always be moving forward, step by step, through the mire of distraction and the mud of self-contentment. An attention must be cultivated that allows for the perceptions of inner and the sensory input of outer, but the wayfarer must navigate between perceived objectivity and subjectivity, and away from the conflation of sensation and feeling.

This is not meant to be solely confined to our perceptions of the Sabbat and the eternal crossroad. Or, alternately, the work of the Sabbat is all-encompassing, and should pervade all aspects of our life. All is grist for the mill, all is fuel for the athanor of transformation. When we confine our craft to ritual alone, or to intellectual musings, we lose valuable opportunity for the cultivation of this awareness. All moments are fertile possiblities, and we must cultivate a relationship between our daily life and our magical praxes. If such awareness is absent or avoided, magic becomes at best fantasy and escapism and at worst posturing and charlatanry, all of which may be poisoned further by self-deceit.

If our pace is too quick and it is to the detriment of the quality of our attention and awareness, a more measured pace can and should be sought. These rhythms will, with experience and consistency, become more swift in process, but there will be moments, seemingly random, that pose great exceptions to this rule. Because it is all too easy to fall into looping frustration and cycles of judgement, we must look again at sensation and perception.

The blurring between the two is especially evident when we experience pain. Often the sensation of pain brings a feeling of anger or sadness, and we give into the pain we feel at that moment. We cede our potential, our humanity, to the sensation of pain, and, in that moment, we are lost. However, when we first observe, not experience, our pain, the act of observing places a distance between sensation and feeling. In this intersection we find the potential for increasing levels of observation that place the pain in a larger context. With this new information, more paths of action open. We release ourselves in greater degrees from the bondage of our mislabeled sensations. This is again the flight of the witch mother, the double edged knife of vantage.

These concentric circles of awareness are not unlike the ritual circles of our arte. While the circles, physical or projected, that delineate different fields of working and spheres of awareness in our rites and associated cosmologies are a cherished part of our repertoire, it is ultimately that which surrounds the mind of each witch that is of the most value. The degree of permeability or resilience we assign them allows us to walk in the world between the extremes of exposure and isolation. Just as we must endeavor at each crossroads to re-examine the inner needs of our path, we must keep attention to the outer that we do not get lost inside ourselves.

The circle's edge hums with sound, yet, in the hendekate direction of center, the Tree of Knowledge grows in silence. Here we may observe the workings of our dual worlds, inner and outer, with less distraction. Here we can re-evaluate our station, and our perception. Here we return to the body for the benefits of sensation as information separate from feeling. For when we can examine the inner world with greater alacrity, the outer world will also reveal itself. This is the gift of the Tree of Knowledge, as here we gain vantage in silence on the wings of the owl.

It is here we meet ourselves before walking into the world; at the crossroads, in the shade of the tree wizened with age and blasted by the jealousy of God, where the owl-as-serpent became mother of the blood. The blood awakens within us a crossroad of rebellion and murder, inviting us to a dream state of two-headed possession where sensation informs, but does not rule; where heresy meets the mirror-mask of orthodoxy; where spirit and matter intersect; where shouts of we unify in the silence of I; where choice and awareness merge.

The keys are ours for the taking. This is the promise, the rock upon which we build, that awareness and choice increase with attention on the same. In each moment is the opportunity to enter heaven or hell, and in that moment, at the center of the crossroad, the witch assumes both blessing and curse as the crossroad incarnate; to walk through the world, but be not of it. We must, as Jesus said to Thomas, *become as passers-by.*

Mysteries of Beast, Blood and Bone

SARAH ANNE LAWLESS

KULLS LINE THE WINDOWSILLS. Skulls float in jars on top of cupboards. Bones boil in pots on the stove, the flesh melting away. Hidden among the drying herbs and roots there are hearts and tongues and eyes. It is not Baba Yaga's hut I describe, but my kitchen. Bone collector, bone washer, animal necromancer, deathwalker, shapeshifter, poisoner, witch ... these are the words people whisper of me and my practices. Some whisper with fear and others with desire. I am an animist, a folk magician, and a rootworker. It is not just herbs I work with in my folk magic, but also skulls and bones, hearts and tongues. I practice the lost art of working with beast, blood, and bone in order to rebirth the ancient nature of Witch as a wild and primal creature; surrounded by spirits, anointed with blood, dressed in hides, and adorned with talismans of bone, tooth, and claw.

The magic of beasts is sympathetic magic, fetiche magic, and death magic, but it is also sensual magic. It is the feel of the Saturn finger dipped in warm blood, of softest fur on barest skin, of sharpest tooth and talon biting in, of a raw heart on the tongue, and the scent of decay deep in the lungs. It is the rendered fat of a flying ointment like smooth silk across the brow, and it is the tactile, dirty, grounding sorcery of the here and now. It is an amoral, carnal, fleshly, and sensory feast of visceral magic combining the sacred and the profane. The magic of beasts belongs to the wild sorcerers who are part human, part spirit, and part animal; the ones who dance the knife's edge between the worlds of life and death, the incarnate and disincarnate.

It is only practical to work with the animals and spirits who share the land where I live, for they have a closer relationship with me than any romanticized exotic animals across the sea. On my altar you will find the spirits of the Pacific Northwest: Orca, Salmon, Black Bear, Black Wolf, Mountain Lion, Mountain Goat, White-Tailed Deer, and wings of the birds who haunt our skies and the tree tops of Hemlock and Red Cedar. Old Woman and Old Man of the Woods whispered to me their names in dreams and one by one the beasts came to me. On my altar are their antlers, horns, bones, skulls, teeth, hides and feathers. The ones I did not find myself ended up in my care through bone collectors, shamans, and hunters.

It is important to state that I do not kill the creatures who come to me; instead, they are brought to me after death by conservation officers, hunters, taxidermists, and from friends as road kill. This is my choice and yet in the future I hope to go with my animist friends who hunt in a sacred manner and help them skin and butcher and then take of the bones and flesh they will not eat or use. When I receive dead beasts, plastic is rolled across the table, knives laid out, and gloves and a mask are worn. The still bodies are smudged with fragrant herbs, anointed with holy water, and blessings of cleansing and release are whispered over them. The bodies may be still but their spirits are not. Sometimes it isn't enough and the animal's spirit must be bargained with; some demanding to be buried whole with nothing taken, some who will only give up a few parts for sacred work and no more, and some who demand an offering or a working before you may proceed. It is best to respect their remains and their demands for they can curse you better than any witch if you anger them. Folly alone will lead you to curse yourself: butchery and preservation require training as dead animals carry disease, bacteria, parasites, and legal issues – it is not something to walk into blindly.

This path is not for everyone; it is not for the weak of stomach or for those who think it is immoral. I grew up with hunters and fishers. I've lived by the sea, I've lived on a farm raising livestock, and I've lived deep in the wildest forests. I was once a professional butcher and cook. It is how I can do what I do. Why follow this path? It should compel you and feed your soul in some way. What is the reward of such bloody work? It is simple, if you want to be a shape-shifter and a walker between worlds, if you want to learn the tongues of beasts, if you want to align yourself more closely than you could ever believe with your animal familiars and the *genius loci*, then you will also need to work closely with death, blood, and bone. Our ancestors were not soft or squeamish and we must not whitewash their memory by imagining they didn't kill the deer used to make their ceremonial costume, the raven for their feathered headdress and cloak, or the bear for its hide to craft their drums and rattles. We must approach our Mighty Dead in full knowledge they killed the swans buried in their sacrificial pits, they killed the mare buried beneath the feasting hall, and they killed the hornless bull for its hide to wrap around their seer so he may dream of invaders' ships. Long have we as the human race worked with animals, their deaths, and their spirits in our rites and ceremonies. Long will our descendants do so after we are dead.

Death will show you a side of your character as yet unknown and your reaction will either gladden you or horrify you. We are so far removed from death in our modern, sterile, clinical world that it is more important than ever as spirit workers to reconnect ourselves and others with death, blood, and bone. I work with death so I can be close to it. Being close to death reminds me I too am a spirit, walking around in a suit of flesh which I may come and go from as I please. When you are close to death you are close to spirits and more easily able to see and commune with them. When you are close to spirits, you are closer to the other worlds where they reside and therefore more easily able to transverse them.

FORMULARY OF THE BEAST

I SHARE my ancestors' belief in sympathetic magic and, when I wish to work more closely with an animal spirit, I need to also work with its remains whether it is a claw, its hide, or its whole skeleton. To practice this magic one must be able to seek out death, for bone collectors and necromancers can sense bones and remains when they pass nearby, be it in the forest or the flea market.

You are what you eat. Sympathetic magic takes this common phrase to a deeper level. To acquire the keen hearing, quick reflexes, and agility of a deer, one would eat venison. To acquire keen eyesight or the ability to fly like a bird, crossing between the other worlds, one would eat poultry. Our ancestors believed to eat a thing is to absorb its powers, spirit, and knowledge into yourself to make you more powerful or wise. To kill a thing is to

take its spirit. Hunters of old would usually let the spirit go and return the bones of a fish to the river it was caught in and the bones of a deer to the forest of its death as a sign of respect so the creature could be reborn again and eaten again.

Not every animal was let go. Some animals were hunted solely for their spirits: for their hides, their bones, for their claws and teeth, for their power, and for their help as an ally, totem, or familiar. Such spirits are asked to willingly offer themselves and stay with you until it is your turn to die. Our ancestors asked permission, not merely of the animal spirits themselves, but of the ruling genius loci, before they hunted or harvested as is evidenced in the hunter's invocations in the *Kalevala*, ancient Latin spells petitioning Artemis, and oral Scottish tales of disrespectful hunters being found dead, killed by a wild shape-shifting crone.

When you bring home any part of an animal with the intention of enlivening it as a fetiche, keep in mind that like any living creature you would have be your pet, you must also be responsible for any spirit you take home – you must accept its wildness and instincts, sate its hunger and thirst, clean it when it becomes soiled, and give it of your love, your energy and your time. The respect, reverence, and care you give a familiar spirit and the fetiche it inhabits is what you will gain in return.

Each part of an animal can be used as a fetiche, a spirit house, a ritual tool, and as a spell ingredient. As a bone collector I save the bones, but as a witch I save the blood, eyes, fats, feet, hearts, skins, teeth, and tongues as well.

> *He layeth corpses at my feet;*
> *not dead slain by warrior's hand*
> *or creatures fit to eat,*
> *but brings me tongue and heart,*
> *skull and bone, tooth and eye*
> *– all to work my grisly witch's art.*

BONES

Fresh bones wet and greasy with fat and blood, smooth white bones stained with earth, dry rough bones eroded by wind and water ... no matter their condition the bones and skulls of a dead animal connect us directly with the creature's spirit and the spirits of all their kind, living and dead. Collect the bones and skulls of animal familiars to ease communion and interaction with them. Gather the bones of animals each from the realms of land, sea, and sky if you wish to better transverse between the worlds and shift between shapes. Become an osteomancer by throwing the bones to divine secrets, foreknowledge, and the keys to your questions. Carve and paint the bones with runes and sigils. Become a charmer and wear a baculum for fertility, virility, sexual prowess, and protection.

The empty eye sockets of skulls watch and guard, apotropaic and undead they never tire of their duty. Hang the skulls of sharp-toothed predators over garden gates and chicken coops to keep out unwanted beasts. Hang them over your own door to keep out unwanted spirits and energies and let them be your fanged bouncers, your hunting hounds. Hang the skulls of horned beasts above a stable, outbuilding, or gate for protection and also to ensure the health and fertility of any livestock or wild game on your land.

The skull is where awareness and the senses dwell. Skulls are the most suited part of a skeleton for a spirit house. Magically cleanse your skull in a ceremony and ask if its spirit wants to continue to dwell in it or if another beast of its kind wishes to volunteer. I prefer the spirit the skull once housed as the connection between the two is much stronger. Consecrate the skull to its purpose as spirit vessel and a tie for that spirit to our middle world. To summon and work with the spirit you can chant:

Black is the colour of womb and tomb;
we meet at night on the dark of the moon.
White is the colour of bone and ash;
to speak to the dead we bathe and fast.
Red is the colour of blood and death;
we rub the bones and give them breath.

Clean the fetiche and leave its spirit offerings on a regular basis for the rest of your life until you pass it on to another or you die. If you must, you can desecrate a spirit vessel in ceremony and release the spirit from the bone.

BLOOD

lood is a sacrifice that feeds the hungry spirits and the insatiable earth. Blood ties us to life and death for we are born in blood and we die when our blood flows through the earth instead of our veins. Blood is holy water, life force, heat, and metal. The spirit dwells in the blood and when you drink of it you are possessed by it, bound to it, and it to you. The earth hungers for blood; the ancient battlefields long to be soaked in red, the mountains cry out for human sacrifice, and the herb garden hungers for dead crows. How they flourish when painted red, how green and juicy the plants grow when fed on the blood of mortals and beasts alike. The whole of nature feeds off death and decay. Leave out offerings of blood or raw meat to the genius loci, to the plants, to the black earth, and see how greedily the spirits claw and bite and devour it. The hungry earth is the easiest way to clean bones. Bone collectors learn to feed their gardens the unwanted flesh of their work so only pure osseous matter is left.

Blood will tie you to living beasts, it will cleanse you like holy water, protect you like an amulet, and lend you increased power and life force for your ceremonies. Blood can heal – trading a life for a life, sickliness for health. Blood can bring you closer to death and your ancestors. Blood can curse too; spilled and spat upon, a life taken in an enemy's name.

Fee fi fo fum, I smell the blood of a Christian man, says the giant. *I smell Russian blood,* says Baba Yaga. The spirits can smell our blood and by it know that we are human. They will want to drink your blood like the hungry earth for not all spirits are amicable towards us mortals. Animal blood will distract them from your scent and feed their hunger ... for the moment. Blood spilled on feather down seems to be a favourite. Is it not why we bathe in cold spring waters, rub and smudge ourselves with fragrant herbs, and adorn ourselves in animal hides? We disguise ourselves as forest creatures to safely travel in and out of the territories of dangerous spirits.

CLAWS AND FEET

LAWS click, dig, and bite deep, shedding blood. Sharp claws and talons have long been worn as protective amulets – wear them about your neck to prevent attacks from the familiar spirits of other magicians and to chase away the evil eye like an owl hunts down a mouse with its eyes upon a corn field. In a trance straddling the worlds shamans use a sharp-clawed bird foot to tear illnesses or elf darts out of a patient's body, to chase away the evil eye, to shield and protect, or to send forth biting curses to rend apart a rival or enemy. Keep the feet, toes, and nails to walk in a beast's footsteps and wear them about your neck for rites of shape-shifting.

EYES

AVE the eyes to see the unseen, to have visions, to dream dreams. Preserve them and keep them to see like the animal and better shift your shape into feather, fur, or silver skin. Eyes to spy: wear them around your neck or place them under you head to see through the eyes of their living kind far away.

Eyes to send the evil eye. Eyes to bind and blind. Eyes to stab and curse. An eye to repel the evil eye. Add to a protection talisman to carry or hide in your car or home. Eyes to watch and warn of dangers. Hang over your door for the worries of this world and place on your altar for dangers from the otherworld. Eyes as offerings to seer spirits and deities of the divinatory arts. Burn them and bury them, the eyes to see the future.

FAT

CREAMY, luscious, succulent fat – it makes such a good and pleasing offering to the gods and spirits. The rendered fats of beasts can be transformed via alchemy into flying ointments, tallow candles, protective ritual grease paints, and potent medicines. Hallucinogenic plant poisons insidiously infuse more thoroughly into animal fats and into your bloodstream than through a vegetable medium. My ointment of bear fat and henbane seed serves me well in my rites of shape-shifting and seership. When I use it I anoint my bear skull as well as myself. I do the same for my crow and owl skulls with my ointment of bird fats infused with feather ashes, the dust of bird bones, solanceæ and artemisias – it aids me in spirit flight and travelling through the worlds in the form of a bird.

Burn down a tallow candle of bear to invoke its spirit or to give offering to a deity or nature spirit whom bear is sacred to. Fat is the food of the gods; burn the fat of pig, goat, deer, bear, cow, and bird as a grand offering. Bury it raw in the woods for the spirits of the wild. Rub fat on a statue to feed its inhabiting spirit.

Mix rendered fats with potent magical herbs, charcoals, and natural pigments to create grease paints to protect your body and soul for your rites of spirit work – especially those of possession and shape-shifting. Rub sacred fats into your untreated wooden ritual tools to feed them, darken them, and strengthen them.

FEATHERS

FEATHERS lend us wings to fly out of body and between the worlds, tucked in the hair or stitched onto the collars and sleeves of cloaks. Feathers connect us to the world of the spirits and can deliver messages between them. Feathers tied to staffs, stangs, wands, ritual pipes, drums, and rattles used in spirit work. Feathers to slice and cut or feathers to caress and heal. Feathers hung for protection when travelling and feathers tucked under the mattress to receive true dreams. Wings sweep away what doesn't suit us and wings cleanse our bodies and souls. Wings wash away emotions and parasitic spirits like a fierce wind. Smudge with a tail fan to help redirect energies so things flow smoothly once more.

HEARTS

HE HEART is one of the seats of the soul. A poet would say a soul is not free from the body until the heart rots, eaten by the earth. To keep a heart is to collect a soul and its power. To hide one's heart like a sorcerer in an ancient tale is to cheat death. To wrap a poultice around a heart is to heal a heart that still beats. To stab a heart is to tear into a soul and let darkness in.

Bake a heart into a salt dough poppet. It is your choice whether the dough contains healing or baneful herbs and whether you cover it in healing poultices or stab it with ill intent. Give a heart the name of your enemy and feed it to your pet or eat it yourself to gain power over them. Prick a fresh heart with pins, needles, or thorns to curse another or to reverse a curse laid upon you. Burn a heart on a fire or bury it in a pit as an offering to your gods or spirits whose currency is souls. Hearts can be dried and saved for later use like any herb in an apothecary. Reanimate a dried heart with red wine and red ochre until it is swollen and bloody once more.

HIDES

UR ANCESTORS wrapped themselves in fur hides to bring on prophetic dreams, to shape-shift into an animal, to journey into the other world, and to call upon their familiar spirits for their power and aid. Bear hides for dreaming, deer hides for transvection, wolf hides for hunting and battle, and seal hides for navigating the mysterious ocean. Furs are tools of magic and can be used as altar cloths, ritual costumes, and sacred blankets.

The rawhide of beasts is the body of our ritual drums and our rattles. We transform skin into musical instruments so the spirits will hear the song of their own flesh and come to us in our time of need. Any creature with skin can become a drum. The hide of each beast sings a different song in a different tune: deer and elk are high and resonant, bear is a deep and thundering roar, and cow and buffalo are soft and deep like their dark liquid eyes.

Save the leather for ritual costumes, for binding your book of arte, and for the crafting of amulets, fetiches, and sacred medicine bundles. Save the skin of a bird to craft from it a crane bag where you will store all your tools, fetiches, and talismans you wish to take with you into other worlds and other forms.

TEETH

eeth to bite and gnaw and scare. Teeth to devour curses, attacking spirits, and meddlesome folk. Teeth to chew and spit back out. Teeth to warn an unruly cub and teeth to put a trickster back in line. Teeth to rip and rend and bloody an enemy. Teeth to give bite to those who lack it and need it. My what big teeth you have, bigger than mine, predator to my prey. A fool stands against one armed to the teeth, but a wiser beast runs away. A tooth carved with a sigil and sung with a rune, carried to protect one from harm. A tooth dipped in venomous herbs to energetically stab and dig in like a serpent's fang – the tooth of a bear, lion, whale, shark, or wolf.

TONGUES

ongues to speak benevolence or malevolence, tongues to bind or cut out, tongues to sweeten others to your cause or to ruin another's. Are there tongues in the crane bag on your altar that you may speak and understand the languages of beasts of land and sea and sky? Do you possess tongues to exchange for your own in the otherworld so the animal spirits will understand you when you speak? I collect the tongues of birds, messengers between the worlds and ferriers of souls, that my own tongue may speak prophecy and knowledge from the other side and that the spirits may hear me when I call out.

I offer this knowledge to those students of the mysteries who truly wish to deepen their relationship with the animal world. Animals have a lot to teach us about magic and wisdom. Long have they been viewed by the human race as guardians, protectors, and teachers proficient in magic, shape-shifting, and communication with the supernatural world. Animals are our familiars, our messengers and intermediaries, our dream companions, our omens, the skulls and feathers on our altars, the skin of our drums and rattles, the antler and bone of our tool handles, the tooth and claw of our fetishes, the tallow in our candles, and the leather of our crane bags. They are furred and feathered gods in the trees, on our dinner plates, and in our homes deserving of our respect, reverence, and a change in our attitudes towards them.

RESOURCES

ELIADE, MIRCEA, *Shamanism: Archaic Techniques of Ecstasy.* Princeton University Press, 1992.

ELLIS DAVIDSON, HILDA, *Roles of the Northern Goddess.* Routledge, 1998.

HARRIS-LOGAN, STUART A., *Singing With Blackbirds: The Survival of Primal Celtic Shamanism in Later Folk Traditions.* Grey House in the Woods, 2006.

JOHNSON, BUFFIE, *Lady of the Beasts: Ancient Images of the Goddess and Her Sacred Animals.* HarperCollins, 1990.

MCINTYRE JORGENSEN, GRACE MIRI, *A Comparative Examination of Northwest Coast Shamanism.* University of British Columbia Department of Anthropology and Sociology, 1970.

Biographies

FRANCIS ASHWOOD is a hermit in the paths of witchcraft native to Southern Spain. He has been nurturing an ascetic practice involving ritual work and communion with the spirits and numina of the Land, as inspired by patron entities in visions, dreamwork and trance. He is acknowledged in other forms of traditional witchcraft of both Italian descent and from the South West of England.

JESSE HATHAWAY DIAZ is a folklorist, reader, artist and performer living in New York City. With initiations in several forms of witchcraft from both Europe and the Americas, he is also a lifelong student of Mexican Curanderismo, an initiated Olosha in Lucumi, and a Tatá Quimbanda

NICHOLAJ DE MATTOS FRISVOLD has been actively involved as a practitioner and wayfarer of the witches' art for more than twenty years. He is the Magister of Via Vera Cruz Nocturna, a conclave of cunning people from a great variety of geographical strands brought into a unique family with its hearth in Brazilian soil. He is also the Magister of the Clan of Tubal Cain's Umbra Lunæ Cuveen, also located in Brazil.

JOHANNES GÅRDBÄCK is a professional folk magic practitioner and Seer living in Gothenburg, Sweden. He serves a worldwide clientele and can be contacted through his website: www.therootdoctor.se

GEMMA GARY lives in the West Country and is a student, practitioner, writer and artist of the Old Craft. Gemma's working interests encompass the witchcraft, folk-magical traditions, folklore and customs of the West Country and beyond.

STUART INMAN studied with Joseph Bearwalker Wilson for several years and shortly before Wilson's death was appointed a Doyen of Toteg Tribe and a Guardian of 1734. After he met JANE SPARKES he began to teach her the elements of the 1734 tradition, but she showed him he also still had a great deal to learn, so they began to develop the Clan of the Entangled Thicket as an expression of the 1734 teachings. Stuart has published several essays on 1734, notably in *The Cauldron* and *Abraxas* and Jane has published articles in *The Hedge Witch*. He is writing a book on 1734 and they are planning a book together that will concentrate on the workings of the Clan of the Entangled Thicket.

SARAH ANNE LAWLESS is a full-time herbalist, writer and artist, living in the Pacific Northwest following a path of bio-regional animism. She practices the arts of folk magic, spiritwork, dreamwalking, and witchcraft in both city and forest. The focus of her magic is in Scoto-Scandinavian folklore, folk religion, and sorcery, living in the New World, she also incorporates Pacific Northwest ethnobotany and folklore into her practice. The heart of her path is honouring and working with the genius loci, whether they are animals, plants, insects, the good folk, or the dead.

TONY MACLEOD is a lifelong student of the mysteries, a West Country boy and freeborn man of England. After many years exploring this island he now finds himself in the wilds of Cornwall, a family man and a faithful servant of the hearth of Tubal Cain. He states: *To serve that which lifted me from the mire is my fate and willingly do I go, with all the love and joy that brings. Gathered home at last, in every sense.*

ANNE MORRIS is a solitary practitioner of Sabbatic Craft in the United States. She lives with and works with a Native American tribe, forging new connections between the working parameters of both Sabbatic Craft and Native American spiritual practice. Anne is currently pursuing her doctorate, studying the nature of art and spiritual practice within the Native American culture. She is an artist, expressing her gnostic dream images through various media, and has written articles published in such diverse publications as the *Journal for the Academic Study of Magic* and *The Cauldron*. She was a member of the Companie Serpent Cross, the outer sodality of the Cultus Sabbati, for eleven years.

SHANI OATES lives in Derbyshire where she is a devoted practitioner of the true art, a mystic, pilgrim, artist, professional photographer and holistic therapist. Her work has been published widely in magazines and journals and in four books with Mandrake of Oxford exploring the mysteries of her Craft. She is the Maid of the Clan of Tubal Cain.

RICHARD PARKINSON is an acknowledged expert on The Society of the Horseman's Word and a practitioner of The Waters of the Moon or toad rite. A lifelong student of esoterica, through careful and extensive study he has acquired an expert knowledge of medieval mysticism and the heretical undercurrents of the Middle Ages. He is a Deacon in the Guild of Eligius, the umbrella guild to which the Horseman's Word and other Word Societies and the Hammermen originally belonged. The Guild was heavily influenced by the Brethren of the Free Spirit and the Bogomils and its philosophy included underground resistance to the Catholic Church during the later Middle Ages in Scotland and the Low Countries.

STEVE PATTERSON is a writer, folklorist, woodcarver and agricultural labourer. He lives and works with his dog in an old granite quarry in a secret location in West Cornwall. He is an initiate of two strands of the Old Craft, one from the East and one from the West. He is a keen supporter of the Museum of Witchcraft in Boscastle, Cornwall and is currently writing a book on the life and works of Cecil Williamson. Otherwise he spends his time concocting sorcerous convocations, getting up to no good, scything, playing psychedelic analogue synths and making beautiful things.

RADOMIR RISTIC is the author of *Balkan Traditional Witchcraft, The Last European Shamans* and *Mystery of Witchcraft*. His articles have appeared in the *Crooked Path Journal*, *The Cauldron* and *Esoteric Source*, and he writes for two Serbian magazines, *Zona* and *Mistika*. He is licensed therapist, chiropractor and instructor in many holistic healing systems.

ARKAITZ O. URBELTZ is a sorgin from one of the few remaining houses of Traditional Craft (*modazaharrak*) in Euskalerria.

XABIER BAKAIKOA URBELTZ is a sorgin from one of the few remaining houses of Traditional Craft in Euskalerria. *Egiak esan eta adiskideak gal; egizu beti on, ez jakinarren non. Aurrera begiratzen ez duena, atzean dago.*

www.ingramcontent.com/pod-product-compliance
Lightning Source LLC
Chambersburg PA
CBHW032034290426
44110CB00012B/800